A Primer
for Playgoers

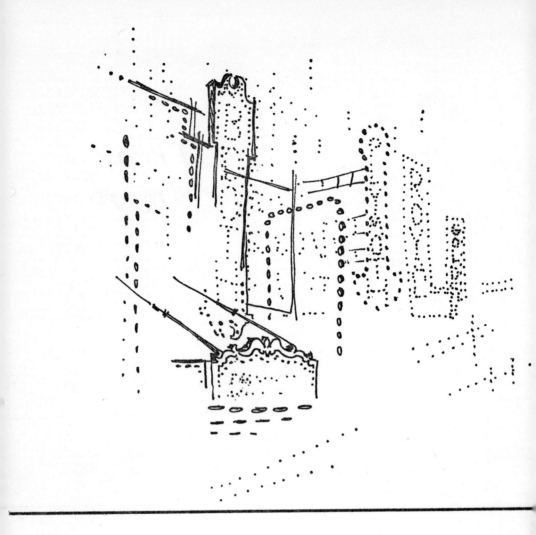

by EDWARD A. WRIGHT

Englewood Cliffs, N.J.   PRENTICE-HALL, INC.

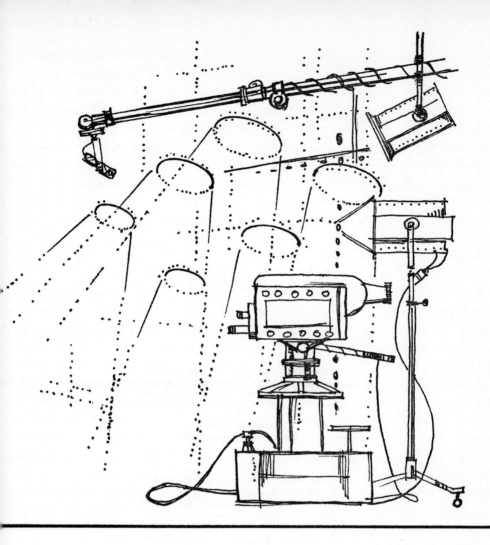

A Primer
for Playgoers

AN INTRODUCTION TO THE UNDERSTANDING AND
APPRECIATION OF CINEMA—STAGE—TELEVISION

First printing .... *January, 1958*
Second printing .... *October 1958*
Third printing .... *March, 1960*
Fourth printing .... *June, 1961*
Fifth printing .... *January, 1963*
Sixth printing .... *February, 1965*

PRINTED IN THE UNITED STATES OF AMERICA
70043–C

To Louise

without whose faith, encouragement, and assistance

these pages could not have been realized

Preface

*I*n a welter of books both good and bad on playwriting, acting, direction, and all phases of play production, the audience and its knowledge of theatre have been largely neglected. No major work for the beginner has appeared that takes into consideration all the dramatic elements in the theatre and treats them solely from the viewpoint of the consumer. There is a need for a book for the novice in the art of understanding the theatre. *A Primer For Playgoers,* therefore, is designed primarily for the audience who will *view* the completed production, rather than those who would create or interpret it.

This book is directed, then, to numerous groups: to those who have been active participants in the noncommercial theatre but who have been too close to develop the feeling of artistic detachment that a critic must have for adequate evaluation; to the countless untrained playgoers who attend school and community theatre performances, as well as the smaller group who have an opportunity to enjoy the professional theatre; to those whose only dramatic fare has been the cinema and, more recently, the television screen; and to those who are beginning their appreciation of the theatre in the classroom.

Through the collection, organization, and presentation of facts, principles, and opinions that have grown out of the theatre's history, the book will develop at least one valid approach to appraising the work of all those artists who have created the drama and brought it to life. At the risk of being both academic and pedantic, it will attempt throughout to give the beginner some generally accepted principles of drama and the theatre. Certainly, one of the earliest lessons a teacher learns is the necessity of giving the beginner some anchor from the very start. As his knowledge and experience develop, the student will learn that these early generalizations have many exceptions; that his appreciation is often enhanced by the artist's deviation from these early principles or assumptions. Training consists of learning the rules. It is experience that teaches us the exceptions.

Although the major portion of our discussions will be directed toward a standard for judging a dramatic production on the legitimate stage, much of what is said can be applied as well to both the motion picture and the television screen. Chapters 7 and 8 endeavor to point out differences that do exist in these two younger areas of dramatic production. One cannot emphasize too strongly, however, the great importance of a solid foundation and full understanding of those principles inherent in the mother of them both—the live and legitimate theatre.

One final admonition: Although every effort will be made to point up those elements that can make for greater understanding of the theatre and all that it has to offer in aesthetic enjoyment, and even though the reader accepts and masters all the facts, opinions, or principles presented, there is no guarantee that dramatic appreciation will follow. Appreciation in itself cannot be taught. That is a by-product, growing out of knowledge and understanding. It comes to the individual only after he has applied, first consciously and later unconsciously, all that he can learn about form and technique, accepted principles and practice. It is an intangible asset that grows with experience and the years. It is the author's fondest hope that through the pages of this book the reader may find a key to this great and enriching experience.

I am most grateful to all those who have permitted themselves to be quoted, but especially to Henry Holt & Company for the generous use of Clayton Hamilton's *The Theory of the Theatre* and to Harper & Brothers for that of John Dolman's *The Art of Play Production.* It was the writing and teaching of these individuals that introduced me to the theatre, and their influence goes beyond direct quotations.

I would be remiss if I were not to mention my most inspiring and helpful teacher and personal friend, the late Elias Day, whose brilliant mind and theatre understanding contributed more to my own knowledge and love of the theatre than any other single individual. Unfortunately, he was too busy during his lifetime to set down any of his thoughts. It is my hope that some of them may be preserved through this work.

I am deeply indebted to Don Swanagan, stage and television designer, who has contributed all the line drawings that appear in the text, and to my colleague, James Hinkle, of the English department, who has helped in editing the manuscript and given invaluable suggestions for its clarification.

Undoubtedly I have borrowed much material from other sources without due credit. If this be true, I ask the pardon of the authors and tender them my thanks. In many years of reading and teaching on a given subject, one tends to merge one's own ideas with what he has read, so that the two become integrally mingled.

E. A. W.

Granville, Ohio

Contents

*A Primer
for Playgoers*

— 1 —

A Theatrical Approach

*I*t is doubtful if ever before in world history, and certainly never in any other single country, so many people could say on a given morning, "I saw a play last night."

In this country the speaker could have been among the one hundred million who sit before a television set from eight to ten o'clock every evening and view one of the seventy-six thousand dramas televised each year; or one of the fifty to seventy million who attend the cinema each week. He may even have witnessed a live stage production in any of the thousands of community or educational theatres—Samuel French has a mailing list of sixty-five thousand amateur producing groups—or one of the one to five hundred (depending on the season of year) touring or stock companies. Or he might have helped make up the audience in one of the twenty-five to fifty on and off-Broadway legitimate theatre productions.

1

It is this latter unfortunate figure that evokes the pessimist's mournful cry: "What is happening to the theatre?" "Is the theatre dying?" "How much longer can the theatre last?"

There is no escaping the fact that each year finds fewer theatre buildings on Broadway. In the past quarter century the number has been reduced from seventy-five to barely twenty-five today. Many have been converted to the use of motion pictures, and in later years others have gone over to radio and television. Furthermore, statistics show that twenty-five years ago there were touring companies appearing in every city of fifteen thousand or more. Today fewer than fifty cities have legitimate theatres available, and at least ten states do not even possess theatre buildings capable of handling a first-class professional production.

A variety of influences have been blamed—the lack of good plays, motion pictures, radio, television, transportation, high prices, the limitations of our present-day realistic theatre—and the list could go on and on. The picture from one viewpoint is indeed dark. It would seem as though the mourners were right.

Before we speak the last rites over the body of the theatre, however, let us look at it from a slightly different and much brighter angle. The past century has witnessed the rise and fall of the actor-manager, stock and repertory companies, the star system, and touring groups, but it has also seen the rise of the community and little theatres and high school, college, and university theatres throughout the land. Literally thousands of theatrical productions are being presented every week by these noncommercial groups, and the calibre of acting, directing, and production are in many instances artistically superior to much that was done by the various commercial theatres of what some like to call the "good old days." The audiences who attend these productions are also playgoers, but the pessimists mentioned earlier have their eyes only on Broadway and the professional theatre.

It is possible that this wider base, this sincerity and enthusiasm so abundant in the noncommercial theatre-worker, this return to the grass roots, may be the beginning of a new renaissance in theatre history. After all, the amateur is the aristocrat of the theatre—for it was he who gave it birth, and he who has frequently kept it alive when the professionals have so debauched the art that public denunciation or the law has closed the theatres.

We need only take a casual glance at the history of the theatre, from its origins in the life of primitive man through its formal organization in Greece seven hundred years before Christ, down through the fall of the Roman Empire, the Dark Ages, and the Renaissance to more recent centuries, to learn that for five thousand years there has been the recurring cry: "The theatre is dying!" This "fabulous invalid" has, strangely enough, been reborn in practically every century and once again is showing a remarkable vitality, for the theatre is immortal not because it never dies, but because it is a phoenix. When a particular theatre comes to an end because it is no longer useful to its audiences, it is replaced by a newer theatre which takes up its work where the predecessor left off.

No, the theatre is neither decadent nor dying. It is merely everchanging, in form and emphasis. The alteration may be in the personnel, physical aspects, styles of acting, scenic background, writing, direction, subject matter, or the fully organized and coordinated production. It may even be that through the marriage of Stage and Science there has come a new theatre for a new age. Certainly the offspring of this union—motion pictures, radio, and television—are showing an amazing amount of life in areas of drama once monopolized by the stage. Yes, the theatre of *yesterday*, we grant, may be gone, but not *the theatre!*

The theatre, in its larger meaning, marches on, and a single production may be witnessed daily by more viewers than saw Burbage, Garrick, Siddons, the Keans, Forrest, Booth, Jefferson, Duse, and Bernhardt in the sum total of their long and successful careers. Even if the new audience in our educational and community theatres were nonexistent, there would still be that far larger one in motion picture houses or before television screens.

In every generation the living stage has been faced with competition in the field of dramatic entertainment. Each time many have found that nowhere was there a wholly satisfactory substitute for the combination of living actors, a good play, and a responsive audience. In the late teens and twenties movies seemed to threaten legitimate theatre, but it survived. Radio gave it further competition in the thirties, but the blind eyes of that medium finally gave way to television in the late forties and early fifties. Now the stage is faced with competition of all three, and they with one another. Each medium has its assets and its liabilities, each its limitations. The offspring, of course, reach millions who could never witness a living stage production, but each must borrow constantly from the parent; for the legitimate theatre is still the main source or foundation of all dramatic principles, as well as the only live, flesh-and-blood, man-to-man entertainment. There and there alone can exist the all-important give and take between artist and audience, the emotion and response that are the very life-blood of dramatic production.

Therefore, valuable and popular as the cinema, radio, and television may be—and they can play an even greater role in our theatre of the future—those in search of dramatic understanding must turn to the living stage to learn the rudiments of theatre art.

Certainly the building of an understanding and discerning audience is fundamental. If we are displeased with what our theatre* is giving us, it is useless to criticize only those who bring us the entertainment. Our criticism should also be of the audience. The reformer who would change the course of the theatre in any of its aspects must first elevate the standards of those who witness the production, for until this powerful group is ready for better dramatic fare, it will not be forthcoming. In their own small way this book and the hundreds of courses being taught in theatre and motion picture appreciation in the high schools and colleges of America may help to bring this about. The real lovers of the theatre are those who know something about it, and those who do know will demand its best. Some national and local organizations have made real progress, but we must never forget that it is the audience that is truly responsible for the calibre of theatre that belongs to any era.

In addition to the pessimists who see no future for the theatre, there are others who question the importance of knowing why

---

* In the word "theatre" we shall henceforth include the motion picture as well as both radio and television.

they enjoy it. They contend: "I enjoy a movie or a play because I like it. I don't know why, and I care less. Enjoyment in itself is enough." This kind of statement often comes from otherwise intelligent persons. The answer to this line of reasoning is that there can be far greater enjoyment in knowing *why* a given play or motion picture has or has not entertained; *why* the acting or direction has been superior or inferior to the play itself; *why* the observer has been moved emotionally or found it dull and uninspired. It can be of great interest to understand why *Hamlet* has lived for three hundred fifty years and *Oedipus Rex* for twenty-five hundred, as compared with many of the modern plays, movies, or television dramas seen in the past twelve months and long since forgotten.

Many of us choose to think of ourselves as educated, and to discriminate is one of the marks of educated people. To number ourselves among that group, we must know as much about as many things as possible. There is a third reason for a better understanding of the theatre—fairness to the artists themselves. Praise or discredit should go to each for the conception and realization of his work. This is where our knowledge of the various forms or techniques comes into use, for we must know something of these as well as the problems surmounted by each artist if we are to bring real appreciation to any work of art.

In summary, then, the primary goals of this book are:

1. To help each individual develop for himself an artistically honest standard for evaluating any dramatic production.

2. To provide a fairer means of judging the work of all those artists whose efforts are being witnessed.

3. To build a better audience, which will in turn demand a better theatre.

To attain these three goals, three sources of information must be used, namely, *facts*, *principles*, and *opinions*. Facts are the most easily recognized. They may consist of dates, names of authors and dramas, definitions of terms, historical material, and so on. Principles, which are often variable and open to question, debate, or change, are a bit more difficult. The individual may accept a principle now and later discard it altogether. A principle is a specific point from which we make our start in analyzing a given piece of work. The fact that certain principles are found in these pages does not imply that they are final answers, nor that the reader must accept them. It does mean that they are precepts upon which the author has arrived at his own opinions or conclusions in dramatic criticism, and can for the present become the anchors the beginner so often needs.

To distinguish between principles and opinions is a more difficult task. It is true that we should arrive at an opinion through the use of certain principles, but where the former ends and the latter begins may at first seem perplexing. Two people may agree on a given principle and arrive at two widely different opinions on the artistic value of a drama, the work of a given actor, the scenery, the direction, or the production. This is due to their different backgrounds, their emotions, and their very natures. It would be folly to say that the author has tried to keep the element of opinion to a minimum. Evaluation of all artistic work is largely opinion, and it would be impossible to deal with any phase of art without personal opinions entering the picture.

The matter of chief importance is that we come to recognize as much as possible the distinctions among these three areas; that we agree, at least in our early efforts at criticism, to use the same principles. We must also come to value and respect the principles and opinions of others, even when they differ radically from our own. The one basic requirement of all criticism, good or bad, is that it should have a sound basis.

Goethe's Three Principles

For a first principle, which can be considered the very base upon which this particular theory of dramatic criticism is founded, we are indebted to the great German playwright, philosopher, and critic, Johann Wolfgang von Goethe (1749-1832). In three simple questions he gives every would-be art critic, young or old, a foundation as sound and as simple as it is profound:

1. What is the artist trying to do?
2. How well has he done it?
3. Is it worth the doing?

What is the artist trying to do? Is the dramatist writing a farce, a melodrama, a tragedy, or a comedy?* Is his goal sheer escape or would he teach us some great lesson? Is this purely a commercial venture or an effort at an artistic production? Are the actors attempting to create characters or to be themselves merely commenting on the role? What has the scenic artist, the costumer, the electrician, or the director had in mind? What is the over-all purpose of the production? These are *facts*. We may not agree with the goals or the artist's methods, but it is his inalienable right to express himself as he chooses.

How well has he done it? This is the critic's opportunity to place his judgment on the degree of success the artist has attained in his efforts. Here we evaluate his technique, his methods, his success in attaining the goals he has set up for himself. We are now concerned with the over-all effectiveness of the work of each artist and of the whole production, and that effectiveness is measured by the *principles* that we have chosen to be the yardsticks of our dramatic knowledge.

Is it worth the doing? Once again the goal of the artist is brought into focus, but now we raise the question of value in time and effort on the part of both artist and viewer. A completely new approach or end may have been presented. The artist may or may not have succeeded in arriving at his goal. We, as the audience, must now say whether or not we feel the end or the means to that end were worth while, and our conclusions are called *opinions*.

Due recognition of these three questions will help to avoid the pitfall of most amateur critics. Too often the novice condemns a motion picture in his effort to compare it with a stage production, or vice versa. He deplores the dramatic program on television without asking why; he bemoans the frothiness of an inconsequential farce because it does not have the stature of a more serious play; he sometimes stands in awe of a dramatic piece built on a

---

* The meaning of these drama types is explained in Chapter 3.

most ambitious scale but not adequately executed by the artist. Again, he frowns upon the very thought of melodrama or farce instead of weighing each in the light of certain accepted principles laid down for them specifically. In short, by answering Goethe's questions, we can escape the common error of condemning or praising without an evaluation of the artist's conception, the medium, the techniques, and the values involved.

The Fine Arts

Although they are often referred to, with one or more mentioned as favorites, it is surprising how many well-educated persons are unable to name all of the fine arts. Webster's dictionary lists them as sculpture, painting, drawing, architecture, dancing, music, poetry, and dramatic art. This would total eight, instead of the commonly listed seven. By many people dramatic art or the theatre has been considered a synthesis of the arts rather than an art in itself. Even a casual analysis of the elements that compose the original seven will point up the fundamental truth that theatre is perhaps the one place where all the various elements meet on common ground. In the acting we find the *bodily movement* and *gesture* that compose the dance. In the speech of the actors and the total sound of the performance we find the *rhythm, melody,* and *harmony* of music. The drama itself, with its *words* and *meter,* is the poetry or literature. The *line, mass,* and *color* of the graphic arts—that is, sculpture, painting, drawing, and architecture—are found in the scenery, lighting effects, and décor of the settings. Since the birth of the theatre it has been closely associated with the aesthetic aspect of man's existence, and in more recent years the importance of unity in the whole dramatic production has developed into the art of the theatre.

In approaching the subject from the historical angle, we find that in every race and in every civilization there is evidence of the dramatic performance being an integral part of the two original arts, dance and music. The dance has often been called the mother of the arts, and music the universal art. Drama came third, for primitive man gave vent to his feelings and emotions through the physical expression of the dance. He soon accompanied it with the rhythm of the tom-tom, and the first drama emerged when dialogue was added. Thus, drama and dramatic art became a part of man's daily life through the unconscious dramas of these primitive men—the dramas of love, hatred, food-getting, initiation, sacrifice, and historical representation.

The Purpose of the Fine Arts

It is said that the basis of all art is religion. Throughout history man has sought something more than the bare essentials of existence, something beyond the preservation of life and the propagation of the race. He has ever been in search of some reason for his existence, some answer to the questions: Who am I? What is truth? Who is God? and the myriad questions that life presents. In this search he has turned to the fine arts, becoming himself a creator. The dramas, music, paintings, cathedrals, sculpture, and other works of art are the only tangible evidence we have from past centuries. Generals, emperors, and kings depart, but Shakespeare, Leonardo, and Bach live on through the medium of their art. Clayton Hamilton has made an interesting point:*

> Art and Nature compete eternally with each other in the great task of making humanity aware of what is true and beautiful and good. They are the two teachers in our schoolroom of a world. . . . It would be difficult to judge decisively whether Art or Nature is the greater teacher. Nature has more to tell us, but Art is better skilled for utterance. Nature has so much to say that she has no patience for articulation. She thrills us with a vague awareness of multitudinous indecipherable messages; but she speaks to us in whispers and in thunders—elusive, indeterminate, discomforting. Art, with less to say, has more patience for the formulation of her messages; she speaks to us in a voice that has been deliberately trained, and her utterance is lucid and precise. She does not try, like Nature, to tell us everything at once.

* Clayton Hamilton, *Theory of the Theatre* (New York: Henry Holt & Co., 1939), p. 426.

She selects, instead, some single definite and little truth to tell us at a time, and exerts herself to speak it clearly. We can never estimate precisely what it is that we have learned from Nature; but whatever Art has spoken to us, we know exactly what we have been told.

Whether we choose to think of the fine arts as an outgrowth of religion, as man's desire to create, or as the product of his efforts to rise above the animal, it is commonly accepted that the artist creates primarily for the purpose of giving us aesthetic pleasure, or pleasure that depends upon the appreciation of beauty.

Defining Beauty

But what *is* beauty? The answer is not a simple one. Even among the Greeks there was a difference of opinion which has only increased throughout the ages, and our modern knowledge of psychology has made the issue even more complicated. The ancients at one time felt that beauty was inherent in the subject matter itself; that the artist's genius lay in his ability to duplicate that beauty. Aristotle found aesthetic pleasure even in the representation of ugliness. To him the beauty lay in the artist's skill, technique, or method. From this we have his theory of *catharsis* or the purging of emotions, sometimes called beauty in ugliness. To Plato beauty was the result of "unity in variety." This meant that many different elements all worked in complete harmony toward the projection of one central theme or idea.

Many modern theorists contend that beauty exists only in the mind of the viewer or hearer; that the artist must strike some note of recognition or suggestion that brings to the observer's mind a pleasurable experience or emotion that gives aesthetic pleasure. Still another theory would place the beauty in the artist's personal interpretation of what he sees. This has given us much of what is called modern art and encompasses the work of both the *impressionist* and the *expressionist*.

There are in addition those who would unite their ethical or religious thinking with their aesthetic sense. They are the followers of John Keats and his belief that "Beauty is truth, truth beauty." Closely allied, but standing by themselves, are those who insist that only the presence of God or an emphasis on their own moral code combined with art can give them aesthetic pleasure. In the theatre these individuals are often called moralists, for they insist upon a great moral theme. They refuse to find beauty or art in the representation or suggestion of anything of which they do not personally approve.

Although the history of art shows that the primary appeal of beauty is to the senses, intellectuals often insist that before an art object can give them aesthetic pleasure it must challenge them to think, or give them a greater understanding of the world's problems. A leader in this field is Eric Bentley, who has expressed these ideas in his book, *The Playwright as Thinker*.*

Someone has said that poetry in its broader sense is defined as that happiness which overcomes us when we become suddenly aware of the presence of the beautiful. We learn that the Greeks sought their poetry in the dialogue. To the Mediaevalists it was found in the theme of the liturgical play, expressing to the masses in their own language the Biblical stories they could not understand in the church Latin. The Renaissance in Italy found its greatest beauty in the scenic backgrounds painted for the theatre by Leonardo da Vinci and other contemporary artists; the English, in the incomparable language of Shakespeare; the French, in the superb pantomime of the *Commedia dell' arte* which finally emerged in Molière's comedy of manners. The realists have found beauty in the completeness of their artistic representation of life on the stage. The expressionist finds it in the imaginativeness of his conception. Thus all these have found poetry and beauty in the theatre, whether it be in the acting, the direction, the setting, the story itself, the work of the technicians, or as it is today, in the harmonious coordination of all these contributing artists.

If the arts are designed to give aesthetic pleasure, and if aesthetic pleasure is an appreciation of the beautiful, with so many divergent opinions on the basic question of what beauty truly is, it is not difficult to understand why, from the very beginning, it will be

* Eric Bentley, *The Playwright as Thinker* (New York: Reynal & Hitchcock, 1946).

impossible to find a common agreement on any art work. There would seem to be only one constant, and that is the agreement that art is based on selection rather than blind representation. A photograph is artistic only when the element of choice or selection is evident through the subject chosen, its arrangement, the lighting, the emphasis, and delicate touches obtained through development and retouching.

These diverse ideas of beauty must also make it clear that the task of the theatre to meet the approval of its devotees is more difficult than in other arts, for while they may appeal to the individual, the theatre is a "group art" and as such must make its appeal to the audience.

This very fact but broadens the meaning of beauty and emphasizes our conviction that art, and certainly the theatre, must never resort to the oft-quoted phrase, "art for art's sake." It is a maxim of this book that such a statement is utterly without validity. Art is the possession of all the people and should exist for and speak to them. Brooks Atkinson, drama editor of *The New York Times*, once said:*

> For art is moribund unless it is firmly rooted in our common heritage and growing out of the needs of human beings. . . . Art must be an integral part of life if it is to survive. Sooner or later the world discards art that no longer expresses human fundamentals, as it has discarded the bogus ostentation of the McKinley period in architecture . . . For art is not a separate chamber of life or the exclusive property of cultivated people. It goes down through the whole structure of life. It is the words we speak and the clothes we wear and the friendships we cultivate in passing and the stamp of the individuality we give to our homes.

Those artists of the theatre who would write or produce for themselves or their own little groups and who look down upon the "common people" are not only ignoring their audience but drawing the cloak of oblivion over the art they profess to love. This responsibility should never discourage experimentation, growth, and change. On the contrary, it may give them birth, for audi-

---

* Brooks Atkinson, "Art For Art's Sake," *The New York Times*, Feb. 19, 1939.

A THEATRICAL APPROACH

ences are willing to learn and are looking for something new. History has shown them to be both receptive and easily adaptable to change, but the theatre artist, more than any other, may be compelled to move slowly. At least, he must never forget that he is the servant of the crowd.

The Theatre's Obligations to the Audience

Let us now consider the obligation of the theatre to its audience, that cosmopolitan group that has paid its admission and surrendered two hours of its time. As an art form and as a teacher, the theatre has definite responsibilities which should now be presented.

It is a truism that the vast majority of theatregoers attend the theatre to be moved emotionally. If the experience can teach them a truth of life, inspire them to do finer things, thrill them with its poetry or literary quality, send them out somehow better equipped to face life, or challenge them intellectually, then truly the experience has been the more worth while, but first and foremost the theatre must give its audience an emotional experience. It was Lessing, the famous German author and critic, who said: "The only unpardonable fault of a tragic poet is that he leaves us cold; if he interests us, he may do as he likes with the little mechanical rules." Throughout history we have found the theatre to be a chapel of emotion, but it has been and should be much more than that.

In exchange for the time given and admission paid, it is the obligation of the theatre to give an audience far more of life than it could have lived in the same period of time. It must accent the lessons and truths it presents and paint the characters so vividly that the audience may come to know and understand them. The story may parallel or differ from their own lives, but it must always furnish the vicarious experience and emotion that only the theatre can give.

Except for a very short period in the nineteenth century, man has always demanded that the theatre as an art must *seem* real rather than *be* real; that it must *reflect* life, not necessarily *be* life;

that it be always an *illusion* of reality. It is in this element of "seeming" that we find the real art of the theatre, though the exact degree has varied throughout the ages and throughout the many types and forms of drama and theatre. Shakespeare's admonition, "Hold the mirror up to nature," supposes a special kind of mirror —one that pictures for the audience just what the artist would have it see, but in that seeing, neither artist nor audience must ever confuse it with life itself.

A fourth obligation of the theatre is always to make the audience *believe* what they see, at least during the time spent in the theatre. The light of the morrow and the process of careful analysis may show up some improbabilities of certain acts or characterizations, but these must never be obvious at the time. The emotion, spirit, and illusion of life must be present.

Finally, the theatre must at all times tell the truth about its people and about life. The moment it lies or the audience no longer believes it, it ceases to exist artistically. This does not mean that plays must be realistic in their style and the settings naturalistic, or even that the subject matter must be close to the actual. A fantasy can be just as true as the most realistic play if the characters in that fantasy and the setting before which it is played *are consistent with the laws of their imagined existence. Alice In Wonderland* and *The Blue Bird* are just as true as the most realistic motion picture, and their truths or themes may be far more lasting in our memories.

To summarize, the theatre's five obligations to its audience are:

1. To move those in attendance emotionally.
2. To give them more of life than they would live in the same period of time.
3. To *seem* real and to create an illusion of life.
4. To make the audience believe what it sees.
5. To give a truthful picture of life through the elements of selection and conventionalization.

The reader will do well to understand these basic requirements, for they are the starting point in any critical analysis of a theatre experience.

The Obligations of the Audience

The *good* playgoer does not look upon the theatre as merely a temporary vacation from his own personal problems. He asks that it be more than mere escape, and he puts no limitations on the artist's conceptions or beliefs, but permits him to use whatever material he may need to tell his story. He does not demand any particular style of entertainment, other than that it be good theatre, whether it is the work of a clown, a Hamlet, a tragedy of Sophocles, or slapstick comedy. When he enters the theatre, he makes a certain surrender to it—not a blind surrender, for he retains his judgment and his taste. He accepts the theatre as make-believe, as a world built for him by many participating in an effort to picture something of life by way of the artist's conception, and as part of the audience he will try to evaluate these efforts.

The good playgoer realizes that the theatre is a synthesis of all the arts and that many individuals are responsible for the production he is to witness. He does not think only in terms of the story, the actors, the scenery, the lighting, or the costumes. He realizes that he may like one aspect of the production and be disappointed in another, and that it is unjust to condemn or praise the whole because of some single contribution. He appreciates the fact that the theatre is capable of moving him in many ways; that it can stir, excite, amuse, teach, or transform, but that the whole experience is a two-way proposition—a game that he, too, must play.

He knows that at the very heart of all theatre pleasure is what Shakespeare called "imaginary puissance," or a sort of temporary half-belief. This half-belief does not demand that he blindly say: "That is Hamlet's castle," or "That is the home of Willy Loman," but that he does not set up in his mind the argument that it is *not* the castle or the home of Willy Loman. Coleridge once said: "True stage illusion consists not in the mind's judging it to be a forest, but in its remission of judgment that it is *not* a forest." Others have called this a suspension of disbelief.

The *poor* theatregoer is sometimes disturbed when he sees

people he knows playing parts that are contrary to his accepted beliefs, as in the case of the college professor who said to the director: "Please don't ever cast one of our fine young people in an objectionable role, for always afterward one is reminded of that character when he meets him on the street," and the mother irate because her son's part required him to swear. In either case the individuals were utterly lacking in any imaginary puissance. They refused to give each actor his right as an artist to *be* an actor, speaking the lines of someone else.

Contrary to this narrow and wholly unjustified viewpoint, the good playgoer gives the actors, the scenic artist, and all those involved with the production the opportunity of taking him into their imaginary world. When actors, technicians, or director have failed to accomplish their goal after the playgoer has given them ample opportunity through his imaginary puissance, or the suspension of disbelief, then he has the right to offer whatever adverse criticism of them as artists that he may desire. It will show more intelligence on his part, however, and give him greater personal pleasure if he is able to tell *why* they have or have not failed to accomplish their goals.

The good playgoer recognizes his own personal prejudices and tries to rise above them. He may not care for a given actor or for a particular type of dramatic event, but he does make an effort to judge each honestly by giving every artist his right to work as he chooses.

The audience's final obligation (or perhaps we should say the very first) is to apply Goethe's three key questions, which have already been discussed and are the fundamental premise of our theory of dramatic criticism.

In summary, it is the obligation of the audience:

1. To enter the theatre with an ample supply of imaginary puissance.

2. To recognize its own personal prejudices.

3. To observe and evaluate the work of *all* the artists who have made the production possible.

4. To give each artist the right to express himself as he desires.

5. To ask—always—Goethe's three questions:

What is the artist trying to do?
How well has he done it?
Is it worth the doing?

What Is Art?

In the last several pages we have enumerated some obligations of both theatre and audience. We have not, however, said what art really is or what the artist actually tries to do. Until these questions are answered we shall have no basis for answering Goethe's three questions.

George Jean Nathan once said that if he were the Secretary of Culture he would burn all the books that attempted to define art. Running the risk of such an appointment, we shall try to do just that and begin with three quotations.

Count Leo Tolstoy has said: "Art is a human activity which is passed on to others causing them to feel and experience what the artist has felt and experienced . . . It is a means of communication between people, uniting them in the same feelings. . . . As soon as the spectators and the hearers are affected by the same feelings which the artist felt—that is art."

Aristotle added something by saying: "The aim of art is to represent not the outward appearance of things, but their inward significance; for this, and not the external mannerism and detail, is true reality."

Francis Bacon said: "Art is man added to nature." By a combination of these three quotations we arrive at the definition we propose to use in our theory of dramatic criticism: *Art is life interpreted through a personality.*

With this definition in mind, let us further accept the principle that art consists of three specific areas: substance, form, and technique. *Substance* is the subject, the material or aspect of life which the artist would present. *Form* is the particular art in which he has chosen to speak as well as the shape or structure in which he will create. *Technique* is the method of fitting or blending the substance into the form. It is the artist's personal means of accomplishing his end and involves the selection and arrangement of his materials for a particular effect. It is the element that distinguishes his work from that of other artists creating in the same medium. It is sometimes called his personal style or quality, for it is essentially the artist's projection of himself.

Let us imagine that an individual has had an experience in life that has given him great personal pleasure by affecting him either emotionally or intellectually. It may have been the discovery of a great truth, the realization of a philosophy, the beauty of a sunset, the song of a bird, or some humorous or serious aspect of daily life. In any event, the participant has an all-consuming desire to reproduce that experience so that it can be shared with others. He must first choose the art through which he will speak, and let us further imagine that of all the possible forms he has chosen the drama. Readers of his drama may find in it what he has meant to say, or they may even discover some further experience of their own which they, too, wish to share. They produce the drama and in turn become the actors and technicians who interpret the characters and create the scenery, costumes, lighting, and other theatrical effects, and the director who envisions and supervises the whole production. Some would call them the interpretative artists and the playwright the creative artist. In a literal sense that may be so, but these artists, too, are creative to a very great extent. Certainly this is true if the definition of art that we have chosen is to hold, for each artist can only present a personalized view of his subject. In whatever he does some facet of his thinking, feeling, and background will be present. The tree an artist paints is not nature's tree—it is his. The characters a playwright creates are not life's characters—they are his. St. Joan, Queen Elizabeth, Abraham Lincoln, Mary of Scotland have appeared countless times in literature. Each creation is different, though patterned after the same model, for each is the sum total of the author's impression, technique, and imagination. In the art of acting, twenty Hamlets will be twenty different people though they speak the same lines, for each actor must create the character through his own experiences and personality. Every artist selects and emphasizes just what he desires us, his audience, to see, for we see life through his eyes. As Brooks Atkinson has further written:*

> Out of his imagination, exultance, despair, revolt or passion he creates a world that has his own coherence and submits it as the truth. For the worlds of art are bewilderingly unlike. The tragic world of Sophocles, the tender, reverent world of Michelangelo, the gamy world of Chaucer, Shakespeare's vast world of intelligence and sensibility, the satirical world of Molière, the human world of Dickens, the mad world of Van Gogh and the luminous world of Manet, the noble world of Beethoven and the nervous world of Stravinsky, the electric world of Shaw, the dark world of O'Neill, the gusty world of O'Casey—these are some of the worlds available.

The moment an artist chooses the fine art best suited to his subject, he begins to work with the other two art areas—form and technique. The playwright tells his story within his own chosen framework with characters, dialogue, and theme all slanted to portray life as he wishes us to see it. The actor creates the role in terms of his own physical, emotional, vocal, and intellectual qualifications. The various technicians sustain the mood, project the story, and enhance the production while the director, as a creator, interpreter, and coordinator, translates all these elements into a single and harmonious whole. All work with a single goal—to share an emotion and thus give an audience the most memorable experience possible.

It is only *after* all these artists have made their individual contributions that the theorist studies their work, and from whatever success they have achieved he deduces the principles or rules that will, in turn, become the guide for evaluating the work of future artists. *While rules must never confine art, art does produce rules.* It was not until almost one hundred years after Aeschylus, Sophocles, and Euripides had composed their great tragedies that Aristotle wrote his *Poetics,* which for centuries became the guide for other playwrights.

Shakespeare and his fellow dramatists, during the late sixteenth century, created an entirely new style of playwriting by dis-

---

* Brooks Atkinson, "Note On Art," *The New York Times,* September 9, 1957.

regarding the unities and formal rules of the Greeks. It was then necessary to set up a new formula that would incorporate this new style, and thus the Romantic School was born. So it was with Henrik Ibsen, who in the mid-nineteenth century became the father of the modern realistic drama. Again in our time various playwrights have gone beyond the limits of the realistic theatre to give us some most interesting, imaginative, and successful scripts.

It is these various forms involved in theatre production with which this book is largely concerned. The playwright with his words and meter must speak through what we shall call the elements of drama: theme, plot, dialogue, mood, character, and spectacle. The play he writes will usually, though not always, fall into one of the four general types: tragedy, melodrama, comedy, and farce. His aesthetic style may be classic, realistic, romantic, naturalistic, impressionistic, fantasy, and so on. The structure of his script will be discussed in terms of its exposition, inciting moment, rising action, turning point, falling action, climax, and conclusion. When the script becomes a real play by being brought to life in the theatre before an audience, each contributing artist will express himself through the form and technique of his contribution.

The actor's particular approach concerns the school and method he has chosen, his emphasis on the various technical, intellectual, and emotional areas of acting. The scene designer's form is reflected in the style of his scenery. It may be realism, simplified realism, impressionism, expressionism, or a combination of several. The costumer and the electrician have likewise worked with certain conventions in mind. Even the director will have approached the whole production with an over-all design that encompasses certain principles or traditions. There is no final authority, no absolute standard, in the theatre. Even now we may be entering a new phase of drama history and perhaps even a new kind of dramatic communication. Television, with its techniques and possibilities, could revolutionize or completely alter the course of what we have previously known as theatre.

It should be emphasized that each artist always has the privilege of casting aside the accepted forms and striking out on his own. The only requirement is that the results should be equally or more effective than the generally accepted way of doing it, for the theatre is the most pragmatic of all the arts. What works best *is* best.

The third area that composes art is technique. A devotee of modern music can recognize the style of almost any leading orchestra or musician. A reader of drama, poety, or fiction will detect the hand of a particular writer after reading a few lines or pages. Actors, painters, designers, architects, composers, and all other artists possess a particular and personal manner of presenting their work, of blending their subject with the form in which they speak.

Alexander Dumas, *fils*, the French playwright, once said: "Technique is so important that it sometimes happens that technique is mistaken for art." We are all familiar with those personalities on the stage or in motion pictures or television who depend too much on their technique or showmanship for success. Such artists usually have a very short professional life, for substance and form are more important. Technique without sincerity or meaning is not enough. Very soon the work seems cold, mechanical, and without life. An old actor summed it all up very well when he said: "Ham acting occurs when the actor gets caught using his technique," and the same test might be applied to all art.

It is fundamental to our premise that the dramatic critic must have some knowledge of the various forms and techniques common to drama and theatre production, both past and present. Then, and only then, can he competently and fairly answer the three questions of Goethe.

Empathy and Aesthetic Distance

From the earliest theatre performance there must have been a relationship between two fundamental principles that are inevitable in the aesthetic experience. The exact names given them by our forefathers are unimportant. In more recent times we have come to think of them as *empathy* and *aesthetic distance*. With the coming of the realistic theatre these principles have taken on much greater importance, and in them one may sometimes find the reason for his appreciation or lack of it. *Empathy* means that the spectator experiences what he observes, both muscularly and emotionally. It happens inside him, although he does not suffer the full physical or emotional strain experienced by the characters on the stage. To him it is a vicarious emotion, though he may even to a small degree participate in the same physical action as the actor.*

In contrast to empathy is a detachment that permits the observer's attention to be held and his emotions to be touched, although he is conscious all the while that he is only a spectator. Herbert S. Langfield has called this principle *aesthetic distance*.** Every theatre production has some planned proportion of these two qualities. We must emphasize that emotion is involved in both. Our interest is there, perhaps even in equal degrees, but in one we are physically involved and in the other we are conscious of the fact that we are observing, not experiencing, what we see. We may be subconsciously evaluating it as a work of art.

The motion pictures have long since sensed the value of empathy and aesthetic distance. Every means of playing upon them has been used. Their melodramas have shown as much of the surface realism and personal physical reactions of the actors as was possible through the use of the close-up. Dramatic scenes are brought so close to reality that little is left to the imagination. A glance to right or left during a particularly strong sequence will show the contorted faces of the audience, the twisted handkerchiefs, and sometimes even overt bodily action. If one has been too similarly involved in the situation to make this observation, he need only recall the muscular tension felt when a given scene has dissolved or faded into one that suddenly changed the emotion. The motion picture has likewise found great use for detachment in its musical extravaganzas, huge spectacles, and historical pan-

---

* During a performance of a mystery-melodrama a dignified and austere middle-aged man had become so involved in the situation being enacted that he unconsciously moved forward and raised his arm at the same moment the mysterious hand on the stage came out of the sliding panel. In doing so, he touched the shoulder of the young lady who sat directly in front of him, and she, being equally empathically moved, screamed uncontrollably. The whole impact of the scene was destroyed, for the distraction of her voice suddenly reminded the audience that they were only spectators observing a play.

** Herbert S. Langfield, *The Aesthetic Attitude* (New York: Harcourt, Brace & Co., 1920), Ch. 3.

oramas where it can excel so brilliantly. In a less artistic instance, empathy is evident at an athletic contest. It has been felt at a football game when the spectator's team has the ball within inches of the goal and less than a minute left to play—his neighbors may almost be pushed from the bleachers in his effort to help the home team.

Empathy is not always so muscularly active. Women may empathize in the leading lady and men in the leading man. Likewise, each may subconsciously feel it in his or her attraction for the player of the opposite sex. For this reason, casting in itself becomes a vital issue, for beauty, grace, stature, voice, personality, and contrasts in coloring all take on their own importance in bringing about the proper empathic response to each player.

A danger of empathy is that one's emotion may be suddenly broken as he is snapped out of the situation he has come to accept or believe. This may be caused by a flickering lamp, a forgotten line or missed cue, a false cry or laugh, an extraneous sound, unstable furniture, or a characterization that the audience is unable to believe. Sometimes broken empathy comes from the audience or auditorium through coughing, a contrary reaction to an emotion by some individual, an overheated room, or some exterior element.

Normally, the melodrama will require a greater degree of empathy. Its loosely drawn characters permit the audience a greater leeway in self-identification, and the very nature of the situations carries a greater emotional force. Of the four play types, the least empathy is found in a farce, for here the spectator rarely wishes or needs to identify himself with the situation he observes. To be actually involved in such circumstances might be unpleasant, but observing them in someone else gives the audience a perspective, and this detachment, coupled with a feeling of superiority, brings about the unrestrained laughter that we associate with farce. The same may also be said for very high comedy and satire.

Empathy is found in varying degrees in comedy and tragedy. Both of these types are built on character, and when well written and performed can be so completely individual or removed from

our own experience that there is little opportunity for self-identification and the empathy it supplies.

A play, if it is to accomplish its purpose, must *happen* in the
audience. The degree to which it does happen is of vast importance
and calls for a careful study by each artist, as well as some analysis
by the spectator if he is to maintain a critical attitude.

Aesthetic distance is not the exact opposite of empathy, for it,
too, involves emotional participation, but participation of a different nature. There is less of the muscular and more of the mental
appreciation, although the personal aesthetic pleasure or enjoyment may be equal in degree. In the theatre it is most evident when
we suddenly applaud a splendid piece of acting or a particular
line. It involves recognizing the work of an artist and still believ-
ing in and being a part of a play, all the while conscious that it *is*
a play and make-believe.

Artists have always been aware of the importance of this detachment. A painter puts his picture in a frame; the sculptor
places his statue on a pedestal; the architect chooses to have his
work set off with space about it. The conventional theatre of
today depends upon an elevated stage, a picture frame created
by the proscenium arch, a curtain, a brightly lighted stage, and a
darkened auditorium. It has not always been thus. Aesthetic distance in the Greek and Shakespearean theatres was sustained by
the language, the nobility of the characters, and the more formal
presentation. During both the Elizabethan and the Restoration
periods in England aesthetic distance was largely destroyed when
spectators sat on the stage and oftentimes participated in the action of the play by answering back and injecting their personal
remarks into the production itself. The same has been true in certain periods of other countries. It was David Garrick in England
who restored it in the middle of the eighteenth century, when the
spectators were driven from the stage.

In the eighteenth and nineteenth centuries, before the day of
the realistic theatre, actors acted as actors and audiences appraised
them and their art as individuals. Playwrights often wrote beautiful or dramatic speeches which were, likewise, praised as just that
by the audience. The "tirade" in the French drama and the

"purple passages" in many plays were applauded by the audience just as was the brilliantly played scene by a particular actor. The works of Corneille and Racine are fine examples of this type of theatre. This was purely aesthetic distance, with the artist's art being judged *as* art. Some actors planned on the applause and consciously played for it. The great Sarah Bernhardt was one of these. On the other hand Mrs. Fiske was often very angry when applause broke the scene. She was more interested in the audience's thinking of her as the character she was playing than as the artist playing the role. The same could be said for most of the playwrights who in the late nineteenth and twentieth centuries wrote in the realistic style.

Today much of the criticism we hear of the arena stage comes from those who are distracted by the proximity of the actors or by the spectators who can be seen on the opposite side of the playing arena. In one sense this might be considered a loss of empathic response, but it also is destructive of aesthetic distance.

Some productions today in our conventional type of theatre make use of entrances down the aisles, and even seat some of the actors among the audience. There are those who want to "put the play in the lap of the audience," and undoubtedly some theatre experiences could be enhanced by so doing. *Hellzapoppin,* with Olson and Johnson, still holds some sort of record in this respect. Entertaining as this piece may have been to many people, no one has ever called it artistic. On the other hand, it is possible to use the entire auditorium as an acting area, if the actor can remain a part of the play and keep the proper and predetermined artistic balance of empathy and aesthetic distance. Too close an empathic contact with the production or the participants can prove embarrassing to the audience.

The type, nature, mood, or style of the play determines how much empathy and how much aesthetic distance is to be sought. That answer lies to some extent in the decision of each artist involved, but more especially with the director whose task it is to balance one against the other artistically. This balance is one of the most important aspects of a theatre production. It involves not only selection and arrangement, but the all-important problem of being just real enough to make the audience share with the players the feelings, emotions, and thoughts of the characters, and yet to possess sufficient detachment to weep without real sorrow; in short, to share the emotions without actually experiencing their unpleasant aspects or becoming over-involved in the production. Therein lies much of the theatre's art.

This last paragraph may very well bring us to another element that is as old as the theatre itself, for it has always been present in varying degrees. This is *theatricalism*.

Theatricalism

The meaning of this term is at once obvious. It implies exaggeration, something overdone, life or nature "theatricalized"; and as such it usually carries a negative connotation. Some writers choose to use the word "magnification" and thus partially avoid such a reaction.

Let us consider this very essential factor in all phases of a theatre production in a thoroughly positive sense and define theatricalism as *exaggeration under control*. When used with taste and discrimination, it supplies a spirit or quality that enhances every phase of the production. When misused or uncontrolled it is not only a distraction but can destroy any admirable ideas, emotions, or qualities the production may wish to emphasize.

All theatre is exaggeration, for it must emphasize and project what it is trying to say. Theatre must be bigger than life if it is to reach an audience. Throughout history this exaggeration or theatricalism has exerted both a good and a bad influence, depending entirely on how and by whom it was used. When it has existed for itself alone, as it did in much of our nineteenth century theatre with its artificially painted settings, the affected lines of the sentimental comedies or slick dramas of the Scribe and Sardou schools, and the declamatory acting where bombast and display were given greater importance than thought or feeling, we do have true examples of the showiness, artificiality, and affectation that the word implies in its derogatory connotation.

On the other hand, we have countless examples in the writings of Sophocles, Shakespeare, Molière, Ibsen and others; in the acting of Garrick, Siddons, Kean, Olivier, Barrymore, and Hayes; and in the settings of Jones, Leonardo, Benton, and Oenslager, when true theatricalism was used with supreme imagination and great sensitivity and sincerity. Then it consisted of the honest selection and emphasis by the artist of those elements from life which he wished to point out. In short, life was theatricalized. In these instances the artists have given the audience an enlargement of life's illusion and meaning and furnished the sheer magic, beauty, and aesthetic joy that can be found in the theatre.

Many of us today feel that our modern theatre, with its great emphasis on realism, has lost much of its power because too many of its workers and some of its audience hold too great a fear of the theatrical and look upon it as a plague, rather than the very soul of theatre which it can and should be.

Walter Kerr in *The New York Herald Tribune* has very aptly expressed this theme:*

> "Theatrical" has, in this day and age, very nearly become a dirty word. We have been obsessed with naturalistic stage deportment for so long that we have got ourselves into the paradoxical position of insisting that the theatre be as untheatrical as possible. We have become suspicious of any voice raised above a whisper, or any gesture more emphatic than that required to light a cigarette, of any facial display beyond the casually raised eyebrow. An overt performance seems to be a dishonest one, a mere ragbag of tricks employed by a calculating actor to conceal his interior poverty. In our enthusiasm for the "realistic" method, we have come to equate sincerity with low gear.

The goal of all theatre has been to give what Aristotle called an imitation of an action. That very word "imitation" means that what the audience sees can never be literally the real thing; something must have been altered. That difference is supplied by the artist's personality, imagination, and creativeness. It is this addition that distinguishes theatre from life—theatricalism, or exaggeration under control.

---

* Walter Kerr, "Don Juan in Hell," *New York Herald Tribune*, November 4, 1951.

Even in our most modern and realistic theatre the language used by the playwright, the settings that would attempt to portray locale, the lighting that strives for realism, and the acting that would portray all emotions and movements in the most literal and life-like manner must use artifice or techniques that can only give an illusion of life rather than life itself. The audience is always conscious of being in a theatre, or at least viewing an imagined situation rather than a real one. Both artist and audience are well aware that this theatre–audience–artist combination creates a relationship very different from the circumstances that would exist in real life. The result is the imitation referred to by Aristotle, which we have chosen to call theatricalism.

The feelings and emotions experienced in life and those experienced in the theatre are the same. The methods of obtaining and expressing those emotions and the effects they have on both artist and audience are vastly different. Gassner has defined these two elements as life's reality and as theatrical reality. He describes the latter as making the most of all the theatre's elements rather than trying to hide or deny them.

We have already seen that one of the theatre's obligations is to portray truth—emotional truth. The principle we would now establish is that the best means of projecting that emotional truth is through theatrical reality or exaggeration under control.

Vaudeville, the musical comedy, the circus, the opera and the works of Shakespeare, Molière, and the Greeks never abandoned their theatricality. The clown, Pierrot, and Pierrette, Charlie Chaplin, Hamlet, Oedipus, and Tartuffe are supreme examples of theatricalism. Their emotions are just as real as are the emotions of Willie Loman or the protagonist in a motion picture or television melodrama. Each is theatrical in its own way and in harmony with the dramatic event of which it is a part.

In each of our theatre mediums today there are many artists —playwrights, actors, designers, and directors—who have each in their own way used theatricalism advantageously. Occasionally the motion picture and television screens have given us productions that have been like a breath of fresh air to those of us almost suffocated by the surface realism that would seem to deny the theatre's theatricality. To recognize and appreciate the artistry of those who have successfully given us emotional truth through theatrical reality is no small part of the drama critic's responsibility.

The Theatrical Approach to Theatre Understanding

Now that some basic principles have been discussed, we come to the matter of just what approach should be made to theatre appreciation. Perhaps this is the place to emphasize that this is a book on *theatre*, rather than *drama* understanding only. The drama is a very important part of the theatre, but it is only one aspect. A written script should therefore always be analyzed in terms of the theatre—the limitations, conceptions, goals, possibilities, and hopes that are so much a part of it. With this in mind let us discard the historical and literary approaches to drama, which have both been treated admirably by many capable authors, and deal essentially with the theatrical approach—that is, to the theatre entire, which is a living art, constantly in the process of evolution. The theatrical approach is an art made possible only in the theatre with the aid of actors, technicians, director, and audience, for the theatre is not to be enjoyed like the lyric, the novel, or the essay in cloistered solitude. It requires a large number of nonliterary elements, and involves the contribution of the crafts as well as the arts. In a very real sense a drama or script is not a play until it is produced by actors on a stage before an audience. The theatre is a cooperative art, for only through the genuine cooperation of the playwright, the actor, the technicians, the director, and finally the audience can there exist the thrilling experience that we know as "good theatre."

It has been said that of all the arts drama is the closest to the people, for it speaks the particular language of the men and women for whom it is set down. It expresses their thoughts and their emotions in understandable terms, and reflects their lives. In it man is able to see himself and his fellowmen. When a drama comes to life as a play in the theatre, we are all able to enjoy a vicarious experience, for the tears we shed there are never really bitter tears, nor is the laughter the same that we experience outside the theatre in association with our friends. It is a world of make-believe that only suggests reality.

A student of the theatre will fail to get the whole picture if he does not constantly take into consideration the fact that a play is written to be performed not in the abstract theatre of an idealist's imagination, but in a theatre of a particular period, with the advantages and limitations of its structure and the contributions of many people. Consequently, the student must know something of the nature of the theatre as it existed in the period in which the play was written or performed, and must keep in mind as vividly as possible the appearance, structure, and atmosphere of the playhouse in that day. The Greek, the Elizabethan, and the modern theatre each call for a particular style of play, setting, and acting. For instance, the invention of the electric light has in the last century changed the whole emphasis of the drama, and brought about a corresponding revolution in the principles of judging it.

The actor himself, through his personality, his ability, his physical equipment, and his temperament, can completely alter the whole production. The total effectiveness of a play is the work of a director who, from a lifeless manuscript, temperamental actors, shabby or elegant scenery, and quarrelsome technicians, may create a few hours of life more glamorous and thrilling, more memorable and meaningful, than any similar time spent outside the theatre.

And always, there is the audience, that cosmopolitan group of people with a diversity of background who have gathered to be entertained, moved, thrilled, or uplifted by the combined efforts of author, actor, director, and technician, and who in the last analysis will judge all their efforts as successful or unsuccessful.

This is the thesis of our whole approach to theatre understanding—namely, that the theatre is really made up of five divisions and that a true evaluation or understanding of any dramatic production must take into account each of the five participants involved. These are:

The Audience and Dramatic Criticism
The Play and the Playwright
The Acting and the Actors
The Background and the Technicians
The Direction and the Director

These areas, and all they imply, are the elements of the theatre. Until the theatregoer has recognized and honestly judged the contributions of every artist involved, he has not really seen the play.

— 2 —

The Audience

and Dramatic Criticism

From one very general point of view, any book on theatre appreciation could begin and end with the audience, for each artist has that all-important body in mind at the conception of his idea through its development and realization. It is the audience whose immediate appreciation and sustained attention he seeks, for it is this body that sits in final judgment of his work. To be sure, the artist finds self-satisfaction simply in creating, in giving an outward expression to the idea, vision, or sound that he has himself known. However, equally important is his desire as an artist to share with his fellow men this joy or ecstasy. The playwright must put it down on paper; the actor must memorize and interpret the lines; the scene designer creates and supervises the background;

32

the electrician and costumer must light and dress the production according to its mood or spirit; and finally, the director must coordinate the work of all into an artistic unit. Each must first have a vision and then express himself creatively. The original desire to share is soon coupled with an equal hope for approval.

Few artists work solely for their own enjoyment. Much as they may deny it, they are hoping for public approval. However, they may not desire material or financial success so much as an understanding and appreciation of what they are trying to do. The artist in the theatre dare not appeal to a single class or segment of society who might more easily understand his language because of its own experience or education. He must always make his appeal to the crowd, who in its make-up, its thinking, its emotional response, and its approval or disapproval is far different from the individuals or small groups to whom many artists in other fields can direct their efforts. The playwright, the actor, and the director must never forget or neglect the audience. And yet this very essential element has been forgotten far too often, or its importance minimized.

The true lover of the theatre considers it a democratic institution that belongs fundamentally to the people. He would criticize just as severely the producers or directors who always cater to the lower dramatic taste and conceive the theatre to exist only as escape as he would those who would sacrifice entertainment and cry out for only intellectual drama or theatre with a message. One is as much in error as the other. The first may talk of "giving them what they want" and "show business," while the other cries out for "art theatre" or "social significance." The former too often demands nothing of his audience, and the latter frequently asks too much. Each is eventually faced with a disappointed and steadily diminishing audience.

The joy of being part of an audience in a crowded theatre at that moment when the lights are dimmed and the curtain rises to disclose a whole new imaginative world is a memorable and thrilling experience. The full house is important not from the viewpoint of the box office alone, vital as that may be, but because that audience is as much a part of the whole production as any individual artist or his contribution. Radio and television usually lack this great advantage of the stage.

Those who choose the theatre fare—regardless of the medium —are faced with a continuous compromise, a constant balancing of the cultural, the intellectual, the artistic, the experimental, and the popular. There is always a place in the theatre for such critics as Eric Bentley, who deplores the popular seemingly because it is popular. We need experimentalists who may envision a new theatre just as did Shakespeare and Ibsen. There is a place for a Brecht, who would break with the basic principle of "illusion" as this book understands the theatre to be. Fry and Eliot, with their poetic freshness, are glorious additions to a prose-stricken drama. But at the same time, it would be folly to look with scorn upon the work of Kaufman, Coward, Krasna, Behrman, Anderson, Williams, Miller, and Hammerstein. It is not only the popularity of their offerings that should be praised; it is their genius at catching the temper of this mass audience and translating it into theatre that is just a little better than they have known before. They, and many like them, may not possess qualities their detractors would have them possess, but they have done a great service in finding new recruits and creating in them an enthusiasm for the theatre.

Psychologists have pointed out that audiences have certain characteristics that make them different from collections of individuals. This principle has been further treated by John Mason Brown* and also by Clayton Hamilton in his essay, "The Psychology of Audiences."** Following is a summation of the metamorphosis which takes place when the average man becomes part of an audience:

> He loses his higher and more personal sensibilities of intellect
>   or character;
> . . . is less intellectual and more emotional;
> . . . is less reasonable and judicious;
> . . . descends several rungs in the ladder—he demands a

---

* John Mason Brown, *The Art of Playgoing* (New York: W. W. Norton & Company, Inc., 1936), pp. 113-137.
** Clayton Hamilton, *Theory of the Theatre* (New York: Henry Holt & Company, Inc., 1939), pp. 18-32.

struggle, is boyishly heroic, carelessly unthinking, easily credulous;

. . . wants to take sides, to hiss, or to applaud;

. . . finds that emotion is contagious, does what his neighbor does;

. . . is more sensuous, loves costumes, color, spectacle;

. . . is more commonplace; demands the love of woman, home, country, right;

. . . is more conservative;

. . . is a little hard of hearing;

. . . is unpredictable.

This theatre audience has been divided into three extremes—the Escapists, the Moralists, and the Artsakists. The escapists want only to forget the responsibilities and problems of their everyday life. They ask only to be amused, and clamor for the lighter plays or musicals. They are referred to as "tired businessmen," although they are found in all professions and sometimes, surprisingly enough, among our most brilliant minds.

Not long after *Death of a Salesman* had completed its road tour, a professor from a large university was heard to condemn it. It had haunted him for days, and he seemed not to be able to put it out of his mind. When asked why he had not liked the play, his answer was: "It had nothing to say." Those within hearing were quick to point out that it said a great deal, with its theme showing that lives built on shallow and ethically unsound foundations will be doomed to failure. The professor readily agreed that he had found all that in the play, but that what troubled him was that there were too many people exactly like that in America. This was an even more astonishing revelation, for it meant that he had completely shut his eyes and mind to the fact that people might sense the theme and realize their own errors. Then came the answer that could have been foreseen had it not come from so distinguished an educator: "To tell you the truth, when I go to the theatre, I want something light and entertaining."

What even this professor did not realize was that "entertain" need not only mean amuse, for it is derived from the Latin word *tenere*, which means "to hold." Consequently, tragedy may be equally as "entertaining" as farce. What he meant was that his only demand so far as the theatre was concerned was "escape."

The second group includes those who demand that the theatre must always uplift, teach a lesson, preach a sermon, picture some part of life of which they personally approve. They would close their eyes to anything with which they did not agree, and insist that only "beautiful and nice clean plays be presented." We find these persons in every community, and they are one of the greatest problems of the director in the noncommercial theatre. Either they blind themselves to the fact that evil does exist in the world, or they refuse to accept the theatre as a reflection of life. In either instance, they are being honest neither with themselves nor with the artists whom they would criticize. This is the group we call "moralists."

The third extreme is made up of those theatregoers who insist on "art for art's sake." They shudder at box-office success, and disdainfully refer to all popular theatre as "show business." They deny that the theatre belongs to the people and would claim it for their own little esoteric groups. They smugly infer that popularity with an audience is only an ingredient of mediocrity and far beneath the true artist. These individuals, whom we call the "art-sakists," like to think of themselves as intellectuals.

To please these three extremes and the millions who lie between is not an easy task, but they all make up that audience out front for whom every theatre artist is working. In *The Art of Playgoing* John Mason Brown says:*

> Stand at the entrance to any theatre when the audience is assembling; look into its multitudinous face; study its varying expressions; attempt to gauge the separate minds which are mere cells in its composite brain; think of the conflicting interests, perceptions, backgrounds, vocabularies, sympathies, standards, convictions, consciences, and levels of sophistication from which his giant body is sprung, and the challenges and difficulties faced by dramatists in presenting such situations, ideas, and characters

---

* John Mason Brown, *The Art of Playgoing* (New York: W. W. Norton & Company, Inc., 1936), pp. 126-27.

as will be comprehensible and acceptable to the crowd even when they are satisfactorily meeting our own quite different individual demands, will be made clearer for us than any textbook or dramatic technique has ever been able to make them.

The variety of what this audience may most appreciate is unlimited. Some may desire the lines of Sophocles or Shakespeare, and others the lines of today's most popular motion picture actress. One may choose a play that propagandizes some religious or social theme, and another an historical romance or biography. To some a line of pretty chorus girls backed by spectacular scenery and accompanied by lively music may have a far greater appeal than the latest tragedy by Miller or poetic drama by T. S. Eliot. One may clamor for revivals of the classics or a dramatization of a famous novel, while his neighbor would prefer the naturalness of Chekhov or the repartee of Noel Coward. There are always those in attendance who would find their greatest pleasure in the preachments of Shaw, the epic theatre of Brecht, the searchings of Pirandello, the time relativity or fourth-dimensional philosophy of J. B. Priestley, or the intellectual challenge demanded of the theatre by Eric Bentley. Practically every theatre audience will include some shading of all these individuals.

The complexity of this all-powerful and cosmopolitan group becomes even more important when we take into consideration the effect they have on any dramatic performance. Every artist who has worked even casually in the theatre knows that the success of a performance is as dependent upon the audience as it is on any individual, from the playwright to the director. The audience must be psychologically right for the play. Robert Sherwood proved on numerous occasions his great ability to sense the pulse of the public. Elmer Rice has in as many instances been just enough ahead of his time to miss the success he has eminently deserved as a dramatist.

No one in the past two centuries was able to make a success of Shakespeare's *Richard II* until in the mid-thirties Maurice Evans sensed the times and gave us one of his most memorable and popular productions just after another English king had abdicated his throne to marry an American woman. On three different occasions in three major cities the author witnessed this production. In each case it was a majestic piece of theatre art that will live in memory, but it was the third performance that will be remembered as the most ecstatic. On that evening everything was electric, from the opening curtain throughout. Even after the curtain calls had been taken and the house lights were on, the audience continued to applaud. Mr. Evans spoke to a small group after that performance. He was as exhilarated as though it were an opening night, although he had played the role for more than four hundred performances and had been lauded by every critic across the country. In answer to the enthusiastic praise, Mr. Evans said: "How could anyone do otherwise with an audience out front like that one?"

If artists of this calibre find the attitude and response of the audience so important, then we as theatregoers should certainly take its contributions into account as we consider the over-all production. The effect of the audience is most easily realized in the motion picture theatre. Ilka Chase tells a story of her grandmother, who never failed to see many times any motion picture in which Miss Chase appeared. It was not uncommon for this little old lady to complain to Miss Chase: "You didn't do nearly as well today as you did the last time I saw it." Without her realizing it, the audience response had affected her judgment of the performance. In this way even in the motion picture no two performances are ever exactly the same. The artists of the production may be constant, but the audience reaction alters the total effect. On the stage there is the further variation due to the subtle changes in the work of the artists involved, and there an even greater responsibility lies with the audience. Howard Lindsay has elaborated on this point in an article which appeared in *The New York Times*. (See Chapter 6, pages 190-92, where this article is quoted in its entirety.)

We must come to the conclusion, therefore, that any critical analysis of a dramatic production where an audience is present must include our estimate of that audience and its contribution to the total effect. This estimate should include our answers to the following questions: What sort of people in general make up the audience? What class do they represent—chronologically, socially, and mentally? Have they come with the proper imaginary puissance, or with the "show me" attitude? Have they displayed an interest and appreciation? Do they seem to understand the play and what the various artists are trying to do? Is their interest held throughout the performance? Is there a definite response of tears, laughter, applause, or silence? Are they emotionally moved, or bored? Do they cough, show restlessness, leave during the performance? Is the applause spontaneous, or politely perfunctory? To the people of what type, group, or age does the play make its greatest appeal? Would you advise your friends to see it and why?

For in the final reckoning of any dramatic production the audience is both the master and the teacher of every artist whose contribution has helped to make up that production.

Pitfalls in Analyzing Dramatic Productions

The theatre has always suffered, and perhaps always will, from the criticism of the inept and inexperienced. Every man, woman, and child considers himself a just critic of what he has witnessed in a theatre. Though each may hesitate to discuss the worth of a musical composition, a painting, the lines of a cathedral, or any of the other arts, none will hesitate a moment to evaluate a dramatic production. He will speak glibly of the play and the acting and oftentimes the setting. This is perhaps the price the theatre must pay for speaking the language of the common man.

One of the dangers in amateur criticism involves a desire to be clever, to say the smart thing or to play with words. The young critic with a pen in his hand and the opportunity to pass judgment often overestimates his own importance. Essential as it is to develop a personal style and to report honestly and frankly his own opinion, it is a basic principle that the critic is not supposed to be creative. It is his duty as a reporter to comment only on what he has seen or heard and to evaluate what in his opinion the artists have accomplished. George Jean Nathan is noted for the fact that he invariably disagrees with the majority opinion, but he has contributed much to the thinking and analysis of our theatre. He has wisely said that the greatest value of dramatic criticism is in the fact that it produces criticism of criticism. When we disagree with an opinion we delve deeper into our thinking to prove the fallacy of that opinion or to substantiate our own.

If a production does not measure up to the artistic standards the artists involved have set for themselves, then we as part of the audience are justified in saying so. The annals of professional criticism are filled with devastating comments by sharp-witted critics who had found the event less than satisfying. On the morning after Tallulah Bankhead's opening performance of *Antony and Cleopatra* John Mason Brown wrote: "Tallulah Bankhead barged down the Nile as Cleopatra last night—and sank." There is also the well-known comment of another critic: "I should not attempt to criticize last night's performance because I saw it under adverse conditions. The curtain was up." Regarding Mae West's performance in *Catherine Was Great* John Chapman said: "The play is a bust, which is one more than Miss West needs."

Clever as these remarks may seem, and apt as they may have been, they do *not* constitute dramatic criticism. Even though they come from the pens of some of our most noted critics, they may be classified under the pitfall of attempting to be clever. Unless some honest reason for the opinion is presented they represent an unjust approach to dramatic criticism. The witty novice in theatre knowledge may often fall into this faulty approach, wisecracking at the expense of analyzing.

The second danger in dramatic criticism lies in the fact that the critic so often cites picayune details or minor accidents in performance rather than searching for the real dramatic values. If ever the old expression about not seeing the forest for the trees is applicable, it is here. The untrained critic will pounce on such small items as a fluffed line, a delayed light cue, a property not wholly authentic, some slight discrepancy in make-up, a ravelling on a costume, or some similar detail not worthy of mention. If such items in the total picture have been so numerous or so blatant as to denote carelessness on the part of the artists or to take precedence over plot, theme, acting, setting, or direction, that is another story. In that case, adverse criticism is justified, although the details themselves need not be mentioned individually.

First nights in any theatre are often chaotic affairs. The nervousness of the entire company and the importance of the event often produce many unforeseen accidents, but the first-line critics never allow these to sway their opinion of the production as a whole. On one New York opening the leading character blacked out during the climactic scene of the play and toppled from his chair to the floor. The son hurried to him with an impromptu line: "Dad, what's the matter? Are you ill?" Members of the cast improvised lines as he was helped back to his chair. After a few moments he recovered enough to complete the scene, but not before the entire audience had realized that this was not a part of the production. On the following morning only one of the nine leading critics even so much as referred to the incident in his notice, and he merely indicated that "Mr. X seemed not to be well last evening but turned in a splendid performance."

This second danger may very easily lead into a third that is typical especially of the novice, although there are seasoned playgoers and professional critics who often seem to have succumbed to it as well. I refer to those persons who never really enjoy a dramatic event because they have become so involved in looking for something wrong that they miss the more valuable points of the art itself. They are the unfortunate souls who have the same trouble as the man in E. B. White's verse:*

> The critic leaves at curtain fall
> To find, in starting to review it,
> He scarcely saw the play at all
> For watching his reactions to it.

The intelligent playgoer soon finds that this is only an early phase in his development. Soon he ceases to think of details and begins to study the play as a whole. Then criticism will take its logical place and become a factor in greater theatre enjoyment. He likewise soon becomes aware that the word "criticism" need not mean adverse. The honest critic also praises.

Now that we have discovered three dangers that may stand in

---

* Copr. 1925, *The New Yorker Magazine, Inc.*

the way of dramatic criticism, let us turn to a more positive approach.

Essences of Dramatic Criticism

George Jean Nathan once said: "Dramatic criticism is an attempt to formulate rules of conduct for that lovable, wayward, charming, wilful vagabond that is the drama."* This definition is most acceptable for our purpose because it is exactly what we are trying to do throughout these pages. The task, however, is a formidable one, especially when we examine the dramatic criticism of both past and present.

Some critics would give their major consideration to the drama itself, and even then from many different and varied angles. Others would only ask that the drama give them an exciting and enriching theatrical experience. Still another group would measure its success not by any artistry, but solely on its popular appeal to any audience.

In a very real sense dramatic criticism can be said to exist on at least three levels, which we shall define as the literary, the theatrical, and the practical. This distinction could be considered somewhat similar to the three extremes that make up the theatre audience, which were discussed on the previous pages.

The literary approach, sometimes called the Aristotelian, is interested primarily in the literary value inherent in the drama itself. Some critics have been most interested in its philosophical or sociological aspects. They would be principally concerned with its impact and contributions in respect to the individual's life and his relationship to the world, his problems and associations with his fellow men. Others have had more interest in the academic aspects of the script that concern the structure of the drama itself—the relationship of form and style or the techniques each artist has used to weld together the substance and form. Others give greater thought to the language of the drama, its characterizations, or its theme.

---

* George J. Nathan, *The Critic and the Drama* (New York: Alfred A. Knopf, Inc., 1922), p. 51.

A further analysis is made from the viewpoint of history. This would take into account the period in which the drama was written and first performed; the size and shape of the physical theatre; and the evolution of the playing area and seating arrangement, as well as the varying demands and moods of the audience during the centuries of the theatre's existence.

In any instance, this first level of dramatic criticism is primarily concerned with the written drama or the work of the playwright, and such an evaluation would be less interested in either its theatrical effectiveness or its popularity with the majority of the audience.

The second level is more interested in what the theatre can do for the drama when it becomes a play; how well it acts; what its psychological impact can be in the theatre. Its followers evaluate the script as a theatre piece as well as a literary work. As aestheticians they are primarily interested in the magic that can be experienced in the theatre through its creativeness and the artistic use of imagination, lighting, scenery and sound, for their interest lies in the beauty it can bring and the effect, aesthetically, it can have on mankind.

The third level is concerned primarily with the practical theatre whose first interest is in making money through the attraction of great crowds. This approach is sometimes referred to as Shubertian or mere "show business." The name is derived from the famous New York producers who for many years made a business of the theatre. It is the criterion used by the publication *Variety*, whose sole test of whether a play is a failure or a success depends on whether the final box-office figures are red or black. The critics who view a production on this level are interested purely in its popular appeal. They demand exciting entertainment, which usually means escape. They insist on attracting great crowds. The theatre they endorse must cater to the masses and could sometimes be accused of sacrificing integrity and truth for popularity and appeal. It is the criticism we hear most frequently of the Broadway theatre, as well as of the motion picture and television.

If Goethe's theory of art criticism is to be our premise, then our effort to formulate rules of dramatic criticism must recognize and evaluate all these various levels—the greatness in drama, the creation of aesthetic enjoyment through theatrical magic, and popular entertainment. It is our conviction that all are occasionally found in a single production; that sometimes none is present and that more often than not there are variations of values even on the same level; that a vulgar piece often pretends to be better than it really is; and that tinsel, spectacle, and applause can often mislead us.

As a first step in formulating a specific approach to dramatic criticism we would refer to John Dolman and his emphasis on the necessity of a critic considering what he calls the seven pillars of the fine arts: *Unity, Emphasis, Rhythm, Balance, Proportion, Harmony,* and *Grace.** Throughout the book these items will be referred to from time to time in reference to the techniques of individual artists. Certainly any critic must have a knowledge and make some application of each in his evaluation of a dramatic production. Here we shall attempt only to define them. Although each does possess a special meaning of its own, there is an inevitable overlapping.

Unity, as the name implies, is a oneness—a singleness of purpose. It would be absurd to place eighteenth century costumes in front of a realistic modern setting. If a director proposes to do Shakespeare in modern dress, he must have sufficient imagination to convey it throughout the production. Plays have been seriously criticized because they lacked a unity in style. The third act of *Our Town,* by Thornton Wilder, was so abrupt a break in this respect that it has never won the wholehearted approval of many authorities. The same is true of *Liliom* by Molnar.

Emphasis is a pointing up or stressing of important points—a singling out of that which is most vital. It may be accomplished by movement, line, mass, color, force, or any other means the artist may wish to employ. Unity and emphasis together afford the most effective means of eliminating both distraction and monotony, the two enemies of attention. In so doing they bring into focus what we call primary or involuntary attention—that which we give automatically and without any effort whatsoever. Its counterpart is sec-

---

* John Dolman, Jr., *The Art of Play Production* (New York: Harper & Brothers, 1946), pp. 54-72. Copyright, 1928, by Harper & Brothers.

ondary or voluntary attention to which we must force ourselves The theatre must always command involuntary attention only.

Rhythm is the recurrence of the accented beat. Rhythm is constantly a part of us—in our breathing, the beating of the heart, the days of the week, the seasons of the year. All are rhythmical, and man knows full contentment when he is in complete rhythm with his surroundings. When he is not, only a sense of "not belonging" can exist. In the theatre we are more conscious of rhythm when it ceases to exist than we are when it is there. A fluffed line, an awkward pause, a break in the flow of the play, too long a wait for an audience reaction, all make one suddenly aware that something has gone wrong. It is this element of rhythm that makes comedy so much more difficult to play than a serious play, for the overt reaction of those out front becomes a part of the over-all rhythm and that may change—if ever so slightly—from performance to performance. Actors must constantly be making adjustments to audience reaction.

Balance and *Proportion* are so closely related that it is difficult to make a distinction. They both indicate an equalizing of forces one against the other. Although it is not wholly true, we do sometimes—at least in the theatre—think of balance as being more visual, and proportion as a quantitative relationship. Using this connotation, we might consider balance as it relates to the stage setting and furniture arrangement, the symmetry and use of line, mass and color in décor. *Proportion* may then be considered the relation of theme to plot, music to story, the two contending forces in the play's conflict, etc. The old melodramas, for example, fall down in proportion because they so "stacked the cards" against the villain and in favor of the hero or heroine.

Harmony is a term with which we are all familiar. In the theatre it is the happy and smooth coordination of all phases of production so that nothing interferes with the basic meaning and purpose of the play. It is the ultimate objective of the artistic dramatic production.

Grace implies the ease and facility with which each artist executes his work and masks his technique. No real art ever shows effort.

Requisites for the Dramatic Critic

The cardinal rule for the beginner in dramatic criticism should be to have some valid reason for whatever opinion he may express. This may not be quite so essential for the critic who has attained a reputation in his field, but all dramatic critics should meet certain tests, and those in this discussion have been paraphrased from the work of the late Bernard Shaw, who was an eminent critic himself before he became better known as the leading English playwright of the twentieth century. To criticize the theatre intelligently Shaw says the good dramatic critic should possess:

1. An awareness of his own prejudices.
2. Some knowledge of the theatre and dramatic history.
3. A sense of the theatre and an appreciation of its possibilities.
4. Some honest standard of theatre evaluation that includes both taste and discrimination.
5. An understanding of the form and techniques involved in the work of each artist in the theatre.

There are many fine professional critics at work in America today. Four with whom the reader should be familiar are Brooks Atkinson of *The New York Times*, Eric Bentley of *The New Republic*, John Gassner, Sterling Professor of Playwriting at Yale University, free-lancer, and our most prolific writer on the theatre, and Walter Kerr of the *New York Herald Tribune*. To familiarize one's self with the writings of such capable men can be most helpful if one wishes to understand the problems of written criticism. It is doubtful if these four topflight critics would completely agree on any production, for each has developed his own standard of evaluation and sees different values in the same event.

Brooks Atkinson, with his fairness, integrity, insight, understanding of the theatre's conventions, and great ability to speak in understandable terms, always sets a high standard of appreciation and demands the best of all those who work in the theatre. He came into the theatre via the journalistic route and is considered the Dean of American theatre critics. He always places great stress on substance and idea. A cornerstone of his whole critical standard is that the play should be optimistic in tone and should show one's genuine faith or respect for mankind with love for his fellow men. He can find greatness in a play because it does profess such a faith, and still be critical of its form. He might criticize another because it lacks that faith in mankind, but recognize the fact that it is very well constructed. He can praise the plot and characterization as well as the theatrical effectiveness, but criticize the fact that it leaves the audience at a dead end, frustrated and in a dilemma. He may praise the inconsequential *Blithe Spirit* or *The Man Who Came to Dinner* as fine pieces of theatre but regret that they lack substance. In fact, Mr. Atkinson has called Noel Coward the "master of the inconsequential." Mr. Atkinson, who seems always to be looking for the best that he can find, would consider a second-rate piece of art with something to say preferable to a first-rate play of diversion.

Eric Bentley, the youngest of the group, received his training in dramatic literature and seems not to have yet developed the "theatre sense" that Mr. Atkinson considers so necessary to dramatic criticism. He is primarily a literary man and a scholar. To him the written drama is by all odds the most important aspect of the whole dramatic experience. This has made him most critical of many current successes. If the play does not read well and thus possess the greatness of drama, he cannot accept its success as a theatrical piece or its popularity with the audience. He has been highly critical of most New York successes, including *Oklahoma* and most of Rodgers and Hammerstein, on this count. He argues that great literary periods are remembered for their playwrights and dramas and not for their theatrical productions. A good play or production, to him, is only as good as the drama on which it is based. He envisions the theatre as an intellectual haven in preference to an emotional one, and thus discounts the values of theatricality. He expects the drama to be a moral and aesthetic force and deplores the work of the playwright who writes chiefly with an audience in mind.

John Gassner is known for the brilliance of his mind, his knowledge of seemingly all subjects and their history, and the constant challenge he demands of the theatre, whose inherent values and weaknesses he understands so well. He is a liberal in that he seems to be ever looking for a new way of approaching or interpreting theatre values. More than any other critic he is able to go to the very heart of the play and find its value as literature *or* as theatre. His vast knowledge of both makes for exciting reading. Of the four perhaps his reaction to a production is the most difficult for one to prophesy.

Walter Kerr, who has been a Broadway playwright and director as well as an actor and college professor of theatre, has a grasp and knowledge of what the drama can be in the theatre. Few critics understand the art of acting and directing as well as he. It is this background, coupled with his flair for expression and his high standards in all phases of production, that make his writing so interesting and so challenging. As can readily be understood, he and Mr. Bentley are poles apart in any critical analysis. Mr. Kerr is a theatre man and as such understands and recognizes the audience as the real master of the theatre. He has faith in that audience and places great stress on the importance of the play's popularity. He has respect for Broadway and its ability to do great things. His "theatre sense" is highly developed, and he sees the drama as a work of art that has not realized itself until it has been successfully done in the theatre. He measures greatness by audience appeal, though he consistently demands integrity, proportion, and clarity in every production. He is convinced that the minority theatre has never produced an important work, and that every great play has come out of a popular playhouse.

With so many imponderables and so much opinion involved, it must already be evident that general agreement on the value of any work of art is well nigh impossible, for all are measured through the imagination, background, personal experiences, and taste of each individual. Furthermore, the world of art is often very complex as it probes the mental, emotional, and spiritual areas of the characters involved and of the observer. The higher the level, the more deeply it delves into the human personality; the deeper it goes, the wider and more unpredictable the response. Two individuals will naturally have widely differing opinions, but each should also have *some reason for his belief*. It should be one of the greatest thrills of the true teacher when a student feels he can and does disagree on the literary or dramatic worth of a given piece, if that student is able to justify his opinion in the light of some valid principles.

This variability is our greatest asset in the field of the arts, for we live in a world where two and two do not always equal four. Various artists may give different interpretations to the same lines, and each be correct from his own view of the role; no two authors will express the same thought in the same manner; no two designers or directors give us the same setting or production, and certainly no two critics receive the same impression. It is this ever-present freshness that makes the theatre so completely entrancing and so ever new. Nor must we forget that each individual has a *right* to his own opinion regarding any phase of the theatre, but that view takes on greater significance if he has sound reasons on which to base his opinion.

Thus far we have discussed the "requisites" of a dramatic critic, and have been concerned with his knowledge, his background, his understanding, his experience and his honesty—those elements he brings to the theatre with him. Let us now consider his duties or obligations as he criticizes a specific production.

If the young critic is called upon to present a written criticism he can benefit from some further advice: he should never tell the story of the performance upon which the report is being made. It is possible to tell the theme and maybe even what the play is about. At no time should any information be revealed that will mar the enjoyment for one who reads the criticism before seeing the event. This would mean, also, that the critic should take it for granted that the reader has not seen the performance. It is always wise to avoid the use of technical or dramatic terms that are not generally known by the average reader.

A critic should always be as objective as possible in his reporting. Where emotion is involved objectivity is very difficult, but the critic should at least report the reaction of the audience—especially if it has differed from his own. He need not mention everyone concerned, but should single out individual efforts that were outstanding in one way or another. Fundamentally, a critic is judging the play and the production on the basis of his own response or reactions to it. It is his duty to be didactic, to make up his mind, to speak his feelings whatever they may be honestly, forthrightly, sincerely.

While a dramatic evaluation may carry more weight because it appears in the morning paper, and seem more authentic due to the prestige of the writer, it is not necessarily more honest or of greater value than that of the average theatregoer if that individual possesses some basic theatre knowledge and has conscientiously followed either the suggestions here listed or some other honest set of principles on dramatic criticism.

Ten points can be of help to the dramatic critic. Of these "Ten Commandments of Dramatic Criticism" the first five have to do with the critic himself, and the last five with the work of the artists he would evaluate. (Many of these items may not, at this moment, be wholly clear, but the remainder of the book proposes to give an explanation of these statements and the many techniques and principles that they involve.)

Ten Commandments of Dramatic Criticism

1. I must constantly, in all my theatre experience, use imaginary puissance.

2. I must know, understand, evaluate, and discount my own prejudices.

3. I must evaluate each of the five areas and the work of all artists involved in the production.

4. I must measure the entire production in terms of life and understand what each artist has personally contributed through and of himself to make or mar the production.

5. I must arrive at every decision only after using Goethe's three principles of artistic criticism.

6. Each and every artist must make crystal clear what he is trying to say through proper emphasis, sincerity, and technique.

7. Each and every artist must work within the medium at hand

THE AUDIENCE AND DRAMATIC CRITICISM

or successfully adapt any elements borrowed from another medium.

8. Each and every artist must cooperate and coordinate his work toward a single goal which is, in turn, the theme or the purpose of the production.

9. Each and every artist must seem real and be wholly believable in his contribution to this production that is a work of art; in short, each must give a picture of life interpreted through his personality.

10. In the final analysis the production may move me, stir me, excite me, amuse me, teach me or transform me, but the one thing it *dare not do* is to bore me. The one thing it *must do* is send me on my way somehow better equipped to face life.

All the verbs used in commandment number ten have been carefully chosen, for it is a basic tenet of our particular theory of dramatic criticism that the theatre exists on several planes and can be many things to many people. There is ample room in our world of theatre for both *Ten Little Indians* and *Waiting for Godot*, for *Auntie Mame* and *Long Day's Journey Into Night*, for *Charley's Aunt* and *Mother Courage*, for *Three Men On A Horse* and *Hamlet*, for *Blithe Spirit* and *Oedipus Rex*, and for all the levels that lie in between.

As individuals we might prefer the theatre that gives us more than mere escape, but at times we might also profit from some purely escapist dramatic fare. We might favor the theatre that is a teacher and an art, but we would not dismiss that which only attempts to amuse or to excite. The release of these emotions can also send us on our way better equipped to face life.

— 3 —

The Play

and the Playwright

*W*ebster defines *drama* as "a composition in prose or verse portraying life or character by means of dialogue and action and designed for theatrical performance," while at least one definition of *play* is "the stage representation of a drama." In an average conversation the two words are often used interchangeably, and the author of a drama is called a playwright as well as a dramatist. This is understandable, for the natural goal of most dramatists is to have their work receive a satisfactory stage production.

The understanding of theatre and drama are two different fields. A novice will soon begin to distinguish between the drama as a work to be read and the play as a production to be seen in the theatre. Although this book is primarily concerned with the play as a theatre piece we must realize that it is also drama, and at least in this chapter deal with the literary approach.

A play has been described as a trap in which the characters are either falling into an inevitable situation or struggling to get out of one. Like many such clever remarks, this soon proves to lack the depth or stature that a definition should possess. It does not go far enough to embrace completely either the theatre or the drama.

Early in the century Clayton Hamilton gave us a definition that is sufficiently comprehensive. If studied carefully, it encompasses an entire theory of the theatre and furnishes a very practical philosophy of dramatic criticism. It is this definition that should be memorized and understood for the remainder of this discussion: *"A play is a story devised to be presented by actors on a stage before an audience."* We shall continue to borrow from Mr. Hamilton's book, *The Theory of the Theatre,** in an attempt to justify briefly each of the five facets included in his definition.

"A play is a story . . ." needs little development, for a play, like the ballad, the novel, the short story, the epic, or any other piece of narrative literature, does have as its chief purpose the telling of a series of incidents that involve certain characters and march forward toward a climax and a conclusion.

". . . devised to be presented . . ." In this second phrase the play departs from all other forms of literature. In choosing the words to be spoken by his characters and in the construction of the conflicts to be presented, the dramatist must continually be conscious of how they will sound rather than of how they will read. Unlike other literary men, he must forego description and translate his thoughts into action and movement, for in addition to the literary quality, the dramatist must consider the pictorial effect, the rhythm of speech, the setting, the properties, the acting, and numerous other arts involved in a production. As a corollary to his writing, the successful playwright must know the limitations of the theatre. This is perhaps the reason that our greatest dramatists—Sophocles, Shakespeare, Molière, and Ibsen—have been men of the theatre, while other great men of literature, such as Scott, Wordsworth,

---

* Clayton Hamilton, *The Theory of the Theatre* (New York: Henry Holt & Company, Inc., 1939), pp. 3-17.

Shelley, Browning, and Tennyson, not versed in the theatre, were able to write only secondary plays, or drama for reading rather than for acting. These plays have been termed "closet dramas."

The playwright must remember that in the theatre the listener is moved by the emotion of the moment and is seldom able to study the language carefully enough to ascertain its full literary quality, although this attribute will add greatly to its permanence and the possibility of its being seen by future generations. Nearly all the greatest dramas of the ages have been great literature as well as good theatre, but a glance at the popular plays of the day, or those with long-run records, will show that literary worth is not of primary importance for momentary success. Any theatre critic realizes that it is unjust to condemn or praise a playwright on his literary value *alone*.

"... *by actors* ..." Here the dramatist is faced with two problems. First, the characters he creates must be vital and interesting individuals with active, dynamic personalities. Not every man or woman of our acquaintance will fit into a play as a character. Each must have a will and a purpose. There must usually be a conflict between men to make a play. Unlike the characters in a novel, the people on the stage must constantly be doing or saying something and reveal themselves through their own acts or lines rather than by exposition on the part of the author or by speeches of the other actors.

Second, the playwright is governed by the actors who are available at the time he creates his roles. It has been said that the plays of a period are no better than the actors available to play in them. Whether or not this is wholly true, we do know that great plays are often written for great actors. Our best argument that Richard Burbage was an excellent actor is found in the fact that Shakespeare wrote for him such roles as Hamlet, Romeo, Macbeth, Othello, and King Lear.

The story is told that when the great Talma lay on his deathbed in France early in the nineteenth century, a young man came to him with the first act of a play. Talma heard the reading of it and in great excitement entreated the young playwright to hurry home and complete it at once. "Here," he said, "is a romantic play fitted to my own talents. No Frenchman has yet been able to succeed in this style, and I have had to appear in translations of Shakespeare all my life. Hurry and finish the play before it is too late." The young man wrote frantically day and night, but before the drama was completed, Talma was dead. The young man was Victor Hugo and the play *Oliver Cromwell*, but no actor has ever been wholly successful in the part, for it was too tailored to the special acting talents of Talma.

Coquelin, for whom Rostand wrote *Cyrano de Bergerac*, did much to mold the character we now know so well. The plays of Sardou were modelled to fit the unique abilities of Sarah Bernhardt. In addition to her magnificent voice, we are told that she superbly portrayed three particular emotions—she could make ardent love; she could be most vindictive; and she could die beautifully. In every play for which she was famous she was given the opportunity to do those three things, and few of the plays for which she is best remembered have been as successful when played by other actresses. Rostand took *L'Aiglon* off the boards and rewrote it to fit Sarah Bernhardt's talents when on the opening night she, as the little Prince, stole the show from Coquelin.

The delightful plays of J. M. Barrie were modelled to the winsomeness of the then prominent Maude Adams. In recent years two distinguished playwrights, Noel Coward and the late Robert Sherwood, have written most successfully for Alfred Lunt and Lynn Fontanne, notably Coward's *Design for Living* and *Quadrille* and Sherwood's *Idiot's Delight* and *There Shall Be No Night*.

America's "starring" age gave us plays tailor-made for great actresses and actors, which is one reason that these plays often do not stand up in revival. A case in point is much of the work of Clyde Fitch and his writings for Richard Mansfield. There are countless instances from theatre history of actors and their abilities influencing the work of the dramatist, but we could not select a better example than the scenario writers of Hollywood in our own day as well as many of those who still center their efforts on Broadway. For this state of affairs we as theatregoers are often responsible, for who has not read a novel or drama and in doing so envisioned some favorite actress or actor in almost every role?

"*. . . on a stage . . .*" This phrase probably governs the context

of the written drama more than any other. It is, at least, one satisfactory explanation for the changes in form and structure that the
drama of every century presents. To judge any drama or dramatist honestly one should have a clear mental picture of the physical
theatre, stage equipment, and actor-audience relationship for which
he wrote. The following line drawings may serve to picture the
evolution of this relationship, as well as the diminishing freedom
of both the playwright and the actor. Further discussion of the
scenic background will be found in Chapter 5.

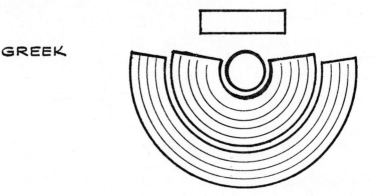

GREEK

The huge open-air theatres of the Greeks, seating fifteen to
twenty thousand persons, called for a particular style of play. Out
of it grew our classic style. The afternoon performances in Shakespeare's Globe Theatre, without scenery or authentic costuming,
necessitated a far more detailed description of the setting in the
lines of the play itself. The appearance of the ghost of Hamlet's
father and Macbeth's murder of Duncan, though both events of
the night, had to be played in the broad light of the day on the
stage of the roofless Globe. The appeal was to the ear rather than
to the eye, and this was a drama of rhetoric. In his lines, and
beautiful lines they were, Shakespeare had to set the time, season,
and locale:

> But, look, the morn, in russet mantle clad,
> Walks o'er the dew of yon high eastward hill.

or

> How sweet the moonlight sleeps upon this bank!

How much greater the imagination of the audience had to be in 1600! Today most of this detail is left to the technical staff.

SHAKESPEAREAN

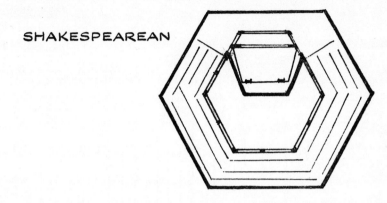

During the seventeenth century, in London's roofed theatres on enclosed stages with painted wings to suggest locality or season, the drama became less romantic in style. The drama of rhetoric gave way to a drama of conversation. Because the audience in the days of Charles II was made up of one class and one group of society, the theatre of the Restoration became a theatre of smart dialogue, clever repartee, and language often considered even by our moderns as quite vulgar. The emphasis fell on writing the type of speech that might be heard in the best social circles of that day.

APRON

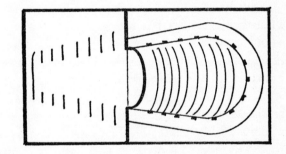

After the Restoration, playwriting in England fell to a very low ebb. The physical theatre was little changed and the plays less vulgar as all classes were once more admitted to the playhouses. Between 1720 and 1860 only three notable plays were written—*She Stoops to Conquer* by Oliver Goldsmith and *The*

Rivals and *The School for Scandal* by Richard Brinsley Sheridan. Each followed the Restoration pattern of prose conversation.

During the eighteenth and nineteenth centuries the stage apron became smaller, and the performance was pushed more and more back of the proscenium arch. The scenery put greater emphasis on the suggestion of locale, although it was still painted, very artificially, on wings and backdrops. It is always difficult to put an exact

WING AND BORDER

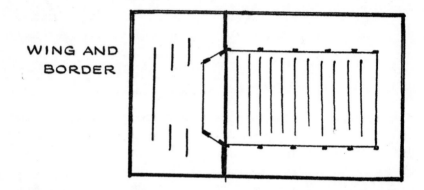

date or locale on the very beginning of a transition. The change begins in many places and in different ways. The "well-made," mechanically constructed play of France was attacked by Zola in his demand for a naturalistic theatre. He demanded that "a slice of life" be placed on the stage. In Norway the young playwright Henrik Ibsen was beginning to write a style of dialogue that sounded very like ordinary conversation. There were also changes in the settings. While the exact date for the first box-set is not known, it is referred to in Germany as early as 1804, and its first appearance in England is generally accepted as 1832. This greater realism in the scenic theatre was soon accompanied by a demand for a more lifelike dialogue. The mirror in this new theatre was expected to reflect life without those purely theatricalized embellishments so common to the plays of Eugene Scribe and Sardou or the artificiality and sentimentality associated with Victorian England.

Arthur Wing Pinero named this three-sided room with the fourth wall missing "the peep-hole" stage, and he with Henry Arthur Jones and Bernard Shaw became the champions for Henrik

Ibsen and what was soon to be known as the realistic drama. Once entrenched, this new style became the reigning one. Improvements in lighting (the new electric light came into practical use in the last fifteen years of the century), improvement in scene-shifting devices such as the sliding or revolving stage, sound recordings, and countless other mechanical assets, all helped give birth to the theatre as we have known it.

BOX

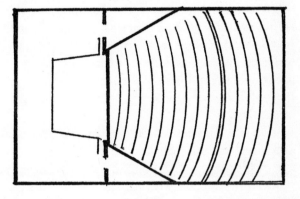

There are many who feel that this style has gone as far as it can go. They believe that the great void in the theatre today is in the

ARENA

area of playwriting, and that the reason lies in the limitations of the realistic style. With the arena stage or theatre-in-the-round growing in popularity, it is highly possible that some new style of playwriting may come into existence, although many contend that any play of any style can fit readily into this means of theatrical presentation. They would point to the fact that this method of seating the audience is far from new, having really been borrowed from the oldest theatre we know—that of the Greeks.

Historically, then, and because of the physical theatre of his period, the dramatist has written for us in the majestic beauty of the Greeks, the poetic power of the Elizabethans, the brilliant and often vulgar dialogue of the Restoration, the artificial and extreme morality of the Victorians, and finally in the language spoken by the modern man in the street. Each playwright writes for the stage of his day, and we must know what it was physically if we are to understand his plays fully. This understanding makes clear the unfairness of comparing the dramas of one century with those of another.

The late Thomas Wood Stevens, famous Shakespearean scholar and director, said: "Shakespeare loses far more than he gains when one of his plays is taken out of the Elizabethan setting and given a modern production with all the accouterments the twentieth century has at its disposal." Mr. Stevens' statement may be open to question, for it tends to limit the production of plays from the past in our modern theatres. However, it does emphasize a very important point. *We should always consider plays of the past not only in terms of the theatre in which they are being given, but also in terms of the theatre for which they were written.*

"*. . . before an audience.*" Although this phrase has already been discussed to some extent in the second chapter, we must not forget that the audiences have differed from century to century and country to country. Neither is it amiss to point out once more that the dramatist, more than any other literary man, writes not for the individual, but for an audience. Others may write for a particular group or class. They may, to some extent, choose their clientele—not so the writer of a play. His appeal must be, as were Shakespeare's and Molière's, to every citizen from the Queen to the orange girl. The poet can compose his work so that it is understood or appreciated only by the most brilliant minds in the world, but for the playwright to do so would be suicide.

The Type of Play

Many argue that a discussion of the type of play is purely an academic matter and of little importance in the realm of appreciation. They see no reason for labeling. This is a perfectly understandable point of view, but in a book of theatre understanding it would seem necessary that some time be given to this subject which has received so much consideration by theorists since Aristotle.

It is true that in some of our current dramas the lines of differentiation have become so thin that there are many plays upon which drama authorities are not able to agree. At times the distinction is almost a personal feeling on the part of the individual. He arrives at his decision on the basis of his own background and experiences, which have made certain phases of the drama take on greater emphasis and importance than others. We cannot always rely on how the playwright himself has labeled it.

It is generally considered that *The Cherry Orchard* by Chekhov is one of the truly great plays of modern times. The author labels it a comedy, but that excellent authority, John Gassner, calls it "a wistful tragedy of personal defeat, symbolic of the decay of a class and a social order." The difference in the point of view and background of author and critic is surely the answer. The play depicts the fall of the old regime in Russia and the rise of the peasant class. Chekhov belonged to this latter group. The theme, however, expresses the tragedy that comes to those who are unable to adjust their lives to a new order and a new world and who must always live in the past, clinging to it long after it is gone. This failure on the part of the protagonist to adjust makes the play a tragedy, in the opinion of Mr. Gassner.

Eugene O'Neill's *Anna Christie* has been variously called a tragedy, a melodrama, and a comedy, depending upon what the individual believes happened to these characters *after* the drama was ended by the playwright. *The Little Foxes*, by Lillian Hellman, has been called both a comedy and a melodrama. Both of these dramas fall into the area of melodrama by this book's criteria.

There are instances in which the direction or production will alter the drama. *Hamlet* with Sir Laurence Olivier in the leading role was more a melodrama than a tragedy in the motion picture production. This very aspect caused it to be a financial failure in England, and had it not been for its tremendous popularity in this country it would have been a fiasco for its producers. However, from the very moment that the voice of the commentator pronounced in the opening sequence: "This is the story of a man who could not make up his mind," we were treated with all the theatrical effects that our modern motion picture facilities could contribute. The atmosphere and spectacle sometimes overpowered the story, the poetry, and even the character of Hamlet, but it did introduce this greatest of all dramas to countless millions who would not have understood it as the stark tragedy written by William Shakespeare.

Death of a Salesman and *Winterset,* in their New York productions directed by Elia Kazan and Guthrie McClintic respectively, and with leading roles created by Lee J. Cobb, Mildred Dunnock, Burgess Meredith, and Margo, were tragedies to all but a few in the audience. The written scripts of these plays, however, have created considerable discussion as to whether they were tragedy or melodrama. Both will be discussed under the latter heading. Some modern tragedies generally accepted as such by our better critics are *Saint Joan* by George Bernard Shaw, *Desire Under the Elms* by Eugene O'Neill, and Garcia Lorca's *Blood Wedding*.

The great majority of dramas and productions do, however, fall easily and logically into one of the four traditional classifications—tragedy, melodrama, comedy, or farce. The very "requirements" that are here listed for each of the four types are arbitrary and may often be open to questioning, even though they are derived from the great dramas of history that have come to be classified in the respective types. These principles can be helpful to the beginner and furnish a challenge to the thinking student who wishes to go further into this subject. They can also lead to some interesting and exciting discussions which will produce further intellectual growth. Finally, such analysis can be downright fun if each individual reserves the right to his own final decision, in the full knowledge that an art need not respect specific boundaries.

Tragedy

Tragedy is the oldest type of drama. It has always ranked as one of the noblest and most artistic works of civilized man. When the theatre was religion and a theatrical performance consisted solely of worshipping the gods, tragedy was the only theatrical type. Even today the world's most superb dramas are found in the works of the three great Greek dramatists, Aeschylus, Sophocles, and Euripides. For sheer beauty of language, nobility of thought, and dramatic structure they have never been equalled, though their work came during the fourth and fifth centuries before Christ. The Greeks, it must be remembered, took their theatre most seriously. The presentation of the religious festival in the spring was an event that all Greece held in reverence. The tragedies, written especially for these religious celebrations, were in keeping with the spirit and humility of the day. These four basic themes appeared over and over again:

1. That everything depends on the gods.
2. The gigantic sin of pride.
3. The dangerous course of the unbalanced man.
4. The positive punishment that must come for all sin.

In each instance the element of conflict was between man and fate or man and the gods. Invariably, it was concerned with some event over which the hero had no control and marched toward an inevitable end with which the audience was acquainted even before the performance began. In reading one of the Greek tragedies one cannot but feel the majesty of their writing and the sincerity of their worship in a faith that rises above any religion as we know it today. They knew no creeds or sects or dogmas. To them the gods were supreme, and religion was an everyday experience. Good fortune or catastrophe was never meaningless; they occurred because some god had been pleased or displeased by man's actions. Their theatre retold these stories as sermons in dramatic terms, and it was an integral part of their daily lives.

To those who know these great tragedies only as dramas and

poetry, it is difficult to explain the majesty and nobility of an adequate presentation. When a production does find its way into some theatre, the audience never fails to marvel at the spirit and beauty that pervades the scene. A few years ago Judith Anderson thrilled audiences across the country with the hauntingly beautiful adaptation by Robinson Jeffers of *Medea,* and brought to a new generation something of the glories of Greece.

The second outstanding period in the production of tragedy was the English Renaissance, with Shakespeare as the leader. His tragedies, though romantic in contrast to the classicism of the Greeks, found the protagonist still struggling with an element which was all-powerful in the end. In this instance, however, it was a weakness within himself. Macbeth's was an uncontrollable ambition; Hamlet's an inability to meet a crisis with action; and Othello's an overpowering jealousy. Always the protagonist was doomed, and the play moved forward relentlessly to personal defeat and usually death for the hero.

In recent times we have known but few really great tragedies. Joseph Wood Krutch feels that the reason lies in the fact that we have lost our respect for the dignity of man; Maxwell Anderson contends that it is in our inability to write great poetry. Many other reasons have been given, but the most logical would seem to be our purely scientific attitude. With our knowledge of psychology, we constantly measure the circumstances in terms of our own background and must analyze the mind of each character before we will accept the action.

Whatever the reason may be, our modern tragedy is not on such a high level of conception or writing. Nevertheless, it still finds the hero in conflict with a force over which he is unable to gain control. It may be his environment, his heredity, or the social conditions of the world in which he lives.

Owing to the progress in our knowledge of psychology, the conflict is often based on the outgrowth of inhibitions, frustrations, and neuroses brought on by our association with persons or institutions about us. Class distinctions, social or moral conventions, our own family relationships, or a change in our environment frequently furnishes the basis of the drama. We need only glance at

THE PLAY AND THE PLAYWRIGHT

some recent dramas of a serious nature to recognize such conflicts, as in *Winterset* by Maxwell Anderson, *The Glass Menagerie*, *Cat On a Hot Tin Roof*, or *A Streetcar Named Desire* by Tennessee Williams, *All My Sons*, or *Death of a Salesman* by Arthur Miller, *Come Back Little Sheba* by William Inge, or *The Emperor Jones*, *The Hairy Ape*, *Desire Under the Elms*, *The Iceman Cometh*, or *Long Day's Journey Into Night* by Eugene O'Neill.

Whereas the Greeks are in conflict with the gods and the Elizabethans with some fault within themselves, the moderns find their conflict with their surroundings, but always the force is greater than the individual and he must go down in defeat.

Great tragedy has always presented the spectacle of a human being shattering himself against insuperable obstacles, because he will not compromise with circumstances or conditions as they exist. Neither he nor the obstacle will alter its course. That conflict awakens pity and fear in the audience because we know he cannot win. These emotions of *pity* and *fear* have been cornerstones in tragedy since the time of the Greeks.

From the days of Aristotle's *Poetics* a very important requirement of all tragedy has been known as *catharsis*, which has been defined as a purification or purgation of the emotions. In the area of psychoanalysis it is known as the elimination of a complex by bringing it to consciousness and affording it expression. John Mason Brown has called it a "spiritual cross-ventilation."

In the art of the theatre this spiritual cleansing is peculiar to tragedy. John Gassner has explained it in modern terms as "enlightenment."* By this he does not mean knowledge gained through the lines of the play or information that may alter its course, as is the case in so many of our modern dramas, beginning with the serious plays of Henrik Ibsen. It is nothing particularly inherent in the action or the dialogue, but rather something won or achieved by the protagonist himself and through him transferred to the audience. It is, in short, an *experience*—not a theme that can be stated—not a "moral tag." Pity and fear and enlightenment grow together in what Mr. Gassner calls a "marriage of emotion and understanding." Enlightenment alone is not enough.

---

* John Gassner, *The Theatre in our Times* (New York: Crown Publishers, Inc., 1954), pp. 51-58.

It must have the collaboration of these two emotions, and this triad must "rise above the perturbing events of the play."

We in the audience, with full knowledge of our frustrations, inhibitions, personal faults, and weaknesses, see those human errors brought out into the open on the stage, and thus we, too, are spiritually cleansed. Mr. Gassner further emphasizes that this is not enough—we must put our own houses in order. Each of us must resolve to go out of the theatre a better man and cast those elements out of our being, if Aristotle's "beauty in ugliness" and Mr. Gassner's "enlightenment" are to have real meaning.

Maxwell Anderson has developed a theory along the same line. He feels that we in the audience watch the protagonist, who has a human fault of which he is not conscious, approach a great crisis, pass through that crisis, and emerge a better man because he has discovered that error and cleansed himself of it. This he calls the "recognition scene."

It is this "enlightenment" that makes tragedy. Sometimes it happens in the audience and sometimes it is only recognized by the audience as it occurs within the protagonist. It is our own interpretation of the presence or absence of this element that brings forth so much debate regarding much of our modern serious drama, especially on the question of whether or not it is tragedy or melodrama. So much depends on our background, knowledge, and sensitivity. A college student, generally considered to be well above average in intelligence, saw nothing in *Long Day's Journey Into Night* by Eugene O'Neill save four hours of a family quarrel. He was bored, angered, highly critical, and unable to understand why it won every award that was given that season for the best play of the year. He simply did not possess the sensitivity, experience, or dramatic knowledge to recognize that the quarreling of the Tyrones was only indicative of more deep-seated elements in each member of the family—the outgrowth of their emotional and psychological environment. Arthur Miller has given us a very satisfactory answer to the question. He is discussing one of the images that came to him, which finally merged into his play *Death of a Salesman.* He says:*

---

* Arthur Miller, *Arthur Miller's Collected Plays* (New York: Viking Press, Inc., 1957), p. 23.

The *Salesman* image was from the beginning absorbed with the conception that nothing in life comes "next" but that everything exists together and at the same time within us; that there is no past to be "brought forward" in a human being, but that he is his past at every moment and that the present is merely that which his past is capable of noticing and smelling and reacting to.

Those who can see beyond the outer and apparent failure of Willy Loman as a salesman and the quarreling of the Tyrone family can experience the enlightenment denied to others.

If we are to study the tragedies from all periods of the past we find there are at least five basic principles common to all tragedies. When a playwright fails to meet *any one* of these demands, his drama is pushed outside the realm of pure tragedy.

Requirements of tragedy. 1. The play must concern a serious subject.

2. The protagonist must be a great figure of heroic proportions, and he must represent more than an individual.

3. The incidents must be absolutely honest and without the element of coincidence or chance. What should happen must happen.

4. The basic emotions are those of pity and fear—pity for the protagonist in his suffering, and fear that the same fate might come to us.

5. In the final analysis the protagonist must meet defeat, but out of that defeat must come enlightenment or the "catharsis" of Aristotle.

These are the principles that this theory of dramatic criticism and many writers of tragedy have generally accepted as sound, and by them *Oedipus the King, Hamlet,* and *Macbeth* can be called tragedies. Many authorities would include *Winterset* and *Death of a Salesman* under the same banner, but there is some difference of opinion regarding these and other serious modern plays. Any of these examples might have failed very obviously as tragedy had the dramatist shown less care in choosing his material or not been wholly honest in its presentation. It is this situation that has opened the question of whether or not the latter two are truly tragedies. The motion picture version of *Winterset* left no doubt. To satisfy the audience the author's script was altered, and in the very last minute of the picture, Mio and Miriamne found a secret path through which they could escape the injustice and the class distinction that was their fate. The spectator left the theatre wondering how long they would be free, where they could go, and if it indicated the sudden abandonment of gangster warfare and miscarried justice. What might have been an excellent tragedy failed utterly at the very last moment because it lacked honesty and truth. The element of chance had been allowed to enter.

This was a frequent error of the motion picture industry until very recently. It has far too often forgotten the principles of artistry for the sake of good box-office receipts. One wonders if more patrons advised their friends to see *Winterset* with its happy ending than would have done so if the more truthful one had been retained.

The motion picture of *Anna Karenina* was made with two endings—the original one and a happy one. Each local motion picture owner was given a choice which his theatre would show. It would be interesting to have a full report on the requests and total audience for each of the two versions. Perhaps in dollars and cents the artistically true version would have come in second best, but from the artist's point of view, it would not be possible to make a picture that could have a choice of *either* ending. There is no quarrel with a happy ending if the whole picture is a melodrama. In that case the escape of Mio and Miriamne in *Winterset* would have been wholly satisfactory, but as Maxwell Anderson conceived the story it was a tragedy, and tragedy demands the honest ending rather than the happy one.

A real artist will not try to mix the element of melodrama with truly tragic circumstances. While no lesser teacher than Shakespeare has shown us that tragedy can often be heightened with comedy, the elements of farce or melodrama have no place in this, the noblest of the genres.

Melodrama

Just as there are degrees in the values of tragedy, so are there in melodrama. The finest melodramas often come so close to tragedy that the distinction is very hard to make. Both *Death of a Salesman* and *Winterset*, which many would call tragedies, are by some standards considered to be melodramas. In our twentieth century such plays as *Ghosts* or *Hedda Gabler*, originally considered trage- dies, now appear to be more like melodramas because of the change in our social and moral thinking from that which existed when Ibsen gave us these two plays. This possibility of a drama's change in type is a weakness in the realistic play that is less likely in the classic or romantic. The former concerns us and our world. The latter concerns authentic people, but they are characters of a fic- tional or imagined world, on a different plane and seemingly not subject to the same details of daily living as those persons in the realistic drama.

Where the tragic writer says: "What is the one thing these peo- ple would do under these circumstances?" the writer of melo- drama says: "What is the most thrilling action I can devise here?" and then: "How can I make it seem logical that the characters would do this?" This often brings about inconsistent characteriza- tions of those involved in the plot. One escapade rapidly follows another, and the excitement that ensues makes it one of the most entertaining and popular types of drama. More than ninety per cent of the serious motion pictures we see are melodramas, and yet they are often so well disguised that a majority of those who see and praise them would be indignant if we suggested that they had seen a melodrama.

Webster defines melodrama as "a kind of drama, commonly romantic and sensational, with both songs and instrumental music interspersed; hence, any romantic and sensational drama, typically with a happy ending." The name grew out of the expression, "drama with music," for melodrama had its origin under those circumstances. The stage later abandoned the music. The motion pictures re-adopted it as part of their own technique, and as one sees the motion picture melodrama today with the almost inevitable musical background, he wonders if the cycle may not have completed itself.

A word in defense is not out of place, for the term melodrama unfortunately is very much in disrepute. This has grown out of those melodramas which came to us in the late nineteenth century, such as *Bertha, the Sewing-Machine Girl, The Streets of New York, Ten Nights in a Barroom, East Lynne,* and hundreds of others. In these plays black was black and white was white. The playwright pitted good against evil, excitement was the key word, and coincidence a commonplace. Because of its connotation many persons feel that to praise a melodrama or to admit a liking for it is a mark of discredit, without realizing that the vast majority of serious plays written since 1900 fall naturally into this type. Both tragedy and melodrama are legitimate methods for planning a serious play, for by either it is possible to give a truthful representation of life. Life itself is divided between chance and character. Melodrama would make more of the chance, while tragedy would place emphasis upon character. Melodrama would show what might happen; tragedy would show what must happen. While tragedy *must tell the truth,* melodrama *must not lie,* and the world knows full well there is a vast difference between those two injunctions! Arthur Miller has said: "When I show you why a man does what he does, I may do it melodramatically; but when I show you why he almost did not do it, I am making drama."* In melodrama there is a chance of victory, for the protagonist is the victim of external circumstances over which he may win; when tragedy exists the protagonist *has within him the power to win,* but is, nevertheless, doomed to failure.

Within the last ten years we have been given many excellent melodramas, both on the stage and on the screen, for they frankly and honestly meet the requirements. Although the element of chance may enter, the plays do not lie. The characters are involved in the most exciting events that can be conceived, and the protagonist may emerge from one situation only to be plunged immedi-

---

* Arthur Miller, "The Nature of Tragedy," *New York Herald Tribune,* March 27, 1949.

ately into another. The whole play is episodic. While the basic emotion may be pity, the element of sentimentality is always present. Sentimentality is said to exist when we are so anxious to experience an emotion vicariously that we do not pause to discriminate just so long as we get the thrill. We sympathize with a child because he is a child or with a pretty girl just because she is pretty and in distress, without analyzing the causes. In reality, neither may really deserve our sympathy. By this definition, sentimentality is said to exist when we are permitted to experience an emotion without paying for it, for the sentimentalist lives on wishful thinking, on emotion rather than reason. He sees just what he wants to see. To him life is a conflict between good and bad, with no in-between. He refuses to apply intelligence and fact to a situation or to think it through. Instead he relies solely on human feeling. Favorite stories show the young man struggling to be honest against the commercially-minded world; the innocence of childhood; downtrodden minority groups; the successful struggles of poor but honest persons; motherhood; the rehabilitation of gamblers, gangsters, women of the streets, and drunkards; and the complete revival of the hardhearted and stingy old man whose soul is saved through the love of a little child. Sentimentality is an important segment of melodrama. There may be fear, but it is of a more temporary or surface variety. We are more interested in the situation and the circumstances than we are in the intricacies of the characters involved. Sentimentality under control can possess great emotional power; out of control it only lies.

The characters in melodrama being as unauthentic as they are, the members of the audience are able to fit themselves into any role and thus receive a greater vicarious enjoyment. The story seems to deal with charmed lives, for the ending is nearly always a happy one. Herein lies the greatest appeal of melodrama to the average motion picture, television, or theatre audience. It furnishes them an excitement and a happiness often denied them in their everyday existence, for more often than not the protagonist wins his struggle. In melodrama there is never the enlightenment that must be present in tragedy.

We must consider *A Streetcar Named Desire* an excellent melodrama, though it does reach what Mr. Gassner has called "the foothills of tragedy." It is splendid serious drama, and possesses a tragic quality. Mr. Gassner points out that in his opinion the same can be said for *Winterset* by Maxwell Anderson, though for different reasons. He questions the presence of enlightenment in the former, while the characterization and theme of *Winterset* as well as the element of chance could keep it from attaining the position of real tragedy. A play evoking pity and fear may approach tragedy but still not attain it. Unquestionably there is a need for some new classification to care for such plays (see pages 83-85), but for our present purpose we shall consider tragedy only as the purest type, and any break with that purity will place the drama in another category.

Requirements of melodrama. As in tragedy, there are five comparable principles which can be considered as basic in the study of any melodrama:

1. It treats of a serious subject.
2. The characters are more loosely drawn than in tragedy and this makes it easier for the audience to identify itself with the characters, thus creating a stronger empathic response.
3. Whereas tragedy must be absolutely honest, the elements of chance and coincidence enter into melodrama. It is episodic and the most exciting incidents possible are brought into the play.
4. There may be an emotion of pity, but it borders on, or is, sentimentality. Fear may be evident, but it is of a more temporary or surface type.
5. There is no real enlightenment even in defeat, and in most instances the protagonist does win his battle.

One can always justify a good melodrama, both as escape and as an artistic theatrical experience. As escape it receives its greatest popularity with the masses, because it permits them to forget their own troubles. Although they may view those of someone else, the experience is a vicarious one. There is no strain or suffering on their part. A brief restudy of empathy and aesthetic distance and their relation to tragedy and melodrama would be helpful.

As critics we should evaluate each type in its own realm of theatrical entertainment, for each should be accepted as a wholly legitimate means of relating a serious story.

The Areas of Comedy

Man is the only animal capable of realizing the miseries of life, and he is the only one who has been given the privilege of knowing how to laugh at those miseries. He likes to make the most of that opportunity, and psychologists have tried to find the reason for his laughter. The elements or areas of comedy have been given us by Alan Reynolds Thompson.* His "ladder of comedy" is our clearest picturization of this subject. If studied carefully it can be most helpful in differentiating between the two types of humor, comedy and farce. The reader must never forget, however, that the artist's treatment or presentation of the material will determine whether it is high farce which borders on comedy or low comedy which borders on farce. This does not imply that one is any better than the other. Each is a legitimate method of presenting a lighter story.

LADDER OF COMEDY

Farce   *High Comedy*
                              6. Comedy of ideas and satire
                        5. Inconsistency of character
                  4. Verbal wit
            3. Plot device
      2. Physical mishap
1. Obscenity

Obscenity, rather than the pun, is considered the lowest form of comedy. It needs no explanation and is very scarce in our own modern theatre, except when combined with one of the higher forms of humor as a necessary part of a specific character or situation. What today would be considered obscene was often evident in the comedy of other periods, and these plays in revival are some-

---

* Alan Reynolds Thompson, *The Anatomy of Drama* (University of California Press, Berkeley, 1946), p. 203.

times made palatable to us only by the deft treatment of actors and directors. Much of *Lysistrata* by Aristophanes or *Volpone* by Jonson and even parts of *Tartuffe* by Molière, as played in Athens, London, or Paris in the days of their writing, would go far beyond what most modern audiences would accept. There have been times in dramatic literature when the digestive processes or the most animalistic elements of love-making were wholly acceptable on the stage. The audience expected and accepted these as a logical part of the play. Many enthusiasts for the "wonderful old plays" would be horrified if they knew what lies behind some of the lines they praise in the classics.

The repartee of the upper classes during the Restoration would be highly shocking to even the most sophisticated audience of the twentieth century. One wonders as he reads some of these dramas how they could ever have been put on the stage. They must be so edited in a modern American production that it is little wonder they lose much of the humor we know they had in their day. These same plays, however, in the hands of an English cast, familiar with the style of writing and capable of catching that style in their playing, not only become hilariously funny but lose any shade of obscenity we find in the reading or detect when handled by less understanding actors. I once saw *The Beaux' Stratagem* by Farquhar in London and was so delighted with every phase of the production that I determined even during the performance to do it sometime in America. It was a great surprise when, a month or so later, the mere relating of the story proved somewhat embarrassing. Upon rereading, even with the imagination of a veteran playgoer and knowledge of its English performance, the drama seemed vulgar. Only then did I fully appreciate the superior treatment and style of the London production.

In recent times New York has accepted and praised plays that many of our noncommercial theatres would not dare attempt, not necessarily because the material suggested obscenity, but because they as actors or producers would be incapable of treating it as well as it had been done by the playwright and trained artists of the professional theatre. *The Voice of the Turtle* in the able hands of John van Druten and the New York cast was free from obscenity because of the subtlety, both in writing and production. What might be considered basically an unsavory situation was treated with such care, honesty, and sincerity that we forgot the situation and accepted the characters and the story. This play could easily be the nemesis of many noncommercial theatres. It looks easy but takes great delicacy in performance lest it appear vulgar and in bad taste, for careful and intelligent treatment by cast and director are the only answer to such situations or lines. If sufficiently capable artists are not available in either the professional or noncommercial theatre, then such dramas had better be left to the readers who will understand them. The theatregoer should recognize and understand such abilities or the lack of them.

Moving up the ladder of comedy, we come to *physical mishap*. This, too, is exactly what it says. The most obvious is the common "pratt-fall," such as having a chair jerked out from under an unsuspecting character, or a banana peel that sends someone sprawling across the stage, the custard pie thrown in the face, the dignified man or woman caught in the stream of water from a hose. Much of what is called slapstick comedy comes in this category. These physical eventualities are found today only in the broadest of farces, or in an occasional motion picture that almost steps out of bounds. When they do appear, the discerning critic cannot refrain from exclaiming: "Oh, no, no, not that, please!" for the distinction is so fine between farce, which we must believe, and burlesque, which we need not believe, that it takes a real artist to know and to keep within these boundaries.

The third step is *plot device*. Shakespeare, whose comedies have never been considered on a par with his tragedies, has often turned to this type of comedy, but has done it most effectively. It involves misunderstandings, cross purposes, inopportune or embarrassing occurrences, mistaken identity, etc. In this area of comedy the author manipulates the characters and situations into the most hilarious combinations. The English are extremely capable in this area, and Noel Coward's *Blithe Spirit* is a good example. Here a remarried widower's deceased wife reappears as a ghost whom he alone can see, and in the resulting situations the audience finds much merriment. In another English farce, *See How They Run*, by Philip King, we find a highly ludicrous situation involving a number of characters in the clothes of the Episcopal clergy, some authentic and some impostors. The frankly contrived situations of mistaken identity provide a perfect example of farce on this level. *John Loves Mary, Dear Ruth, Brother Rat,* and many others of our most popular farces fall into this category, where the author has built his play by setting up a series of ludicrous situations that he is able to make his audience believe.

The next step is *verbal wit.* Even in reading, this dialogue will seem very humorous and as a play will send an audience into gales of laughter the first time it is heard. In the English language few playwrights have surpassed Oscar Wilde and his great gift at this sort of comedy. He is known for such epigrams as: "To love oneself is the beginning of a lifelong romance"; "Wicked women bother one. Good women bore one. That is the only difference between them"; "There's nothing in the world like the devotion of a married woman. It's a thing no married man knows anything about"; "Experience is the name everybody gives to their mistakes"; and one as modern as "Spies are of no use nowadays. The newspapers do their work instead." His *The Importance of Being Earnest* is considered our most perfect example of verbal wit, although Wilde by his treatment has almost made the play a comedy, as will be pointed out later in this chapter.

In America George Kaufman, Moss Hart, and S. N. Behrman are known for their wit in such plays as *The Man Who Came to Dinner, You Can't Take It With You, First Lady,* and others. Like Wilde, they, too, occasionally treat the characters who will speak the lines so that the distinction between farce and comedy is difficult to make.

These four elements of comedy—obscenity, physical mishap, plot device, and verbal wit—are considered the basic materials of farce. The fact that they are ranked low on the ladder of comedy does not mean that they should be considered any the less artistic. In most of the examples that have been given, the authors have been able *by their treatment* to lift the farcical material to a high degree of artistry. We could point out many plays that have failed because the same material had received inadequate treatment, and the plays were for that reason undistinguished. It is very important that we be able to recognize the material itself and also the treatment it has received by the artist. These are separate entities.

Before we turn to the last two steps, let us first summarize briefly an essay written on comedy by William Congreve in 1696. Even today it possesses great validity in helping us to distinguish between the materials of farce and comedy. Congreve emphasized that the following five items should not be considered humor:

1. *Wit,* which is only an ability to quip smartly or to say the right thing at the right time, be it satirical or facetious.

2. *Folly,* which involves doing the foolish thing. He points out that we laugh at a monkey or at man making a monkey of himself or at low thoughts.

3. *Man's personal defects,* such as blindness, deafness, or infirmities brought on by age.

4. *External habit,* which includes singularity of man's speech or dialect, his clothes, behavior, profession, or nationality.

5. *Affectation,* which is pretense without truth or sincerity.

After listing these items as not constituting humor, Congreve points out that, although we may laugh at them, real humor exists only when it grows out of the man and his character. Using Congreve's theory of humor and substituting the word "comedy" for "humor," we may now consider the last two steps on the ladder of comedy—inconsistency of character and comedy of ideas. These two belong wholly in the realm of comedy, for each is dependent upon character.

A superior example of the first, *inconsistency of character,* is found in *The Late George Apley.* The opening of the second scene, when this stuffy family returns to the drawing room after the Thanksgiving dinner, is one of the most humorous of modern scenes. An equally splendid example comes later in the same play when George Apley, a staid conservative Bostonian of the late nineteenth century, is appalled to find his son is enamored of a young girl from that "foreign" city of Worcester, Massachusetts, forty miles distant, and again when he determines to be "liberal" and condescends to smoke a cigarette with the young man in whom his daughter is interested. The lines he speaks and the business of handling the cigarette make for one of the finest comedy scenes in memory, at least with Leo Carroll in the George Apley role. Characters completely out of their locale, deliberately doing things wholly foreign to their natures, can create real comedy. This material is basically a long way removed from what we consider to be farce.

In the theatre, as in life, man has attained the pinnacle of humor when he reaches what Mr. Thompson has called a *comedy of ideas* or *satire*. These qualities of humor are found in man's ability to laugh at that which is most serious or closest to his heart—his family, his friends, his religion, his politics, his country, himself. One is said to have a real sense of humor when he can appreciate the humor of his own pretensions and shortcomings. This is sometimes called high comedy and may be defined as a criticism of life, though we must point out that farce, too, by its treatment is often raised to the level of satire. Sometimes the laughter may be violent and angry and again delightful, tongue-in-cheek, accompanied by an intensity of purpose because the characters involved, and we as an audience, realize the seriousness of their acts and thoughts as well as the humor involved in them.

One of the finest examples in America is found in *I'd Rather Be Right,* in which George M. Cohan portrayed the role of Franklin D. Roosevelt at the very peak of Roosevelt's popularity in the late 1930's. In this play authors and production lampooned the administration and our whole governmental system in a way that no other country would have tolerated, with the possible exception of Great Britain. In that country, some half century ago, Gilbert and Sullivan made a great contribution with their satirical treatment of English government officials.

The proximity of farce to comedy is exemplified by the common denominator of the highest comedy and the lowest farcical material—they both demand a sense of detachment on the part of the audience. Both frown upon sentiment or sentimentality, and neither will tolerate the audience identifying itself with what it sees on the stage. Both high comedy and farce regard life objectively, and either can be a strong agent toward eliminating social injustice or the individual's deflections in his own personal habits. As Molière has wisely said—and demonstrated—"People do not mind being wicked, but they object to being made ridiculous."

It must be kept in mind that even though Mr. Thompson's ladder indicates farce and comedy materials as belonging to different levels, the highest comedy could be made to appear the lowest of farce, or the most blatant farce could by its treatment be lifted into the realm of comedy. This is by way of saying that nothing in itself need be labeled as either, but that the treatment of the artists may make the material one or the other.

The diagram and discussion will bear careful study and analysis, for if they are understood by the reader they can be of great assistance in distinguishing between comedy and farce.

Comedy

Comedy is the most miscellaneous of all the dramatic forms and therefore the most difficult to define. There are some who, when in doubt, measure a given play as tragedy, melodrama, or farce, and when it has failed to meet any of these requirements, call it comedy. We know that it must present believable and understandable characters; that the situations should be both possible and probable; that it should treat the individual and his personal problems; and that it should concern the lighter side of life. While a comedy may often use a serious subject as its substance, such as infidelity, war, communism, tolerance, religion, marriage, or divorce, it does treat that subject more lightly than does tragedy or melodrama. In comedy the protagonist has the power to alter the immediate obstacle in his way.

Much of comedy is based on incidents occurring in the life of others which provoke laughter in us, but which we would find unpleasant if they happened to us. In this special brand of comedy it is the element of perspective that gives us the detachment we need. The seriousness with which the characters involved attack the problem provokes us to laughter. This is exemplified by the cartoon of the father leading his small son toward the woodshed and carrying a paddle in one hand. The caption reads: "Dad, you know we're both going to laugh at this about thirty years from now." Perspective is a vital factor in comedy.

In comedy the protagonist usually overcomes his obstacles, but the means of his success should be logical with the laws of life. We may, as an audience, laugh at the situations even while we sympathize with the characters. A common belief is that comedies have a happy conclusion as compared with tragedy. The ending must be honest in the spirit of the play, and in that sense is happy, but three great comedies that do not end happily—in the general connotation of that word—are *The Misanthrope* by Molière, *Volpone* by Jonson, and *Cyrano de Bergerac* by Rostand.

Historically, the Greeks revelled in a rollicking sort of humor with much biting satire. The Romans leaned toward buffoonery and ingenious plots. The Elizabethans gave us the romantic comedy of Shakespeare with its lyrical poetry and light-hearted stories of love and adventure, and in addition the comedy of Ben Jonson with its bitter satire and ridicule of the man in the street.

Molière is considered to be the greatest writer of comedy who has ever lived. His was the most skillful satire, and his plays are said to have evoked the "thoughtful laughter" that is the final and true test of comedy. This is in contrast with the "thoughtless laughter" brought forth by farcical elements. Various names have been given this phase of comedy, such as "comedy of manners," "high comedy," "artificial comedy," and "intellectual comedy," but the purpose is to satirize the social customs of the upper classes. They create thoughtful laughter, though they may not stir our emotions very deeply. Sheldon Cheney has said:*

> True comedy arises rather out of character, usually the clash of foibles in character against common-sense truth; out of the vices and weaknesses of human nature held up to ridicule. If at the same time sympathy is aroused, the play borders on sentimental comedy. What is generally accepted as essential comedy, "high" comedy, is the satiric sort, untinged with sympathetic appeal.

---

* Sheldon Cheney, *The Theatre* (New York: Longmans, Green & Company, 1930), pp. 329-330.

THE PLAY AND THE PLAYWRIGHT

After Molière the Restoration comedy brought forth the "comedy of manners" of which much has already been written. In modern times Bernard Shaw is considered a leader in comedy. In his hands Molière's comedy of ideas became the comedy of propaganda, but his grasp of character and his brilliant mind again made us appreciate the value of "thoughtful laughter."

No one would question that comedy is one of the most popular of all the types, being challenged only by farce. If man wants escape he can usually find it through laughter, and too often he does not care how it is provoked.

The requirements of comedy. A survey of the best comedies in twenty-five hundred years of theatre shows that comedy:

1. Treats its subject in a lighter vein even though the subject may be a serious one.
2. Provokes what can be defined as "thoughtful laughter."
3. Is both possible and probable.
4. Grows out of character rather than situation.
5. Is honest in its portrayal of life.

Farce

A common error is to use the word "comedy" while thinking in terms of farce. Farce is to comedy what melodrama is to tragedy. It consists of exaggerated incidents and characters with a domination of plot and only a pretense of reality. More often than not it develops on a series of misunderstandings between the characters involved. The generalization is still good that comedy is both possible and probable, while farce is possible but not very probable. Farce has been called a purely mathematical sequence of laughs. The object of the author is to make the audience believe only for the moment. The incidents come rapidly, and the whole play is very episodic. The audience is given very little time to think, because farce portrays the strictly ludicrous in life. If the spectators did analyze the action, believability would be sacrificed. Farce depends upon extreme improbability that usually grows out of someone's mental or physical distress. It is a paradox that this type of humor has always flourished most in ages of great cultural activity and refinement. The reason lies in the fact that farce, though improbable, is usually based on logic and objectivity, qualities which are an integral part of education and culture.

The author of a farce usually asks the audience to grant him a few improbabilities at the very beginning, but from this point on he proceeds in a world of reality. It is often true that a farce exists when the whole story would evaporate and the play be concluded if at any time each character of the story were to tell the whole truth. However, it is our acceptance of this opening improbability or this lack of knowledge shared by all the characters that makes the series of events so highly enjoyable.

While observing a farce in production we should, with a modicum of imaginary puissance, believe what we are watching. We may not believe the story or the characters once out of the theatre, and perhaps not even during the intermissions, but while the actual performance is on there must be a sense of believability—at least in a detached, fairy-story degree. *Blithe Spirit, The Taming of the Shrew, Arsenic and Old Lace, Three Men On A Horse,* or *Auntie Mame* would all lose much of their charm without such belief.

The Importance of Being Earnest is one of our best farces, though at times the treatment does approach comedy. In it we see what would happen if a man were to invent an invalid brother who needs his help whenever the man desires to avoid some unsavory engagement, and what would happen if one of his friends decided to impersonate that mythical brother. The story is told that on its opening in London the audience was fairly screaming with laughter during the whole of Act I at the author's witty dialogue, but Oscar Wilde was frantically walking the floor backstage. When in Act II Earnest enters, walks to the front, and utters the one word, "Dead!" the audience burst into applause, and Mr. Wilde for the first time relaxed. "At last," he said, "they believe in the characters and are interested in what they are doing. Until now I feared they were only laughing at the lines."

Another famous English farce is *Charley's Aunt*, made by Ray Bolger into the very popular musical comedy, *Where's Charley.*

As a popular stage piece this has had a truly amazing career. Ludicrous as it is in content, an audience is ready to accept the improbabilities and howl with laughter in temporary belief—*if* the players attack these improbable situations with sincerity. Measured by the tests which follow, this play becomes an almost perfect example of farce.

The dialogue of farce may run from the epigram of Oscar Wilde to the "gag" in the most recent radio or television script. In either instance any speech could be given to almost any character in the play, for the lines have no special relationship to character but exist for the laugh value they may possess. We can see the logic of this fact when we realize that the term *farce* comes to us from the Latin word meaning "to stuff."

Like melodrama, farce is most delightful when done well. The motion pictures lean heavily to this type and in it have done some of their most superior work. Some years ago there was an influx of English farces, notably those of Alec Guinness, which added much to our appreciation of their value.

The requirements of farce. The qualities of farce that have been most constant through the ages show that it:

1. Has as its object riotous laughter and escape.

2. Asks the audience to accept certain improbabilities, but from that point proceeds in a life-like manner.

3. Is possible, but not very probable.

4. Is dominated by situation rather than character, and calls for little or no thought.

5. Must move very rapidly in an episodic manner, and is believable only for the moment.

The Plea for Further Types

The four generally accepted types of drama have now been discussed and we should be able to fit a given play into one of them. For years, however, there have been strong cries for further classifications that would more accurately describe many of our modern dramas. We have already hinted at such a need in showing the difference of opinion on many scripts that lie close to a borderline between types. So many times the decision by a given critic will depend on his own interpretation or what he reads into the script due to his own background or thinking. Connotation is most prevalent in all the arts. Likewise it is not uncommon, in production, for one type to appear in another classification—and do so very successfully. Neither must we deny that the playwrights themselves may frequently break away from a pure type and they must be granted this freedom. In doing so they may use such terms as drama, serious-drama, comedy-drama, farce-comedy, tragi-comedy, and so forth. Writers cannot, however, always be relied upon to have classified their own plays correctly. One of our most popular farces, *Arsenic and Old Lace,* was written by its author as serious drama. It was only after he had failed to sell it to a producer that Lindsay and Crouse stumbled upon the script and saw in it, with only slight alterations, the laughing qualities that it proved to possess in such abundance.

The writer of melodrama may want to picture the serious side of a situation, but does not feel man should always be doomed. The characters may be deeply affected, but not destroyed. The situations are serious, and the truth of tragedy is present without its inevitability.

Some plays of this nature were discussed under tragedy and melodrama. They are the troublesome ones to classify in a manner satisfactory to all. Mr. Gassner would place them in the "foothills of tragedy." Others who particularly dislike the term melodrama call them *serious dramas.* Many modern dramas such as *Our Town, Journey's End, The Little Foxes, Ghosts, Hedda Gabler, Outward Bound, The Diary of Anne Frank, A Streetcar Named Desire,* and *The Silver Cord* would fit admirably into such a category. The debate regarding the type of such plays as *Winterset* and *Death of a Salesman* or *Anna Christie* might be resolved. The French would instantly classify these plays under a term which they call *drame.* From this some authors have derived the word drama as a distinct type, although the English-speaking countries have never accepted this narrower definition.

By the same token, a play might have the general attitude of comedy without its accompanying humor. These might be called *comedy dramas*. They move us deeply, and their conclusions may not be completely happy ones. *Green Pastures, Cyrano de Bergerac, What Price Glory, Candida, Point of No Return,* and *The Rainmaker* might be cited as examples.

A farce-comedy follows the same pattern as above with a leaning toward farce, though George Jean Nathan's famous remark might well be considered; in his facetious manner he said that a farce-comedy was so named by its author when he realized that it wasn't quite funny enough to be called a farce but was too ridiculous to be classed as a comedy.

With a full realization that many plays are difficult to fit into any pattern, we do feel that further classifications could go on and on until they had no meaning whatsoever. For this discussion it would seem wiser to think in terms of only the four traditionally accepted types, keeping in mind the playwright's freedom and recognizing that difference of opinion is inevitable. Exceptions to any of our principles will always be present, but the majority of dramas will fall into one of these types.

The Style of the Play

We have already discussed the personal style of the artist. His literary approach is known as the *aesthetic* style and includes the classic, romantic, naturalistic, realistic, fantastic, expressionistic, etc. Each has dominating characteristics which will be explained. Basically, however, the aesthetic style follows one of two routes. The playwright in his effort to picture life does it by suggestion or by imitation. The great literature of past centuries has been more by suggestion, but since Henrik Ibsen and the birth of the modern drama, playwrights have used varying degrees of imitation.

A criticism often made by the beginner regarding Shakespeare or the Greeks is that their language does not sound "natural" or "real." This criticism stems from a misunderstanding of the words "reality" and "realism." The first refers to life itself; the second is an aesthetic term used to denote the artist's style in portraying that reality. The realistic writer attempts, by imitation, to picture the life we live and know. In the classic style of the Greeks and the romantic style of Shakespeare the characters were just as natural and just as real in the worlds of imagination these playwrights portrayed through suggestion.

Shakespeare spoke of "holding the mirror up to nature," and he must have felt in 1600 that he was doing just that, but it was the nature of his romantic world, not the realistic world of our modern school. Reality in the theatre meant something different to the Elizabethan from what it does to our modern audience. Shakespeare's characters were not of the street or next-door variety. They were romantic, imagined characters who were drawn so well that they became real individuals in a world of theatre or imagination rather than in a world of reality. Shakespeare made it sound quite natural for Macbeth, on hearing of his wife's death, to speak the beautiful lines:

> Tomorrow, and tomorrow, and tomorrow,
> Creeps in this petty pace from day to day
> To the last syllable of recorded time,
> And all our yesterdays have lighted fools
> The way to dusty death. Out, out, brief candle!
> Life's but a walking shadow, a poor player
> That struts and frets his hour upon the stage
> And then is heard no more; it is a tale
> Told by an idiot, full of sound and fury,
> Signifying nothing.

Likewise, it was real in Shakespeare's world for Lorenzo to say:

> The moon shines bright: in such a night as this,
> When the sweet wind did gently kiss the trees
> And they did make no noise, . . .
>
> . . . .
>
> In such a night
> Stood Dido with a willow in her hand
> Upon the wild sea banks and waft her love
> To come again to Carthage.

In contrast to the beauty of Lorenzo's speech, the modern boy in a realistic play of the twentieth century might easily say: "Wow!

What a night for lovin'!" In Shakespeare's day Lorenzo sounded just as "real"; and there is no question which words possess more literary and aesthetic value.

It is small wonder that some students of our generation question the reality of Shakespeare's speech, if they measure it by the yardstick used in our realistic theatre rather than the one by which he wrote in his romantic one. They have known only the realism of radio, stage, motion picture, and television in their generation, and they do not realize that this realistic style with which they are familiar is only one small segment of the world's literature and that the vast majority of our drama is nonrealistic and falls into the aesthetic styles known as classic, romantic, fantastic, symbolic, and, in more recent times, expressionistic. An honest evaluation of any play demands a knowledge of the style of writing at the time of its creation. As in modes of dress, so styles of writing have changed from country to country, each being the accepted mode of theatrical expression in its particular era.

The classic tradition was given us by the Greeks. It has a certain worship of form and orderliness. As a part of the Greeks' religious worship, the theatre was formal. It conformed to the unities of time, place, and action, which meant that the play considered a single unified action and took place within twenty-four hours, and in one setting or locality. A chorus was usually employed to give the necessary exposition, set the scene, and introduce the characters. It was a theatre of verse. The Greeks held steadfastly to one mood and did not feel that comedy should be mixed with tragedy. Aeschylus, Sophocles, and Euripides were the greatest playwrights in this style, and their works still stand among the finest drama in all dramatic history. They *were* the theatre of tragedy during the fourth and fifth centuries before Christ, and a truly noble theatre it was. The English have never taken very strongly to the classic tradition. Addison's *Cato* is about the only example of strict classicism. In America Eugene O'Neill borrowed from the Greek stories, but wrote more in the realistic style. When Robert Turney wrote a modern version of classic style in *Daughters of Atreus,* it promised more in its reading than was realized in its New York production. Anouilh's *Antigone* and Robinson Jeffers' *Medea* are other notable examples of the Greek style translated into modern terms.

It was the Elizabethans who introduced the romantic tradition. The words "romantic" and "romanticism" as used here have no connection with romantic love or the love of man and woman. They refer rather to the dramatist's general style of expression and the principles involved in his dramatic construction. Romanticism is the tradition in which Shakespeare is supreme, and his plays serve as ideal examples of true romanticism in dramatic history. The writing itself is indifferent to form and order. It disregards tradition and scorns the practical everyday life. The stories are light, interesting, and believable but on a plane of imaginative grandeur. The characters revolt against a sense of reality and represent the idealistic and imaginative side of man. They live what seem to be charmed lives with a great exuberance in a world of the theatre rather than a world of reality. Their language is beautiful and reflects life as we should like to imagine it but would rarely experience. Man's existence is filled with excitement, suspense, and success. The setting is usually in some faraway or fictitious place, and the dramatist envisions the whole of life through rose-tinted glasses.

Sheldon Cheney has given us a superior definition of romanticism:*

> If we accept a broad definition of romanticism we may visualize the dramatist as far-riding in imagination, unhampered in shaping theatric action and in choice of characters, writing with constant reference to the deeper life of the human spirit, utilizing every resource of physical staging and acting, choosing prose, or verse or silence, and drenching the world in sensuous beauty.

This is truly a drama of freedom, a drama of beauty and imagination and a drama worthy of the theatre. A good example of romanticism in our modern theatre is *Cyrano de Bergerac* by Edmond Rostand.

Until early in the nineteenth century the French dramatists attempted to follow the Greeks and Romans in what is considered a neoclassic style. During the early nineteenth century there grew

---

* Sheldon Cheney, *The Theatre* (New York: Longmans, Green & Company, 1930), p. 411.

THE PLAY AND THE PLAYWRIGHT

up a school of Romanticists in France, but they followed a far narrower interpretation of that tradition than is found in the Cheney definition quoted above, or in any of Shakespeare's plays. Their works were sentimental and bombastic, attempting not to picture life but rather to use the theatre as an escape from life. Their plays were shallow in conception, seeking contrast in characters, situations, and language. Their characters represented all classes, but the protagonist more often than not was an illegitimate child, a criminal, or an outcast. Their conflicts pitted innocence against vice, and the language was florid and the speech most common. They were seeking liberalism in literature, but they failed to lift the theatre with their writings.

This false romanticism of the French theatre became so artificial that in about 1880 it ran up against a serious revolt. The revolutionists, Zola and Becque, fought for the naturalistic theatre, and cried out for freedom, life, and naturalness in contrast to the artificiality that had grown out of the French romanticism. The answer was Naturalism. This was merely the swinging of the pendulum to the opposite extreme. The theatre became more scientific than artistic in its effort to present life exactly as it was without any effort to theatricalize it. Zola called out for "a slice of life." He would have that slice of life put on the stage, and pictured for an audience without any thought of selection or even dramatic technique. The Théâtre Libre in Paris with André Antoine as its leader became the center of this movement, and naturalism was the spirit of the day. It had a greater grasp on France and Russia than on any other country. As a style it was short-lived, for all true artists soon come to realize the basic principle that art is not representation but selection, and that great theatre is a *conventionalized* representation of life rather than an exact duplication of it.

Out of naturalism grew the realistic theatre. This, too, pictures life, but not in stark photographic detail. Rather it selects, arranges, and discards. It speaks the language of the people and is free from the rules of the classic or the imagination of the romantic. It stresses the practical everyday details and pictures the ugliness as well as the beauty of life. Man's problems are discussed, and the characters are those we meet in our daily life, but it is not always a systematic picture, for it is colored by the feelings and the beliefs of the dramatist. This is the style that has been predominant for some seventy-five years—a short period in the span of history.

Expressionism is a more recent style and appeared as a reaction against realism. It resembles none of the other styles, and its strongest tools include the use of the abstract, the author's impression and distortion, and a strong emphasis on mood. The scenes do not always follow in logical order or tell the story in the accepted manner. They become increasingly imaginative and sometimes even grotesque. Quite frequently only the thoughts of the character are portrayed, or the audience is given a distorted view of the action as seen through the eyes of the protagonist. Eugene O'Neill used this style in such plays as *The Hairy Ape, The Great God Brown,* and *Days Without End.* In each case, particularly with the use of masks, he moved away from the realistic theatre. Elmer Rice's *The Adding Machine,* Kaufman and Connelly's *Beggar On Horseback,* and some of the later work of William Saroyan are further examples. Expressionism often deals with modern social problems and is more often than not serious in nature. It is still in an experimental stage and not as firmly established as are those styles previously mentioned. *Death of a Salesman* was a most happy combination of realism and expressionism, shifting from the reality of the Loman life in realism to Willie's own thoughts, feelings, and imagination through expressionism.

Symbolism and fantasy are two additional styles. The first tells two stories at once. *Everyman* with its symbolic characters is an example, and *The Blue Bird* by Maeterlinck a more recent one. Fantasy is purely in a world of the imagination and make-believe and has few limits by which it is bound. Familiar examples of fantasy are *Tobias and the Angel* by James Bridie, *Mrs. McThing* by Mary Chase, *Blithe Spirit* by Noel Coward, and *On Borrowed Time* by Paul Osborn. The television screen has occasionally given us some very interesting fantasies when its producers dared move away from realism.

In any given drama it is essential to know the aesthetic style in which the author has written. It is the method he has felt was best for telling his story at that particular time. While the classic and the romantic are the two basic forms in which we find our greatest plays, theatregoers of today are more familiar with the realistic. Some who are partial to experimentation and novelty may find great joy and satisfaction in the remaining styles, some of which, as we have noted, are still in the process of development.

In summary, each author tries to picture life in his own particular manner or through his own personality. If he chooses the method of suggestion he may turn to the styles of classicism, romanticism, fantasy, expressionism, or symbolism. If, however, he prefers to picture life by imitation, he will employ naturalism or realism.

A few years ago there appeared a letter to the editor of a metropolitan newspaper in which a young critic was trying to compare the stage production of *Cyrano de Bergerac* in its romantic style to a very successful motion picture produced in the realistic manner. The writer was crying out for more of the latter and wondering why anyone could possibly favor the "unreality and artificiality" of *Cyrano de Bergerac*. Such a comparison is grossly unfair from every viewpoint and could never be made by a well-informed theatregoer. In these productions the authors had chosen different styles in which to tell their stories. The romanticist chose to suggest life and the realist to imitate it. Each was a means of giving the audience a vicarious experience. Each has value as an artistic medium of expression. An individual may prefer one or the other, and that preference is based upon his personality, education, standards, tastes, background, experiences, and even moods of the moment. Although the theatre—in its greater sense—may have lost something in discarding the romantic style for the realistic, it has also gained something. Today we are able to discuss our own social problems and to see characters on the stage who might live next door. Without our realistic tradition we could not have had *The Cherry Orchard, Street Scene, Waiting for Lefty, Death of a Salesman, A Streetcar Named Desire, The Diary of Anne Frank,* or in a more humorous vein, *Life With Father, Arsenic and Old Lace, Mr. Roberts,* or *Auntie Mame.* For the opportunity to know these plays, however, we have traded the dignity and power of the word as well as the exaltation of language and emotion that can be found in the suggestive styles. The price we have paid for our realism has been an over-all littleness of conception, language, and character. This we must not allow ourselves to forget when we loudly proclaim our desire for realism in the theatre.

The Structure of the Play

Now that we have discussed the type and style, we must try to analyze some of the mechanics involved in the actual writing of a play. An interesting analysis of this phase has been given us by Arthur Wing Pinero, an English playwright of the late nineteenth century. Mr. Pinero would divide this aspect of the playwright's work into two areas, the *strategy* and the *tactics*, which together make up the play's structure.

Strategy is the over-all pattern or plan of the play. It normally begins with the *exposition*, which tells us who the characters are, their relationships to each other, what has happened previously, or what is occurring at this time. Any material that we may need to make us aware of the status quo when the curtain went up is included in the exposition. Occasionally, as in a mystery play, these explanations may be scattered throughout the play, and the final bit given us only at the conclusion. This was largely true in *Death of a Salesman*. In most dramas this phase ends with the *inciting moment*, or that instant when the equilibrium is upset, when we as readers or audience recognize a change in the status quo and realize that this is what the play is going to be about. Something happens to change the situation as it is. The next step in the strategy is the *rising action*, which consists of conflicts and crises building to a peak when one of the two contending forces suddenly gets an advantage over the other. This moment in the theatre is called the *turning point*, and in a modern play more often than not comes at or near the end of the second act. It is that crisis in the dramatic action of the play which leads directly to the climactic moment and makes it inevitable. After the turning point comes what has been called the *falling action,* although the term is a misnomer, for interest must never lag at this point. There is usually a slight decline or at least a plateau in the dramatic action until some new element enters the picture which furnishes the intensity to the *climax,* which is the peak of our interest and includes the answer to the final question of the play. The *conclusion* is a tying together of the various minor aspects, if this has not already been done, and ends with the fall of the final curtain. The reader will note that in the theatre we make a distinction between the turning point and the climax. This is often not done by those who consider the drama for its literary values rather than its theatrical effectiveness. To them the terms are used interchangeably. Milton Marx has made such a fine differentiation between turning point and climax that he is quoted here in full:*

> An analogy [between turning point and climax] may help to make the distinction clear. The *turning point* in a man's career would be that action or event that ultimately leads to failure or success—winning the first big law case or successfully performing the first big surgical operation, deciding to become a criminal by an embezzlement or a forgery, choosing between retaining a throne or marrying for love. The *climax* to the lawyer's career might be his appointment to the bench of the Supreme Court; that of the doctor, the saving of the life of some personage after everyone else had failed, or perhaps nationwide recognition at a celebration commemorating many years of service; the climax of the criminal's career might be a life sentence to prison; that of a king who gave up his throne so that he could marry the woman on whom he had set his heart might be some subsequent achievement for his country that would list his name among its greatest heroes.

The importance of the climax in a play can hardly be overemphasized. It is the very essence of the structure, for without a climax there is no play. Many playwrights have admitted writing the climax first and then the rest of the play—in other words,

---

* Milton Marx, *The Enjoyment of Drama* (New York: Appleton-Century-Crofts, Inc., 1940), p. 79.

writing it backwards. The climax must be the final culmination of everything that has been said or done by the characters during the production. It pulls all the threads together, for the whole play must have built to this moment. It is the solution of whatever conflict may have existed.

One of the most common weaknesses in playwriting is for the dramatist to permit his characters to do something at this crucial moment that is not wholly consistent with their natures as the audience has come to know them. A strong character dare not become suddenly weak or a weak one show a great strength he has never suggested before this moment. Any characteristic or action on the part of an individual during the climax must have been amply motivated during the earlier scenes. The climax of necessity comes very close to the end of the play, for after this moment the play is over. There are occasions when two characters or two stories are almost equal in interest, and in these cases there may be what is called an *anticlimax* when the second, usually the lesser of the two, is culminated.

If we were to make an historical analysis of strategy in the period of the Greeks and of Shakespeare and of our modern times, we would find considerable variation in the strategy. The Greek playwright gave most of his time to the falling action. His exposition, inciting moment, and rising action were furnished by the chorus or by messengers and quickly introduced. Shakespeare and most Elizabethan writers were concerned with balancing the play's dramatic action. The turning point of a five-act play came in the third act. In our modern drama we are concerned mostly with the rising action, which means that the turning point is usually much nearer the climax and the conclusion. Quite often the climax is practically the conclusion as well.

The reader should by no means take the following diagrams* too seriously. They serve only in a general way to give a pictorial outline upon which prominent playwrights of each period have worked. We would emphasize that their purpose is to show the course of the play's *dramatic action* rather than the intensity of

---

* Adapted from *The Enjoyment of Drama*, by Milton Marx, pp. 76 and 77. Appleton-Century-Crofts, 1940.

THE PLAY AND THE PLAYWRIGHT

GREEK PLAY

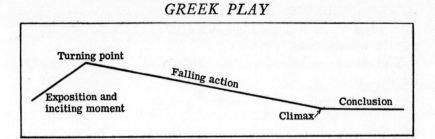

SHAKESPEAREAN PLAY

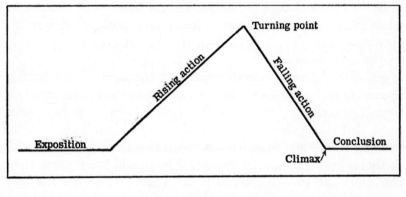

MODERN PLAY

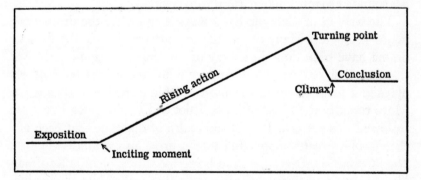

interest or of the emotional response on the part of an observer.

Whereas strategy is essentially literary, the tactics of the drama are theatrical. The two abilities do not always go hand in hand. Shakespeare and the Greeks excelled in the former and sometimes fell down in the latter. Our modern playwrights are quite often most adept at the theatrical but lack artistry in the general laying out of the whole play.

The *tactics* are defined as the methods used by the dramatist to implement the strategy. They involve getting his characters on and off the stage, giving the audience just the information it should have at any given time, and furnishing incidents that will keep the play alive. They include the language of the characters, their motivations, the filling in of their backgrounds, and the selection of any details that will implement the over-all strategy.

In the Greek theatre the exposition was handled by the chorus, while Shakespeare often had it given as a prologue before the opening of the play. The modern writers have constantly sought a new means of presenting this necessary information. At one time it was done by two servants discussing the lives of the leading characters as the curtain rose on Act I. Others have used travelers, confidantes, diaries, or letters. The best exposition is considered to be that which no one recognizes as exposition. This is called "edging it in," and is at its best when one in the audience suddenly realizes that now he knows all he should know about these characters and the situation as it exists but that he has not been aware of the information being given him as such, for the dialogue has sounded so much like natural conversation.

The writing of dialogue has always been one of the dramatist's major problems. Many of our literary masterpieces in the field of drama have been done in poetry of one form or another. It was this fact that led Maxwell Anderson to compose several of his plays in a form of verse, the most notable of which is *Winterset*. More recently the plays of T. S. Eliot and Christopher Fry have followed this pattern. It is in the realm of dialogue that each author has his greatest opportunity to express his own individuality. Noel Coward is often accused of being too smart. George Kaufman likes to turn a phrase or display a wit that makes him distinctive, but decreases the individuality of his characters. George Bernard Shaw and Oscar Wilde too often speak for the characters of their plays, rather than permit the characters to be personalities in their own right.

The personal style of the playwright in respect to his writing of dialogue is something to be especially noticed, for conversation is a very important part of the playwright's tactics. It must always sound "real" and "natural" in the style chosen. In the realistic school it must never be ordinary conversation, but it must always look and sound as if it were. In the romantic or classical school it must follow the lofty or poetic quality of that imagined life. It is the stilted and unnatural language found in most of the plays of the nineteenth century, especially the Victorian Era in England or the late nineteenth and early twentieth century in America, that makes them seem so false and artificial today.

It is the task of the playwright in his tactics to motivate both the action and the speech of each of his characters. A lack of motivation will cause us to question a play more readily than any other factor, unless it is the untruthfulness of the dialogue.

A final test of the playwright's tactics is how well he has defined the characters of his play, whether they are individuals in whom we can believe or whether they are merely stock or stereotyped characters chosen for his purpose. Such types include characters classed as the hayseed farmer, dumb blonde, shopgirl, truck driver, obnoxious child, or gossipy old man or woman. These are often referred to as geometric types. When characters of this kind appear over and over again, they become stereotypes, or a copy of a copy, and show little imagination on the part of the playwright.

Analyzing the strategy and tactics of the drama itself and being able to understand the various aspects of its structure is always an interesting study. To understand just how the playwright has gone about his job and managed to tell his story in a logical and believable manner is no small part of understanding his form and technique.

The Meaning, Nature, and Value of the Play

Thus far we have been concerned purely with the drama's technical aspects. Now let us consider the author's meaning, the nature of the story he has presented, and the values it has as a piece of literature—in short, the aspects of the play that we will remember as an audience. Aristotle called drama "an imitation of an action." Cicero defined it as "copy of life, a mirror of custom, a reflection of truth." Nicoll insisted that it must "arouse, stimulate, or startle us." If a man discusses a play with a friend, he will not often start with the style, structure, or even type. He is more likely to talk about the *characterizations*, the *dialogue*, the *story*, the *theme*, and the impact it had on him as an individual.

Theme and plot. It has often been said that the plot is the body and the theme the soul of a play. Most plays have a conflict of some kind, which may be between individuals, between man and society, man and some superior force, or man and himself. If this conflict can also teach some generally accepted truth of life, the play will have taken on a deeper and more permanent quality. That generally accepted truth is called the theme. Few of us would demand that every play teach a lesson. It is enough for some plays merely to furnish an escape or amuse the audience for an evening.

If an author chooses to write the fluff and smart repartee so often given us by Noel Coward, S. N. Behrman, or Terrence Rattigan, he should be given that privilege. If he chooses to write the poetic drama of Christopher Fry or T. S. Eliot, then we should accept the play on its own terms. We need not prefer it nor praise it nor go to see it, but we should not try to compare the work of the poetic playwright to that of the escapist or the discussion plays of Ibsen, Bernard Shaw, or Galsworthy. This was once expressed superbly by Bernard Shaw himself when he answered a critic who complained that *Odette* was not a great play: "Its author never meant it to be a great play. The question is how does it rank with the type of play it is trying to be?"

Albright, Halstead, and Mitchell have expressed this very well in their use of the two words *autonomous* and *heteronomous* drama.* Autonomous drama exists primarily to delight, amuse, entertain, or move an audience emotionally. Heteronomous drama

---

* H. D. Albright, William P. Halstead, and Lee Mitchell, *Principles of Theatre Art* (Boston: Houghton Mifflin Company, 1955), pp. 7-8.

would stir an audience to some overt action, demonstrate or teach, further some propaganda or persuade. It would use the theatre to achieve an end that could have been realized equally as well in some other medium. It must also use the principles of dramatic art that will hold the attention of the audience. Bernard Shaw was a master with the heteronomous play—so great a genius that his plays often are as theatrically effective as they are thought provoking. One readily realizes that many of our best dramas offer instruction along the lines of morality, politics, psychology, or sociology. In fact, it is often difficult to tell just what the primary purpose of the author might have been, but this is part of the critic's responsibility.

We can readily see that few dramas are wholly either one or the other. An extremely heteronomous play would lack artistic qualities, seem inconclusive or over-long or short. The wholly autonomous play might be very exciting or amusing, but fail to project any intellectual value and thus be very quickly forgotten.

To endure, a play should have a theme. It is sometimes suggested in the title as in *Loyalties, Justice, Strife,* or *You Can't Take It With You.* At other times it is found in a speech from the play itself, as in *Craig's Wife* when the aunt says to Mrs. Craig: "People who live to themselves are often left to themselves." Sometimes it is not so obvious but calls for closer study.

If the author has done his job, we should be able to state the theme of his play in general terms and in a single sentence. The theme of *Hamlet* is the failure of a youth of poetic temperament to cope with circumstances that demand action. The theme of *Macbeth* is that too much ambition leads to destruction; of *A Streetcar Named Desire,* that he who strives hardest to find happiness oftentimes finds the least; of *Death of a Salesman,* the fallacy of building a life on shallow or false foundations; and of *Green Pastures,* that even God must change with the universe.

In many instances several persons may get different themes from the same play, each of which constitutes a logical truth. The same theme may be found in several plays. For example, the Hamlet theme is found also in *L'Aiglon, Petrified Forest, Key Largo,* and numerous others.

The statement of the play in specific terms is the plot or story. John Van Druten has pointed out an interesting distinction between these two words: the story is defined as the listing of the events that happen in their relation to time, while the plot explains *why* these events occurred.* It is the plot with which we are now concerned, the reasons behind the actions of the characters involved. Plot and theme should go hand in hand. If the theme is one of nobility or dignity, the plot itself must concern events and characters that measure up to that theme. As we analyze many plays, we find that some possess an excellent theme, but are supported by an inconsequential plot. A fine example of a satisfactory theme and a weak plot came to us in the 1920's in a comedy called *Abie's Irish Rose.* It held the stage for many years in a continuous New York run. The theme was a good one, namely, that a Jewish boy and an Irish Catholic girl should be able to marry and find real happiness. However, that theme was portrayed through a plot so thin and with such stock or even stereotyped characters and situations that neither could measure up to the seriousness or truth of the theme. This weakness was even more obvious when an attempt was made to revive the play twenty years later.

Examples of the more frequent fault of superior plot and little or no theme come to us in much of the work of the popular playwright, Noel Coward. He is known for his cleverness at making the most apt remark at the right moment. His plots are unquestionably original and extremely witty in their conception. His plays are very successful, and he has a large following, but more often than not, they are utterly lacking in a theme or truth that will withstand more than momentary analysis. Such plays as *Design For Living, Private Lives, Hay Fever,* and *Blithe Spirit* are delightful, but ephemeral. An audience could believe them only while they were being witnessed in the theatre. The same criticisms might be given of two of our American playwrights so popular in our day—George Kaufman and S. N. Behrman. Each is able to give us a dialogue purely distinctive and plots cleverly enough contrived. Mr. Behrman, we are told, has great fun writ-

---

* John Van Druten, *Playwright at Work* (New York: Harper & Brothers, 1953), p. 30.

ing his friends and himself into his plays. Usually his chief aim is to present amusing contradictions of psychology as in *Wines of Choice, Biography,* or *No Time for Comedy.* George Kaufman, at his best, can give us *The Royal Family* or *You Can't Take It With You,* but too often he does sacrifice theme for an interesting plot and clever lines, as in *The Man Who Came to Dinner* or *George Washington Slept Here.* We are assured escape and momentary amusement, but when the play is analyzed for a truth of life or a theme, we either find one so thin that we shall not long remember it, or we fail to find one at all. Consequently these authors, although among our most popular, surely will not endure as artists, nor are their plays likely to be revived a hundred years hence. They but emphasize more strongly the axiom that a good plot or conflict is needed for transitory success, but a theme is more likely to assure a play of long life. As always, however, one could easily name exceptions. Few of Shakespeare's comedies possess really worthy themes. *Charley's Aunt* and *The Importance of Being Earnest* are frequently revived, as are such pieces as *Pierre Patelin* or *Gammer Gurton's Needle.*

The coordination of theme and plot is the author's problem. This has already been referred to as proportion in playwriting. It is the balancing of one against the other. Neither should get out of control. If the plot is too strong, we run to poor melodrama or farce, and if the theme is predominant, we run to the propaganda play.

During war times or great emergencies we get more than our share of propaganda scripts. The cruelty of the enemy and the justness of ourselves are themes driven home so consistently and forcefully that we weary of them. The one-reel propaganda films that the government issued during the Second World War on *Air Raid Precautions, Buying Bonds, Doing Your Bit, The Black Market, The Home Front,* and so on, often brought moans from the motion picture audience because the theme was completely out of balance with the story with which they tried to support it.

Such old plays as *Ten Nights in a Barroom* or most of our so-called religious dramas are other examples of propaganda plays because undue emphasis is placed on the theme, and the plot does not carry its full weight.

In addition to discovering the theme and evaluating the plot, the dramatic critic must also consider the playwright's treatment. It has been pointed out that the same theme is found in many plays. Much of the artistry, then, may be found in the manner in which the author has handled his material.

A casual comparison of Bernard Shaw and John Galsworthy will show the former blasting away, taking sides, and ardently preaching his beliefs. Galsworthy, on the other hand, with similar subjects, would weigh one side against the other with all the care of a judge and try to avoid any evidence of giving his own opinion or of working for a theatrical effect. Even his curtain lines would lack the dramatic or theatrical value that another playwright would try to find for them.

When in 1938 the Playwright's Company was organized in New York, the personalities of its five members were analyzed by many writers, and it was generally conceded that they represented five very different types. Any one might have hit upon a single theme, but each would have treated that theme in a different manner. Maxwell Anderson was the poet and Sidney Howard the aristocrat; S. N. Behrman was the introvert, Elmer Rice, the firebrand; Robert Sherwood was the craftsman. If we were to pick a theme at random—for example, one that has been used frequently in other plays, namely, that "the liberal of today is the conservative of tomorrow"—it would be interesting to contemplate what each of these five playwrights would do with its treatment. The chances are that Anderson would treat it loftily and with considerable seriousness. Sidney Howard, whose untimely death occurred shortly after the organization was formed, might have seen in it a conflict between capital and labor and through it would have developed sharp characterizations. S. N. Behrman would have thrown his emphasis on the dialogue, and his conflict, minor as it would be, might have taken place in a Park Avenue apartment with professional artists as the leading characters. Elmer Rice would have castigated society in one way or another with the dynamite of indictment and a touch of patriotism, while Robert Sherwood would have more carefully built a conflict or story based on current events and thus injected a journalistic as well as a possible literary flavor. These are, of course, all suppositions, but they are in keeping with the styles or personalities of each of these playwrights, and we as critics must always consider the treatment or point of view along with the theme and plot. It is the playwright's comment.

The greatest single criticism of our theatre today is that our playwrights speak, but far too often have nothing to say. They lack purpose, skimming over the surface and not really getting at the reason for or motive behind the characters' acts. This is indeed a weakness if the theatre is to meet its obligations as set forth in Chapter 1.

Literature or journalism. Does this play possess the qualities of permanence that make it literature, or is it merely entertainment for the moment? Is it only "good theatre" because it discusses a question, tells a story, or presents a theme that the public is demanding, or does it portray a universal truth?

Why is it that so many plays we call "modern" seem to be so lifeless when they are revived after fifty, thirty, or even twenty years? We instantly apply the word "old-fashioned" or "dated" and let it go at that. Then there are other plays from the Greeks, from Shakespeare and many others of his period, even from the Restoration, and certainly from the works of Molière which, when given an adequate production in our modern times, have something about them that thrills us in the theatre.

The question is readily answered by those who have made a closer study of drama. The Greeks and Shakespeare were careful in selecting their materials. They always looked for some inkling of eternity. Their topics were removed from their period. In short, they were out of time and out of place. There was no date on them, and thus they wrote not of an age, but for all time.

Likewise, they were extremely careful to avoid ideas or questions for debate. They went along with the crowd and refrained from discussing problems of their own everyday world. The Greek writers of comedy were not so wise. They chose personalities and situations of their period, and consequently we are unable in the twentieth century, save in a few plays, to understand much of what was extremely humorous to them.

Ibsen chose in many of his social dramas to take a definite stand on current issues and problems that faced his generation. His plays had their influence, their points were made, and now another generation has come to accept as natural the very standards for which he fought. Ibsen's social plays seem unimportant to an audience not interested in the trends of dramatic literature or in the theatre. Though this influence was valuable to mankind and sociologically the world is better for having had an Ibsen, his plays have suffered in the sense of becoming dated. On the other hand Shakespeare, Racine, and Corneille were careful to avoid issues that might provoke debate in the audience. They talked only of those accepted beliefs of their day. They aroused no antagonism and presented no controversial ideas—sociological, political, or moral.

One method of weighing a play is to examine it for its literary or its journalistic qualities. These two means of expressing man's thoughts or beliefs are worlds apart in their objectives. Literature does not attempt to be novel or new or unusual. Its goal is not to shock its audience, but to reveal for them some truth that the author must share with them. Journalism seeks to be timely, to bring the people the news or events of the moment, to tell them what they most want at this particular time, and what is most timely today is usually doomed to be most untimely tomorrow. Certainly nothing is so dated as last week's newspaper—but at that time it was something we awaited with keen anticipation. To a great extent Ibsen and Shaw and Dumas were journalistic so far as material was concerned, but as artists the first two were able to raise, through their treatment, the general level of their finished work.

To the journalist facts are important as facts. The war news, the political convention or campaign, the doings of our neighbors, unusual tidbits of local, national, or international importance are read and discussed today, but considered out-of-date tomorrow. In direct contradiction, the literary man is interested not in the facts as facts, but only insofar as they represent recurrent truths of human existence. The journalistic writer hurries to his typewriter and gets out his daily article because the public wants him to speak. There may really not be a story worthy of his time, but he has so much space to fill. He may have nothing of importance to say, but there is a deadline to meet. The public and the subscribers expect their paper or their magazine at a certain time each day, week, or month. The journalist writes because his public demands it. This is also true in nearly all the radio and television drama we hear and see today, which may partially excuse its general low calibre. On the other hand, the writer of literature writes, not to meet a constant demand or a deadline, but because he has something to say. Journalism is motivated externally, and literature grows out of an inward impulse on the part of the writer himself.

The average person purchases the newspaper or reads the article that expresses his views. Editors, in turn, often find what the public wants and give that to them, regardless of whether or not it is what they need to be told. Majorities are often favored, for journalism is an enterprise, a business, a profession. In contrast, literature is a religion, and the author has a greater freedom for expressing his own ideas. The market and the royalties may be smaller, but he is permitted clearer thinking. On many important issues of the past we can, in the light of time, see that the majorities were wrong and the minorities right.

Many of our most successful New York productions are little more than dramatized newspapers. When an author selects a subject because he feels the audience wants him to talk about it rather than because he personally has a story or a truth to tell, it is usually journalistic.

A study of our New York stage over a number of years will show the drama running along strangely similar lines in any given season. A play appears and achieves some success. Instantly other writers, anxious to participate in the banquet table of that particular season, rush to their typewriters. In one season the offerings run to mysteries, in others to newspaper offices, to musical versions of recent plays, to dramas of historical or biographical backgrounds, to peace plays, to war stories, to discussions of special social problems, to nationalistic or patriotic themes, to propaganda on some current discussion or belief. In each instance the professional critics begin to complain very shortly that they would like a change from the diet, but so long as the audiences attend, the journalistic playwright will continue at work.

Now and then a play that has a journalistic bent may also possess a truth that has literary qualities as well. When Russia attacked Finland, Robert Sherwood was so moved by the injustice of a great nation turning on a smaller one that he put his strong resentment into *There Shall Be No Night*. With Lynn Fontanne and Alfred Lunt it attained great success both in New York and on the road. It was extremely timely, for the events were occurring at that very moment. Then the tables changed, and Russia joined the Allied cause. Mr. Sherwood, now sensing that the political regime in Finland was not as he had thought it to be, closed the play's run. Journalistically, it had become dated, but as literature its theme told a universal truth, namely, that "there shall be no night when man's intelligence has reached the point where he realizes the futility of war." Because of the theme, and because it was equally true regardless of the countries involved, he revised the play, making Greece the country attacked and Italy the aggressor. Early in 1957 the same play was again revised and presented on television with Hungary as its background.

After the first revision Mr. Sherwood was criticized for insincerity and accused of journalistic writing or jumping on the bandwagon of popularity, but we must remember that the world was changing rapidly and with it Mr. Sherwood's thinking. Was it not possible that the basic theme of the play was of greater truth and significance than the conflict, surface acts, and personalities involved in the plot? The illustration is given to show that in the hands of a good craftsman as well as an artist, a journalistic play may also possess literary qualities.

A play, then, might be both literary and journalistic, but the one that is envisioned in an "out of time—out of place" atmosphere has a greater opportunity of living than one specifically dated by events, characters, or debatable issues.

Morality or immorality. There are undoubtedly those who would question the inclusion of this section under the play and the playwright. They might easily consider the whole discussion as a matter of taste rather than morality, or point out that one of the world's eternally unanswered questions is: "What is moral?" Any individual's personal ideas of what is right or wrong— bigoted, narrow, broad, or free as they may be—grow out of his own background, experiences, training, thinking, and religious beliefs, and these conceptions are influenced by time, by country, and by community; they vary from family to family, and even within the family group itself.

This lack of any absolute standard only makes the playwright's task more complex. The community or educational theatre frequently finds its selection of plays greatly limited on this account. Even the professional field is often threatened with censorship. The motion picture and television are constantly faced with what they can do and say and what they dare not. It is most important that some artistically honest criteria be found for determining the morality of a play if we are to answer criticism intelligently when it is presented by the more vocal segment of the audience whose personal moral codes may not be compatible with what the playwright has written.

A long dissertation could be written on freedom for the artist or on a plea for broadmindedness on the part of the audience, but neither would help to answer the fundamental criticism that a given play or some part of it is immoral. What we must establish is some basic and honest measuring stick in the hope that the intelligent theatregoer can evaluate what he sees and hears and thus decide for himself. Few would deny our premise that the theatre is a reflection of life. It follows logically that its duty, then, is to picture life truthfully as well as artistically. It must not show only one phase of life or the little segment with which an individual approves, but *all* life of *all* classes and groups and personalities and ages. We do not necessarily agree with the man who said: "Good plays are only written about bad people," but we do contend that if some evil does not appear in a play to conflict and contrast with the good, we do not have a very satisfactory play. It is *only* when the supposed evil succeeds or is praised as such that the play can justly be called immoral by any honest standard.

That times and ideas change is illustrated in the fact that Ibsen's *Doll's House* and *Ghosts* were considered most immoral when first written. Mrs. Fiske was so desirous of playing the role of Nora that she first enacted it on an improvised stage in the lobby of an hotel. She had been denied the use of a theatre because the audiences of England and America were not ready to accept the idea of a woman's leaving her family and home. The conservative critic, William Winter, condemned *Hedda Gabler, Rosmersholm,* and *Ghosts* on the grounds that they were immoral. His premise was that the subjects discussed had no place in the theatre. His cry was:

> There are halls to be hired. There is an audience for the lecturer, if lecturing would serve any good purpose. There are societies of learned men who study sociology and are ever ready to accept illumination on the subject from anyone who can provide it. Why inflict the stage with inquiry as to "original sin" or the consequence of ancestral wickedness or the moral obliquity resultant from hereditary diseases or the various forms of corruption incident to vice and crime? Since when did the theatre become a proper place for a clinic of horrors and the vivisection of moral ailments?

In opposition to him Harrison Grey Fiske, through the *New York Dramatic Mirror,* spoke the feelings of his wife and himself in saying:

> Truth will not down, and the speaker of it must sooner or later be heard. Ibsen is the apostle of truth, and his drama means something that is human.

History has proved Fiske to be right and Winter in error, for Henrik Ibsen's plays have withstood the test of time. Today their themes are so generally accepted that they are written into the laws of our land. It is difficult for us to believe they were ever considered immoral. Unquestionably they have been great factors in enlightening a public on issues that needed to be brought into the open for discussion. One of the obligations of an audience today, as in Ibsen's day, is to question in their own minds the validity of their own code of ethics or their own thinking on moral issues.

Today the items most often condemned by this small segment of the audience are the elements of swearing, drinking, and any suggestion of sex deviation or laxity. Why an audience, conscious of the fact that these "sins" do exist in the world and that one or more of them may even be practised by their own acquaintances or friends, should frown upon their appearance in the theatre is beyond comprehension. The fact that they do is common knowledge. Like the proverbial ostrich, these individuals would bury their heads in the sand or close their eyes to the things they do not want to see. They would judge the world by their own individual codes of morality and on that basis would rate themselves as above reproach. By those same codes, they would devaluate the moral standards of those who do not believe exactly as they. Such so-called "sins" need not be endorsed, but they should be recognized as existing in life, and if the artist is to portray life he may need to include them. If the character is a swearing or a drinking man, it is more moral and honest to picture him thus than to lie about his character. The audience need only remember that the playwright is writing about a particular character, not all men, and should see and understand that character as an individual. In short, it is the obligation of the audience *to judge the characters of a play in terms of life.*

Ibsen does not say that all women should leave their husbands, but that Nora—this one woman who is not permitted to be an adult, have a personality, or live a life of her own—does have the right to walk out of her home and leave her family.

Just so long as the author has a true insight into the lives of his characters and pictures them as they are, the play is moral. If he makes his audience admire a vile character or invents excuses for situations that have no excuse, lauds the villainy within the characters, allows weakness to be rewarded, or lies in any way about his characters, then we may say the play is immoral.

We hear much about the coarseness in the plays of the Restoration and how they portrayed the bawdiness of the times. In spite of their apparent lewdness, they did portray truth and pictured life as it was. It was Charles Lamb who pointed out that, in spite of the audience being shocked at what the characters did and said, it was always made very evident that no good person was permitted to suffer on the stage and that the characters lived "in a world of themselves—almost a fairyland, and in their own world the creatures are not so bad."

Chicago prohibited the playing of *Tobacco Road* with Henry Hull in the leading role on the ground that it was an immoral play. Any intelligent and honest person who saw Mr. Hull in this play must have felt that this prohibition on the grounds of immorality was unjust. Both Mr. Hull and the entire company made of that play a truthful, and for that reason a moral, picture of life along Tobacco Road. After the language of the first few minutes had come to be associated with the characters as they were, one forgot the profanity as profanity. The play was conceived honestly, and the characters played with sincerity. It was far more moral for the author to employ the language he did than to have substituted something less fitting. It should be emphasized, however, that the discussion here concerns the production starring Henry Hull. Had the Chicago authorities forbidden the appearance of the same play as performed by some later companies, the ruling could have been more easily understood, for in their effort to capitalize on the publicity given the prohibition in Chicago and their appeal to a less discerning audience, these later companies reduced the play to uninhibited farce. They played it solely for laughs rather than the near tragedy intended. They made the most of all profanity and unsavory situations. All the aspects of the play that had been criticized were emphasized for sheer effect, rather than as character traits of the unfortunate individuals portrayed by the playwright.

One may not personally like swearing. With rare recent exceptions (and Clark Gable's classic "I just don't give a damn!" as *Gone With the Wind*'s tag line) the movies have steadfastly censored any strong slang or profanity, and have thus played beautifully into the hands of those provincials who choose to believe that swearing does not exist. However, on the subject of drinking, equally as taboo to some in the audiences, the motion pictures have not only gone all the way, but have even carried it to the point of making it appear that by way of excess drinking one might even accomplish a goal otherwise unattainable. Television has followed the motion pictures very closely.

The whole question of morality is as involved as human nature itself, but the basis for determining morality in the theatre should be one of honest and objective analysis. Such an approach would demand that since a play purposes to give a picture of life, we must always measure the play *in terms of life*. With this fundamental principle in mind we may then ask three specific questions:

1. Has the playwright lied about these characters? If at any point he has, he should be condemned. If he has been truthful about them, he should be praised, and the play is essentially moral.

2. Has the author permitted any evil or wrong to be rewarded? Have the wicked achieved their goal because of or through their wickedness? If so, the play may be left open to the charge of being an immoral play.

3. Has the author, in this play, clouded in the minds of his audience their basic beliefs in the idea of what is right and what is wrong? If he has, then the play may be, again, open to the charge of being immoral.

If we have been completely honest in judging a play in terms of life rather than our own conception of what we believe life should be, and may still answer any of these three questions in the affirmative—then we have the right personally to consider this play as immoral. The mere presence of material we do not approve does not in itself constitute immorality by any just or artistic standard.

Finally, we would further emphasize that the artistic merits of a play are not necessarily affected by a decision as to its morality or immorality. The purpose of this discussion has been to find a terminology. We have merely presented what we considered basically honest criteria for evaluating the work of a playwright when his effort may not agree with the moral or religious beliefs of some of its audience.

The Final Tests of a Great Play

Can this play stand alone, or is its success dependent upon the work of the actors, the technicians, the director, or the over-all production? What are some simple tests of a great play? So often we in the audience are carried away by the theatre's own contributions that we are unable to distinguish between them and the inherent values of the drama itself. Sardou in his time and Clyde Fitch in his were thought to be far greater playwrights than they are considered today. They were fortunate in having available for their roles the divine Sarah Bernhardt and the great Richard Mansfield, respectively. These actors made the plays appear to have far greater meaning than they have shown themselves to possess since the death of these actors. Likewise, the acting of Joseph Jefferson made *Rip Van Winkle* known as a great play. When Jefferson was no longer able to appear in the role it came to be recognized as very mediocre, and since his death it has rarely been produced—certainly never with the success enjoyed by that superior comedian. Very often the convincingness of the acting will hide the weakness of the writing.

In the same manner, a magnificent production can easily blind the sensibilities of the average audience. An excellent comment on this is a remark by Tallulah Bankhead to the late Alexander Woollcott. They were attending an extravaganza that might call forth all the Hollywood adjectives in regard to its setting, its lighting, its expensive costumes, the beauty of the chorus, and the magnitude of the entire production. As the performance unfolded in all its splendor, Miss Bankhead is said to have whispered to Mr. Woollcott: "You know, Alec, there is less in this than meets the eye."

The theatre must substitute spectacle as a last resort and only when the playwright has not introduced enough of the human element to hold the attention of an audience.

A translation of Aristotle's *Poetics* would, in modern terms, list six elements of the drama. They are: plot or story, idea or theme, mood or atmosphere, character, dialogue, and spectacle. Most

THE PLAY AND THE PLAYWRIGHT

BROOKS ATKINSON, Drama
Critic, *The New York Times*

ERIC BENTLEY, Drama Critic, *The New Republic*. Eric Bentley, with the Israeli actress, Orna Porat, and the Broadway star, Uta Hagen. Both actresses have starred in Brecht's *Good Woman of Setzuan*, the latter in Eric Bentley's production of the play in New York. *Photo by Mike Zwerling.*

JOHN GASSNER, Drama Critic
and Sterling Professor of Playwriting at Yale University. *Photo by
Roy Schaff.*

WALTER KERR, Drama Critic, *New York
Herald Tribune*

KATHARINE CORNELL. *Photo by Dorothy Wilding.*

MAURICE EVANS. *Photo by Friedman-Engeler.*

These actors are generally considered in the school known as Interpreters and Commenters.

ETHEL BARRYMORE. *Photo by Vandamm Studio.*

HELEN HAYES

PAUL MUNI

FLORENCE ELDRIDGE and FREDERIC MARCH

The actors on these two pages are generally considered in the school known **as** Impersonators.

ERIC PORTMAN and MARGARET LEIGHTON, as they appeared in the performance of "Table Number Seven" in the production of *Separate Tables*.

ERIC PORTMAN and MARGARET LEIGHTON, as they appeared in the performance of "Table by the Window" in the production of *Separate Tables*.

JAMES CAGNEY, who portrayed the role of the late Lon Chaney in the motion picture *The Man of a Thousand Faces.*

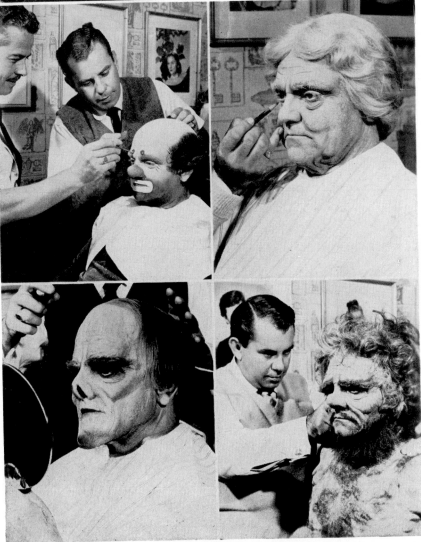

Make-up director Bud Westmore is shown making up four of the twenty-two characterizations which James Cagney re-enacted. At top, a clown and the old woman in *The Unholy Three.* At bottom, Erik, from *Phantom of the Opera,* and Quasimodo, from *The Hunchback of Notre Dame.*

LIFE WITH MOTHER, by Howard Lindsay and Russel Crouse. Original design for Acts 1 and 2, by Donald Oenslager. (*Realism*)

SABRINA FAIR, by Samuel Taylor. Valley Players Summer Theatre. Designer: Don Swanagan. (*Realism*)

STREET SCENE, by Elmer Rice. Denison University. Designer: Richard G. Adams. Photographer: Rolan Thompson. (*Realism*)

WINTERSET, by Maxwell Anderson. Denison University. Designer: Bernard O. A. Bailey.
Photographer: Rolan Thompson. (*Realism*)

DEATH OF A SALESMAN, by Arthur Miller. State University of Iowa. Designer: A. S. Gillette. (*Simplified Realism and Simultaneous Setting*)

MISALLIANCE, by George Bernard Shaw. State University of Iowa. Designer: A. S. Gillette. (*Simplified Realism*)

THE LADY'S NOT FOR BURNING, by Christopher Fry. Denison Summer Theatre. Designer: Don Swanagan. Photographer: Rolan Thompson. (*Simplified Realism*)

THE MADWOMAN OF CHAILLOT, by Jean Giraudoux. Denison University. Designer: Don Swanagan. Photographer: Rolan Thompson. (*Simplified Realism*)

LE BOURGEOIS GENTILHOMME, by Molière. Designer: Donald Oenslager. Photographer: Peter Juley. (*Impressionism*)

THUNDER ROCK, by Robert Ardrey. Temple University Theatre. Designer: Martin Zipin.
Photographer: Richard R. Frame. (*Impressionism*)

THE SKIN OF OUR TEETH, by Thornton Wilder. Tulane University. Designer: George Hendrickson. (*Impressionism*)

THE WANHOPE BUILDING, by John Finch. Temple University Theatre. Designer: Clemen M. Peck. Photographer: Richard R. Frame. (*Impressionism*)

THE EMPEROR JONES, by Eugene O'Neill. Voodoo Scene designed by Donald Oenslager.
Photographer: Peter A. Juley and Son. (*Expressionism*)

BRAND, by Henrik Ibsen. Near the old church. Designer: Donald Oenslager. Photographer: Peter A. Juley. (*Expressionism*)

ONDINE, by Jean Giraudoux. State University of Iowa. Designer: A. S. Gillette. (*Expressionism*)

TARTUFFE, by Molière. Temple University Theatre. Designer: Clemen M. Peck. Photographer: Richard G. Frame. (*Theatricalism*)

THE POOR SOLDIER, by John O'Keefe. Denison University. Designer: Don Swanagan. Photographer: Rolan Thompson. (*Theatricalism*)

BERNARDINE, by Mary Chase, Denison Summer Theatre. Designer: David Rounds. Photographer: Rolan Thompson. (*Theatricalism*)

SHE STOOPS TO CONQUER, by Oliver Goldsmith. Tulane University Theatre. Designer: George Hendrickson. (*Theatricalism*)

A STREETCAR NAMED DESIRE, by Tennessee Williams. Michiana Summer Theatre. Designer: Richard G. Smith. (*Formalism*)

THE CRUCIBLE, by Arthur Miller. Tulane University Theatre. Designer: George Hendrickson. (*Formalism*)

FRANK CAPRA. Motion Picture Credits: *It Happened One Night, Mr. Deeds Goes to Town, Lost Horizon, You Can't Take It with You, Mr. Smith Goes to Washington, It's a Wonderful Life.*

HAROLD CLURMAN. Stage Credits: *Golden Boy, The Member of the Wedding, Bus Stop, Tiger at the Gates, Waltz of the Toreadors.*

JOHN CROMWELL. Stage Credits: *The Insect Comedy, Tarnish, The Queen's Husband, The Silver Cord, Lucky Sam McCarver.* Motion Picture Credits: *Of Human Bondage, So Ends Our Night, Abe Lincoln in Illinois.*

MORTON DaCOSTA. Stage Credits: *No Time for Sergeants, Plain and Fancy, Auntie Mame, The Music Man.*

CECIL B. DeMILLE. Motion Picture Credits: More than seventy films, including: *The King of Kings, The Sign of the Cross, The Ten Commandments.*

GEORGE ROY HILL. Television Credits: *A Night to Remember, Billy Budd, Good Old Charley Fay, The Helen Morgan Show.* Stage Credits: *Look Homeward Angel.*

JOHN HUSTON. *Photo by Burt Glinn.* Motion Picture Credits: *The Red Badge of Courage, The Maltese Falcon, The Treasure of Sierra Madre, Asphalt Jungle, African Queen, Moulin Rouge, Moby Dick.*

GARSON KANIN. Stage Credits: *The Diary of Anne Frank, Born Yesterday, Years Ago, A Hole in the Head.* Motion Picture Credits: *The Great Man Votes; Tom, Dick, and Harry.*

ELIA KAZAN. *Photo by Floyd Mc-Carthy.* Stage Credits: *A Streetcar Named Desire, Death of a Salesman, Tea and Sympathy.* Motion Picture Credits: *Baby Doll, East of Eden, On the Waterfront, The Music Man.*

ROBERT LEWIS. *Photo by Fried-man-Abeles.* Stage Credits: *Briga-doon, The Teahouse of the August Moon, Witness for the Prosecution, Jamaica.*

GUTHRIE McCLINTIC. *Photo by Roderick MacArthur.* Stage Credits: *Winterset, Romeo and Juliet* with Katharine Cornell, *Yellow Jack, Saint Joan* with Katharine Cornell.

ROUBEN MAMOULIAN. *Photo by Alexander Bender.* Stage Credits: *Porgy, Wings Over Europe, Porgy and Bess, Oklahoma!, Carousel, Lost in the Stars.* Motion Picture Credits: *Applause, City Streets, Dr. Jekyll and Mr. Hyde* with Frederic March and Miriam Hopkins, *Love Me Tonight, Becky Sharp, Blood and Sand, Silk Stockings.*

DELBERT MANN. Motion Picture Credits: *Marty, The Bachelor Party, Desire Under the Elms, Separate Tables.* Television Credits: *Marty, Our Town, Yellow Jack, The Petrified Forest, Lee at Gettysburg, The Day Lincoln Was Shot, Darkness at Noon.*

GEORGE SCHAEFER. Stage Credits: *Man and Superman*, Army production of *Hamlet.* Television Credits: *The Lark, Cradle Song, The Green Pastures.*

ALAN SCHNEIDER. *Photo by Lee Salisbury.* Stage Credits: *Anastasia, The Remarkable Mr. Pennypacker, The Skin of Our Teeth* (Paris edition).

dramas will emphasize one, two, or three of these elements. A very important step in our understanding of the playwright's work will be to recognize just where he has focused his attention.

The drama itself is only one of the many elements with which we shall be concerned when it becomes a theatre production, but it is the starting point. It is this playwright's work that all the other artists in the theatre must interpret for the approval of the audience. They will use every means within their power, but must always come back to what the drama itself is—what it says, where its emphasis lies, what the characters would have us feel, and in total what the playwright was essentially trying to say or do.

Although every playwright must be given the opportunity of writing as he desires—and many times a playwright is not trying to write a great play—it is only fitting that in concluding this chapter we list what this particular theory of dramatic criticism would consider the tests of a really great play.

First, it should have done more than merely hold our interest or entertain us for the moment. It must have been really effective in some very definite respect such as moving us emotionally with its beauty or with its truth, and it must have had sufficient strength to sway our thoughts. To fall down on any of these points is to weaken its right to this distinction. Joseph Mersand has summarized what we would endorse as five very pertinent requirements of the truly great play. These are his questions:*

Does the play
  . . . possess universality of appeal in time and space?
  . . . create living characters in convincing situations?
  . . . stir, move, enrich, or transform us?
  . . . express its thought in beautiful or appropriate language?
  . . . teach life's meaning and strengthen our own hand in facing life's problems?

---

* Joseph Mersand, *The Play's the Thing* (New York: Chapbooks, 1941-1948), pp. 32-39.

—4—

Acting

and the Actors

*T*he art of acting is one of the most fascinating areas of human endeavor. From earliest childhood we find ourselves escaping into the realm of "let's pretend." There are few persons who are not convinced that they could act. Ask someone to play the piano, paint a picture, design a costume, or build a set, and he will probably answer: "Oh, I couldn't. I have no training. I wouldn't know how to begin." But ask the same person to take a part in a play! There may be a momentary hesitation, but there will also be a reaction of pleasure. Though he may decline, it will be on the grounds of previous commitments or lack of time in a busy schedule—not from a feeling of incompetence in handling the part. The principal reason for this situation is that good acting

looks so easy and so natural. The finer the performance, the surer the uninitiated will be that "all one has to do is to learn his lines, get on the stage, and be himself." How very far from the real truth of the matter this is!

George Jean Nathan has said: "Criticism of acting amounts to little more, save on its highest levels, than a reflection of the critic's notion of himself in the actor's role." George Kelly has expressed this universal phenomenon in an interesting little comedy entitled *The Flattering Word*. The theme is that to make a friend you need only tell a person he should be an actor, for that truly is the flattering word.

Acting is a splendid means of self-expression. It permits the individual the opportunity of getting out of himself, being someone else, living in his imagination, and experiencing emotions and situations often denied him in his everyday existence. To those on the side lines the life of the actor would seem to be a round of interesting experiences, public acclaim, applause, curtain calls, easy living, and personal freedom. Actors are always in a position of prominence. To the general public they possess a beauty, a charm, and a personality not often found in their own mundane lives. It is little wonder that from afar the actor's life looks so fascinating.

The truth, however, is quite the contrary, for the profession is far from an easy one. It involves hard work and serious training, vocally, physically, and mentally. It demands personal sacrifices, for the theatre is a jealous mistress. It requires God-given talent and an ability that entails long hours of study and intense concentration, great imagination, persistence, and determination. These are the requisites not recognized by those who claim that anyone can act. Historically, acting is one of the most ephemeral aspects of the theatre, but at the moment of its existence it may be the most rewarding. Once the actor's performance is concluded, it lives only in the memory, and when the last individual who witnessed the genius of Edwin Booth or Joseph Jefferson is dead, the contributions made to man's aesthetic pleasure by these artists will have gone out of the world forever.

During and immediately after a given performance it is often the work of the actor that commands the greatest attention. It is

not unusual for the playwright, technicians, and director to be completely overshadowed by the performance of some actor which electrifies the audience. History abounds in exciting stories about the great moments on the stage of such actors as Kean, Forrest, Booth, Cooke, Bernhardt, Duse, Garrick, Burbage, Siddons, Matthews, the Barrymores, and many others. All these artists had their triumphs, heard their applause, took their bows, read their notices, and were heroes of the hour, but the future will find these moments recorded only in books or in the memories of those who were privileged to witness the performance. We have photographs of the scenery and costumes, and we can read the play, but the work of the actor lives only for the moment. In the twentieth century we have perfected a method of recording the voices and action of these artists. For those who have seen the actual performance, these recordings or pictures can rekindle the flame, but for those who have only the mechanical reproduction, the all-important human quality is lacking.

Just as good acting is more difficult to attain than it would appear to the average theatregoer, so is its evaluation. Critics of the past have not been able to agree upon the relative merits of our greatest actors. If experienced critics are divided in their opinion on the work of the giants, then it must follow that lesser critics might find greater difficulty in agreeing on the art of lesser actors. One need only read the major critics of the New York papers the morning after an opening to understand that even the most experienced professionals may run the gamut in their evaluations of the actor's work. Every player may be mentioned in one or more of the reviews, but his work may have been ranked from high praise through the cursory dismissal of being "adequate in the role" to downright adverse criticism. There are many reasons for this, but it would seem to have been stated as clearly and concisely as possible by an old and well-established actor who once said: "Don't ever forget that acting is a matter of opinion." Acting is based primarily on emotion, and emotions will always cloud an objective viewpoint.

Perhaps nowhere in the theatre is the element of prejudice more involved than in the analysis of acting. We like or dislike

ACTING AND THE ACTORS

an actor, although it may be impossible to give any logical reason for our view. These prejudices are often purely psychological in their nature. Many of our most popular actors of the day have attained their status not through talent or imaginative acting, but only because of a personality, appearance, or charm that has caught the imagination of a large segment of the population and thus won for them great reputations as actors. Although these individuals —and many could be named without difficulty—rank high in general esteem, they are utterly lacking in dramatic talent and owe their current success only to these public prejudices by which they have been elevated to their prominent position.

John Mason Brown has called these the actors of understatement. They have reached their position not through artistic merit, but because they are fortunate enough to possess a particular quality that is in demand at the moment. This may be a laugh, a walk, an ability to wear clothes (or not to wear them), a peculiar charm, or some unique physical or vocal characteristic.

Recently a representative from one of the major motion picture studios visited a summer theatre company as a talent scout. On his arrival he questioned the director: "What do you have for me?" The director began to enumerate the particular talents of two young men, and the scout asked about their height. When informed that they were about five feet eight or nine inches, he shook his head and said: "Sorry, we are only interested in men who are six feet or six feet two, and look as if they might have been born in Iowa or Texas." Following the evening performance, where he had been particularly impressed by the acting talents of a very attractive, dark-complexioned young man, the scout approached him and said: "You have a great talent, and ten years ago I would have given you a screen test, for at that time the public wanted your type."

We would not adversely criticize these individuals who have attained a certain success, but it is important that an honest understanding of their work should include an ability to explain why they have become so popular.

Another reason for the difficulties of dramatic criticism is the rapid evolution of acting style. We need only observe a ten-year-

old motion picture to realize that acting changes almost as rapidly as does the style in dress.

Furthermore, the individual acting in the theatre may change from performance to performance in the same play. It may be altered by the physical or mental changes in an individual actor or by these same variables in other members of the company. It can come also from the reaction of the audience. Helen Hayes has said that her acting varies considerably for matinees which are attended largely by women, for the evening performances early in the week, and for the holiday crowds on the weekends. The reader is once more referred to the article by Howard Lindsay in Chapter 6.

A featured player who has worked for years with one of our current stars has said that this actor's greatness is never fully realized except by the opening night audiences, either in New York or on the road. The over-all pattern is the same, and he may never give what could be called a bad performance, but the little nuances, that extra something that lifts and captivates an audience, are not always so sure to be present as on opening nights. This is not intentional on the part of the actor; it is just that the critics and first night audience bring to him an added stimulus. In an effort to keep the actors ever on their toes, *Variety Magazine*, a publication of the theatre, does a series of what it calls "follow-up reviews," by which plays are covered after they have been running for several months or a year. They often find the acting greatly altered from the earlier performances.

It is wholly unjust to engage in group discussion on the work of any actor in the legitimate theatre unless the participants have attended the same performance. Furthermore, it is often difficult to distinguish between the actor and his role. How often an actor has been praised for speaking witty lines when the credit really belongs to the playwright! How often an actor has been criticized adversely when the author has given him an unsympathetic part or one that merely supports or "feeds" the protagonist or some more popular character so far as the audience is concerned. Such parts are often referred to as "thankless roles," for the actor often receives little credit for what is a fine piece of acting. A third

equally common fallacy is to bestow more praise on a mediocre actor especially suited to his role than on a vastly superior artist not so well cast.

Even though we may understand and agree that the actor's sole job is to interpret the role as it has been given him, we may as critics vary widely in our opinions of his interpretation. It is here that we must once more be reminded of the importance of judging the acting only through an application of the three principles of Goethe. Even in so doing we must not forget that the actor is different from any other artist, for he is his own instrument and his own medium. His profession is to be someone else, but always to do so in terms of himself. His work will always be the result of his looks, size, age, figure, voice, temperament, and personality, for actors are people who are appraised as works of art. Henry Irving once said: "What makes a popular actor?—physique. What makes a great actor?—imagination and sensibility."

Even professional critics are frequently fooled by an actor's personal qualities which, though an important part, are not the whole of acting. After John Kerr's third Broadway appearance Eric Bentley wrote in his criticism: "When I praised Mr. Kerr in two earlier plays, I thought I was praising acting. I now wonder if I was really praising a certain sort of personality—perhaps only a certain sort of sex appeal emanating from a pouting, indolent, insolent sort of face and a helpless, dead voice. In the next role he undertakes, let Mr. Kerr prove me wrong."*

The Nature of Acting

Some recognized critics refuse to define acting at all. They agree only that acting is never an imitation, but rather that the actor is a translator—not literally but imaginatively—that he re-presents the character conceived by the playwright by allowing that character to pass through his own personality, and thus he (the actor) adds something mystic to the performance.

In our search for some principles on the subject of acting, let us

* Eric Bentley, *What Is Theatre?* (Boston: Beacon Press, 1956), p. 6.

turn to a few definitions that are most commonly used. The first that comes to mind is: "Acting is make-believe." On the surface this seems wholly logical and simple. If it were sufficiently complete to cover the art of acting, it would be a happy solution. Certainly acting is make-believe, but it is much more! If it were that alone, then the most perfect actors in the world would be a group of children happily imagining a situation of their own choosing. Who has not watched such a drama as a group of youngsters playing house, cops and robbers, cowboys and Indians, or any number of similar make-believe situations? They are completely at ease and very natural in their voices and actions, for their imaginations are working in high gear.

If, however, this same group of children is placed on a stage or asked to enact the same lines from a memorized script, they immediately become frightened, didactic in their delivery, stiff in their actions, self-conscious in their approach, utterly devoid of emotion, and ineffective as actors. What do they lack? Technique!

So our first definition falls short. It fails at once to make acting an art because it has eliminated the very essence of all art. "Fine acting," says Sarah Bernhardt, "is not a gift of the gods. It is the ultimate result of a willingness to acquire technique by constant attention to petty details. No actor ever became great overnight who had not spent weary months in the acquisition of technique."

Another definition also carries some truth and is quite satisfactory for one school of acting. It says that "Acting is the art of throwing away your own personality, taking on that of another, and making that assumption seem real to the audience."

In the days of the old stock company, when each actor was required to play a new role every week and sometimes more than one role in a single play, always submerging his own personality, this might have been a logical answer. A member of the audience once praised Edwin Forrest in his role as Lear by saying: "I felt that you acted King Lear magnificently." Mr. Forrest angrily replied: "Acted! By God, I *am* Lear!" There are many other great actors now and in the past who might find this definition sufficient to encompass their work. They are often called the impersonators. On the other hand, there is always an abundance of fine actors who

could not begin to meet the requirements of this definition, for their own personality is too evident.

It would at once rule out many of our present-day actors who never pretend to lose their own identity. In discussing the play or picture in which they have appeared, we find ourselves using their names rather than those of the characters they would have us believe they were playing. They only act themselves and are often called personality actors.

Many will remember the cartoon showing three questions on a school blackboard with answers written by movie-going little Johnny:

> Who invented the telephone? . . . Don Ameche.
> Who issued the Emancipation Proclamation? . . . Raymond Massey.
> Who invented the incandescent lamp? . . . Spencer Tracy.

One of the most severe criticisms of personality acting in the motion pictures is that it too often forgets the actor's major problem: *characterization*. However, we must still recognize personality actors as actors, and to do so we must search for a broader definition.

A third answer is the simple statement: "Acting is consciously doing on the stage the things people do unconsciously in everyday life." This is valid as long as we are concerned with the realistic school, but the classic actor, or the Shakespearean actor, and the actor in fantasy or expressionistic plays would be wholly lost doing what he would do in everyday life. It is far too limited in its scope.

Rather than searching further for a definition, here is a combination of several generally accepted definitions that attempts to bring into its meaning all the elements we have been discussing.

Acting is the art of creating an illusion of naturalness and reality that is suited to the play, to the period, and to the character that is being represented.

This definition seems to encompass the technique, the various schools of acting, the element of illusion so necessary in the theatre, and the unity of the acting with the play and style—all vastly important considerations, one or more of which had been omitted in each of the other definitions.

The word "art" implies control, selection, form, and technique. "Creating an illusion of naturalness and reality" establishes our principle of holding a mirror up to life and still making it *seem* real rather than *be* real. "Suited to the play" gives a free rein to the style of the actor's performance. "Period and character being represented" furnishes the final freedom of creation in character delineation and use of the actor's own physical and imaginative assets.

The Schools of Acting

In our search for a satisfactory definition of acting we have mentioned those actors who in a large sense seemed always to play themselves—the personality actors—and those who would cast off their own personality and adopt that of another person—the impersonator. In essence we have already classified actors into two groups. There are few actors whom we could place wholly in one or the other, and it is doubtful if many actors consciously think of themselves as belonging to either school. Actors in their study are more likely to talk about their approach to a role, their personal style of acting, one of the many "methods," or even the age-old discussion of *feeling* versus *not feeling* the part.

For the sake of classification, we might say that acting falls, roughly, into two general schools: (1) those personality actors whose performances nearly always approach a close resemblance to themselves as we know them, who belong especially to the realistic theatre and interpret a part in terms of their own personality; (2) those actors who seem always to lose their own identity or personality in the character, not necessarily through make-up, but by the alteration in their body, voice, physical movement, and all outward characteristics. They seem to *become* the character they portray by disguising their own personality to fit the part. The first group we shall call the *Interpreters* and *Commenters*, which implies much more art than just being a personality actor, and the second, the *Impersonators*. To clarify as simply as

possible, the first brings the character of the play to himself and makes it over to fit his own personal characteristics, but also *interprets* or *comments* on the role. The second goes to the character and makes himself over as much as possible to be like the character he envisions the dramatist as having created. Either school is an acceptable approach to acting. The actor's talents, personality, training, physique, background, voice, and temperament all contribute to the school he consciously or unconsciously chooses. The demands of the role also help to determine the method. We, as an audience, need only decide which he has followed and then give our estimate of his success.

Just as the playwright chooses the type or style that best fits his material, so must the actor follow the method most satisfactory for him. The answer is often made easier when the author has written a part with a particular actor in mind, or when the director has resorted to what is called type-casting, or casting the actor who comes closest to the role, physically and emotionally, as he feels it was intended by the playwright. In this case it is many times necessary to see an actor play several roles before it is possible to determine which of the two schools he has followed.

The reader may well be asking what this "comment" entails, and the answer is not an easy one, for it is based on how each actor is able most subtly to give us his own feelings about the character and all that that character is saying or doing. The actor must not only discover, interpret, and project the feelings and emotions so that they are wholly clear to the audience, but he must enhance that interpretation with his own particular talents, understanding, experience, personality, and charm. The character must have taken on new dimensions as it passed through him to the audience. Ethel Barrymore was one of our greatest actresses in this school. Her voice always possessed that same deep quality, and the familiar gestures or mannerisms that we associated with her were present. She created a style that was peculiarly hers in every role, and still every part she played had its own individuality. In thinking back over the roles she made famous, each had its own characteristics, and though the great artistry of Ethel Barrymore was ever present, it never got in the way of the character. The same can be said

for Lynn Fontanne, Alfred Lunt, Katharine Cornell, and Maurice Evans. The school of interpretation and comment is especially evident in the work of Tallulah Bankhead, who has given us some fine acting during her career, but the personality of the actress is always a great part of her characterization. The vast majority of our motion picture and television actors are interpreters in varying degrees The great emphasis that has been put on type-casting is largely responsible for the general predominance of this school of acting.

In the school of impersonation our best illustration is the English actor, Alec Guinness. Anyone who has seen *Kind Hearts and Coronets* needs no further clarification. Any two of the following pictures, *The Man in the White Suit, The Lavender Hill Mob, The Prisoner,* and *Oliver Twist,* will show how completely the personality of this actor is lost and that of the character takes over.

Helen Hayes would seem to be the impersonator as much as any actress in our theatre today. To remember her as Victoria Regina, Mary of Scotland, Mrs. McThing, and the mousy little librarian in *Happy Birthday* is to remember four completely different persons. Not only were their emotions and personalities different, but their physical and vocal characteristics were equally as individualistic. The same can be said for Paul Muni as Zola, Louis Pasteur, or the fugitive from a chain gang in the motion pictures. On the stage he is remembered for his memorable characterizations in *Counsellor at Law, They Knew What They Wanted,* and *Inherit the Wind.* Each character is so distinctly different that it is difficult to believe they were played by the same man. Frederic March, Florence Eldridge, and the late Lon Chaney (played by James Cagney in the motion picture *The Man of a Thousand Faces*) are impersonators. This school was most brilliantly exemplified in the acting of Eric Portman and Margaret Leighton in the New York and London productions of *Separate Tables,* by Terrence Rattigan.

In commenting on the acting of Edwin Booth, Otis Skinner once said:*

---

* From *Footlights and Spotlights,* by Otis Skinner, copyright © 1924, 1951, used by special permission of the publishers, The Bobbs-Merrill Company, Inc. P. 93.

ACTING AND THE ACTORS

Booth had power of suggestion to the mind of the spectator, never losing his own personality in the assumption, but nevertheless conveying the impression that he was the character. It was never with the dominating force of Edwin Forrest who exclaimed: "By God! I *am* Lear!" The alchemy of Booth's art was more profound and subtle. Although a small, even a frail man, I could swear that at times in *Othello* and in *Macbeth* he was seven feet tall. Cardinal Richelieu was a physical giant; Shylock appeared shortened to stubbiness; Iago, small, lithe, dangerous, and radiant with devilish beauty.

Photographs used as illustrations for either the impersonator or the interpreter in a series of roles might easily confuse the reader. The subtlety of characterization cannot be expressed by a static picture. It is far more than the mere photograph of facial make-up. The distinction must be observed or felt in the physical and vocal attributes of the artist. It is inherent in his walk, his gestures, his stance, the inflections and delicate nuances of his voice, the shadings of his personality and that of the character he portrays. It lies in the spirit and mood of his attack, for characterization—the actor's major job—possesses dimensions that can never be caught by any single photograph.

The Areas of Acting

After deciding whether the actor has chosen to be an interpreter or an impersonator, we can, as an audience, turn to the next issue, namely, the three areas of acting.

In the first chapter we discussed the meaning of the term "technique," which was defined as the means to an end. In acting, it includes developing a "stage sense," for there are rules and principles of conduct that must be observed on the stage. It also means having an "audience sense," which is the actor's consciousness of the audience and its reaction without his ever permitting the audience to realize it. The actor's technique is a mastery of his own physical, mental, and emotional properties which will always assure his giving a satisfactory performance even when faced with

discomforts, sorrow, illness, or similar distractions. It is the element which, when most perfected, the audience calls naturalness or ease.

For the sake of clarity we might say that technique falls roughly into three areas:

The Technical or Physical
The Mental or Intellectual
The Emotional or Spiritual

The technical or physical is similar, in a way, to the scales one must master in music. It involves the way an actor gets about the stage—walks, sits, gestures, moves, handles himself and the properties. It includes his breathing, vocal training, and projection. It is the ease and convincingness with which he can *do* all that the audience sees and hears. All these attributes are basic to the actor's work. They can be taught and must be mastered before an actor can be really effective, for he must first be master of himself; his body and voice must be fully controlled.

The second area concerns the actor's mental approach to the role. He must have analyzed the character from every angle—understood his thoughts, feelings, and actions, his relationship to the play and the other characters. Again his approach is not of as much importance to us as are the results—whether or not he is able to project a well-rounded, honest, and believable character who would actually do and say the things we as an audience see and hear.

We have many actors who are highly successful in mastering these two areas. In the commercial as well as the noncommercial theatre there are those who never go beyond and who are considered "good actors." They are often referred to as "technicians" and even sometimes rise to stardom, but they rarely attain the status of "great actors."

The third and most vital area of acting technique is the emotional or the spiritual. Unfortunately, there are many actors who never attain this height, and it is extremely doubtful whether it can be taught. It involves the "imagination and sensibility" that Henry Irving had in mind when he spoke of great actors. It is what Ellen Terry meant when she said: "There are those

actors who can *only* do what they are taught, and there are those who can not be taught, but can be helped by suggestion to work out things for themselves."

David Belasco, a famous director of the early twentieth century, had it in mind when he said:

> The first word and the last word in acting is temperament. There must be heart, heart, heart. Soul is only a glow. The definite thing is the heart, the capacity to feel. Intelligence is desirable, but it is secondary. The merely brainy actor is never a great actor on the stage. The heart is greater than the brain.

Mr. Belasco developed many well-known actors, and for years held a prominent place in the American theatre as manager and director. One of his protégés was Frances Starr, a really fine actress. She was once asked if she could remember one admonition or direction that Mr. Belasco had given her which seemed most helpful, and Miss Starr answered without hesitation: "Yes, I remember his saying many times, 'Frances, listen with your eyes and speak with your heart.'" Helen Hayes has often referred to this same quality as "human warmth."

No one has ever sensed this third area as an audience in the theatre without being conscious of it. The experience may have lasted but an instant, or it may have pervaded a scene or an entire play. It may have been evident in only one actor, as is sometimes true in the community or educational theatre, but it is a quality that lifts the actor to a higher plane of creation and gives the spectator a special excitement or pleasure far above the ordinary. It furnishes those wonderful experiences in the theatre that one carries in his memory for years. Instances of its presence are legion in the annals of theatre history and stories about the great actors of the past, but there is not room to recite them here. If one has known the experience, the point is clear—if not, further discussion would not necessarily be of help.

As was said in the first chapter, all arts are translations of some phase of life in which one thing is expressed in terms of another, but in that translation *something must appear that was not there before.* Acting uses a human being as the medium and by that

means translates life as it is *plus* the elements of thought (selection) and action (drama or theatre), both of which have grown out of life.

At its base acting possesses certain fundamentals that make it a craft as well as the possibility of becoming an art. These fundamentals must be mastered. Their mastery makes it possible for any real gift the individual may possess to shine through. These basic requirements—the craft—are often developed to a high degree when there is no really great quality present. In such instances we may talk of good actors, but not of great artists. It is often these practitioners who fall back upon a personality or some physical qualification as the source of popularity, but we must not confuse this with art. By the same token, genius is sometimes lost to the world if the potential artist has not first mastered these fundamentals.

In this book we have chosen, because of a long association with actors and with the theatre, to give the two words *ability* and *talent* definitions that may not be wholly acceptable to either the dictionary or some schools of psychology. *Ability* we would define as a willingness to endure long study, tireless rehearsals, personal sacrifice, and the ordeals of completely mastering voice, body, and emotions. *Talent* is that crowning quality that, if not actually God-given, has come to the individual through no effort on his part. It is this gift that composes the third area, and it must be recognized, nurtured, and trained. Rarely are these two qualities found in a single individual.

To possess ability—the willingness to work and to sacrifice—is most commendable. To have talent is a minor miracle. To waste that talent due to the lack of ability is indeed tragic. The happy combination of the two, an inner radiance plus the acquisition of technique, can spell genius.

John Mason Brown has made a classification of actors that fits our discussion on schools and areas of acting most admirably:*

> There are the bad or indifferent players who cannot act, and who are unable to be themselves on a stage.

---

* John Mason Brown, *The Art of Playgoing* (New York: W. W. Norton & Company, Inc., 1936), pp. 193-94.

There are the character actors who are excellent at all sorts of eccentric types, but who can neither be themselves nor act themselves in public.

There are the suave or tough, the charming or the brusque, the handsome or the portly "straight" actors whose only, but whose quite considerable, talent it is to be their off-stage selves on stage. They are among the most delightful and serviceable contributors to our theatre of understatement.

Then there are the precious few, standing at the top of their profession, whose high gift it is to act themselves, to adapt their spirits to the spirits of the parts they are playing, to possess and then to be possessed by the characters they project, and to give them the benefit of their beauty and their intelligence, their sympathy and their virtuosity, their poetry and their inner radiance, their imagination and their glamour.

The Actor and Theatre Form

One of the earliest and most fundamental decisions the actor and director must make for each production concerns the theatre form and the actor's performance. Will it be presentational (audience centered) or representational (stage centered)? Will it be non-illusionistic (no attempt to give the impression that these events are actually occurring) or illusionistic (that these lines and these emotions are all very real, the characters mean what they say and do, the events are actually happening)? Some schools of drama prefer to consider this intent on the part of the actor as another style. We prefer to consider it as a separate entity and call it theatre form, for it can vary and yet be found within any given style. Although the playwright's script may suggest the proper approach, it is the director's decision and the actor's performance that make it evident to the audience.

In the theatre of the Greeks, Shakespeare, Molière, the Restoration, and the eighteenth and nineteenth centuries, the form was essentially presentational. The large audience, outdoor performances, and the aesthetic styles of all these periods made it practically mandatory. The play was presented straight *to* the audience,

almost as if it were another character in the drama without lines to speak. The audience, in effect, was taken into the confidence of the actors. Such information as it should have was given out directly by the chorus, a soliloquy, or later an aside. This form is common today in musical comedy, the vaudeville act, or the television skit with two comedians engaged in a verbal feud, but centering the whole of it directly to the audience. We call it presentational theatre. The old melodrama with the villain walking down to the footlights and confiding his thoughts to the audience was an exaggeration of this form.

Presentational drama can be either illusionistic or nonillusionistic. Certainly great actors of the past in the roles of Oedipus, Electra, Agamemnon, Hamlet, Macbeth, King Lear, and even Tartuffe intended that the audience should believe what it saw and should receive the impression that this situation actually existed and that the emotions and incidents were all very real. They were, then, presentational and illusionistic. This same technique—presentational and illusionistic—is still used by the monologist, as exemplified by Cornelia Otis Skinner and the late Ruth Draper in their one-woman shows.

On the other hand, many comedies such as *The Rivals* and *She Stoops To Conquer* and much of the eighteenth and nineteenth century sentimental drama might easily have been meant to give the impression of only a group of actors, rather than characters, telling a story. This is the great charm of the Restoration comedies. Each actor takes on the vocal and physical characteristics of the character he portrays, but the actor is always present. It is almost as if he is speaking in the third person. This treatment or form is called presentational and is nonillusionistic.

When the theatre moved indoors, the scenic background became more realistic, the lighting improved and with it the intimacy of the production, and there was a greater emphasis on the effort to give the impression of reality. The style leaned more and more toward realism or naturalism, and thus the representational form came into existence. The audience ceased to receive the direct attention of the actors. The play was stage centered. The actors spoke only to each other. It was directed *at* the audience instead

of *to* it. Eventually, an imaginary fourth wall was erected and the audience was, figuratively, looking through that wall at the actors. The actor's goal was to make the audience believe he was the character he pretended to be and that the story was actually occurring. The form is called representational and is illusionistic.

A play, then, can be presentational and nonillusionistic or presentational and illusionistic or representational and illusionistic. It is difficult to imagine a performance that is representational and nonillusionistic, though that might sometimes occur. Occasionally, there may appear to be several different combinations of theatre form in the same production. In this instance it is the predominant over-all effect that should determine the classification.

Some plays can be nearly ruined because the actors have not understood, mastered, or settled on a consistent approach as far as the form is concerned. An ultra-realistic modern play that depends upon the audience's belief and empathic response could have its very point shattered if one of the actors should suddenly step out of the illusionistic into the nonillusionistic form.

Interpretation, spirit, intent, director's and actors' goals, and the playwright's purpose all help in dictating exactly how the actor will consider his role in respect to the audience. For our purpose it is necessary only that we understand the meaning of these theatre forms so that we can judge more accurately what the actor is trying to do insofar as his audience relationship is concerned.

What the Audience Should Look For

Thus far we have talked more or less in generalities about acting. It is now important that we consider some specific items in the work of the individual actor. No two persons will necessarily look for the same things, and it is doubtful if many will be conscious during the performance of the exact points as they are here discussed. Their noticeability might very easily be distracting to the audience or an indication of overdisplay of technique on the part of the actor. It is often only in memory that we realize just what it was the actor did to make us criticize him favorably or adversely.

As has already been stressed, it is one of our first obligations as an audience to take with us not only our imaginary puissance, but also an attitude of critical discernment which again includes Goethe's three principles. Next, we must ask in what general style and theatre form the actor is playing. The use of his voice and body will vary widely in the performance of a classical, romantic, realistic, or expressionistic role. Today we would consider the acting of Garrick, Peg Woffington, Talma, Rachel, or even the great Sarah Bernhardt extremely odd and very much overdone. The recordings of so recent an actor as the late John Barrymore in the role of Hamlet will bring smiles from our present-day college students, yet John Barrymore is considered by many to have been one of the two greatest Hamlets of this century, matched only by John Gielgud. Death, indeed, is a blessing to the actor, for his prestige can be destroyed by the rapid evolution of his art.

If we know the actor personally, as in many school and community productions, it is important that we try to forget that fact and give him the opportunity of creating a character. If we have seen him before in another role, we should make an effort to put that out of our mind and think of him in what he is now trying to do. At the same time, we should try to separate him as an actor from the role he is playing, asking ourselves what he is doing or not doing to make that assumption easy or difficult.

To understand adequately the art of a given actor, it is our own responsibility to: (1) possess imaginary puissance and observe Goethe's advice; (2) understand the general style in which the actor is working; and (3) dissociate the actor from our previous knowledge of him and from the role he is playing. Only then can we evaluate his acting honestly and impartially.

In analyzing the work of the individual actor or the over-all effect of an entire cast, there are six questions which should be considered. The first deals with the actor's personal qualifications —what he brings to the role. The next four come from the writings of Crafton and Royer and concern the performance itself. They can be most helpful in pinpointing details that might otherwise evade us. The final question deals with the actor's cooperative ability and unselfishness. It has taken on greater importance since the theatre began to demand a unified production.

These six yardsticks for measuring the actor's work can be of assistance in the discussion of any dramatic event, whether it be stage, motion picture or television. They are:

1. What does the actor bring to the role in voice, body, personality, or as an individual?
2. Is his acting fresh?
3. Is his acting restrained?
4. Is his acting easy?
5. Is his acting convincing?
6. Does the actor fit into the production as an integral part of the whole?

What does the actor bring to the role in voice, body, personality, or as an individual? It may be imagination, a dynamic outgoing personality, temperament, a quality or style that is peculiarly his own, a voice or body that distinguishes him, or an authority that makes him master of all he does or is supposed to be. On the other hand, many of these attributes may be negative. Above all else, each actor—on the stage—must be a distinct personality. Off the stage, he may be as ordinary as any citizen, but on the stage he must bring something definite to the role, and we as an audience must recognize and appreciate just what that something is. It has been said, and nowhere is it more valid than in the actor, that personality is an aura that surrounds those individuals "who are capable of doing some single thing extremely well and with consummate grace."

Let us first consider his *authority.* Does the actor have a complete command over his body, voice, and emotions? Is he above the role, or is he so involved in it that he lacks adequate control? An actor should be two persons—the artist and the character. The artist should ever be in the ascendancy, guiding and controlling the character he is presenting with a firm hand. It is evident in the way the actor handles emergencies, such as a late entrance, a missed cue, an accident on the stage, or an unnecessary disturbance in the audience. It is always evident in the actor's command of what we have already called "stage" and "audience" sense.

How effective is the actor with the use of his *voice* and *body?* The voice must be pleasant in its pitch and its quality. The force must be adequate to be heard throughout the auditorium. There is

never an excuse for inaudibility. He must always speak without strain. The actor's diction, which includes articulation, enunciation, and pronunciation, should be sharp and clear, but must never attract attention to itself. Unless it is a part of his characterization, it must show no evidence of dialect or any particular section of the country. Any false or artificial note will instantly stamp him as insincere. He should have sufficient command of his vocal powers to give the subtle meanings that make for originality in line readings.

Regardless of how many times one may have seen *Macbeth*, he can never forget the completely new meaning that Judith Anderson brought as Lady Macbeth to those two simple words in the scene just before the murder when she said: "We, fail? !" Another unforgettable interpretation was given in the performance of Helen Hayes in *Twelfth Night*, after she received the ring from Olivia and realized that Olivia had fallen in love with her. She spoke those familiar lines, "She loves me," but gave them an inflection that expressed surprise, flattery, concern, and a wonder that one had never suspected the lines to possess.

S. N. Behrman relates a similar experience of his own:*

> In London I saw Dame Edith Evans as Cleopatra in Shakespeare's play. She played it for high comedy. In an early scene Cleopatra is informed by Antony that his wife, Fulvia, is dead. Cleopatra's line is: "Can Fulvia die?" The Dame's reading of that line was delicious; it sent a ripple of laughter through the audience. She read it with a rising inflection of incredulity and pleasure, with a peculiar overtone of the last word which raced you through Cleopatra's mind. You heard her also saying: "Well! Evidently I have always underestimated Fulvia. I never suspected that she had the resource or the tact for a gesture like this!" Ever since then, when I see this play, I listen for the actress who plays Cleopatra to read this line; usually it comes out as a simple request for information, like: "Do you play canasta?"

The unusual shadings which reveal hidden connotations in a line indicate not only a brilliance of conception, but a voice highly trained in the art of expression.

* S. N. Behrman, "Query: What Makes Comedy High," *The New York Times*, March 30, 1952.

The actor's body must be completely coordinated. His movements must be graceful and his gestures used only to augment the voice. What he does physically must be effortless and never attract attention to itself, unless that is the specific demand of the play. Every movement and gesture on the stage must have a purpose and a meaning. The slightest twitch of a finger or an unnecessary shift of the weight can become a distracting element.

Does he possess an *individual style* or *quality* that distinguishes him as an actor? Individual style does not mean the use of individual vocal or physical mannerisms as such. Rather it implies the use of the actor's own body and voice *adapted* to the character he portrays, but adapted with intelligence and imagination as well as originality. It is the lending of his own instruments of interpretation to the role so well expressed by Mr. Brown in his fourth classification of actors on pages 128, 129. It is more than the actor just being himself; it is what the actor consciously does with himself. No wise actor ever attempts to copy any part of the style which is associated with another. Imitation is the kiss of death to any real artist—no personal style is of any value unless it belongs to the actor as an individual and to him alone.

What special characteristics does this actor possess to make him excel? What does he do that is distinctive? To have seen George M. Cohan or Margaret Anglin take the audience into their confidence without ever seeming to break through the proscenium arch was to have witnessed one of the most unusual techniques in the modern theatre. No one has ever seemed to quite capture Miss Anglin's unique manner in this respect. Each person in the audience seemed suddenly to become the character on the stage to whom she was speaking, and yet her performance remained realistic, representational, and wholly illusionistic. It was the perfect example of a really great artist's ability to break through and show an exception to any basic principle.

What we call a distinctive quality of the actor may be a warmth, a coldness, a dry sense of humor, a winsomeness, or any other personal attribute that distinguishes this particular actor. It may be something we feel or hear or see. It may lie in the quality of voice as with Ethel Barrymore, or in a great talent for walking as

with William Courtney, or in a tremendous personal charm so evident in Mary Martin, or the human warmth of Helen Hayes. Whatever talent this particular actor possesses, it is worthy of being recognized, for it is part of him and his art.

Sincerity is a valuable quality. Sometimes it may be so great a part of the individual actor that it all but takes precedence over important principles already mentioned. In a certain performance of Saroyan's *Hello, Out There*, presented by college freshmen, there was evidence of this point. The young girl had a polish, a depth of emotion, a voice, and a feeling that aroused the audience to great admiration. She had developed a stage and audience sense that held great promise for her and suggested a native talent with some acquisition of technique. The young boy lacked all these qualities, but his performance portrayed a sincerity, a youthfulness, a wonder that made the lines of the play take on a completely new meaning. His wistfulness, his failure to understand just why he seemed always just to miss the things he wanted most in life pulled at the heartstrings of the audience. The actor was utterly without technique and might not have been very powerful in any other role, but here he possessed a spontaneity and an unabashed sincerity that made him very exciting. This *special* quality was deserving of praise, and the discerning critic will seek and point out just such examples of talent.

The actor's authority, his command of voice and body, his personal style or quality, and the sum total of his personality are the attributes he brings to the role as an individual. As we have said before, he is his own instrument and must be so considered and evaluated.

Is his acting fresh? Regardless of what the printed program may say, the events on the stage or screen are supposed to be happening now! No matter what period in history is being presented by playwright and actors, we have the right to demand that it give us what William Gillette called "the illusion of the first time." It is most important in the actor's work that each speech, each look, each action carry with it the evidence of its never having been said or done before.

Mary Martin on her five hundredth performance in *South*

Pacific was so fresh and so new that it seemed as if she were experiencing every emotion and speaking each line for the very first time. Another important member of the company read each comedy line with the full knowledge, and practically with an official announcement, that here is a big laugh—get ready!—it's coming!!—here it is, and—bam!!! Then he settled back complacently until the reaction had subsided and awaited the next response which he knew so well would come. It was obvious to the least critical analysis that his inspiration was gone and that the task of performing the role had fallen into mere routine.

This "illusion of the first time" should be noticed in how the actor comes into a room, locates an object, reacts to the lines spoken by other members of the company, and in the tone of his voice. It can be especially evident in the fleeting expression of the eyes and face that appears just before the actor speaks a line. It is seen in the position of hands and feet, and attitude of the body. Not only is it of vital importance to the art of the actor, but also to sustaining the "half-faith" of the audience. It is the great test of the actor's thoroughness, his honesty, and his sincerity. Each audience has the right to demand this freshness, this illusion of the first time.

Observe how an actor makes an entrance or an exit. How many times one has seen a character merely come on or leave the stage. It is so obvious that he has been standing outside the door waiting for his cue, or that since the author has not given him further lines, he might just as well leave. On the other hand, great moments can be remembered in the theatre when an actor has made his entrance or exit truly meaningful.

The first entrance of Maude Adams in her revival of *The Merchant of Venice* can never be forgotten. Even though she was past sixty, it was as if ten thousand watts of light had suddenly been turned on. True, at this age, she was not able to sustain that excitement throughout the performance. The same was true of Mrs. Fiske in her revival of *Becky Sharp*. To those who had not seen these great actresses in their prime, it was a revelation of what they must have been.

During the performance of an otherwise undistinguished pro-

duction of *The Silver Box* by Galsworthy, Ethel Barrymore provided a further illustration of a memorable exit. At that point where the wife realizes that it is her husband who is the thief and must soon be taken by the law, she turns and quietly walks off the stage. In that exit and without a word, she portrayed the disillusionment, sorrow, and wreckage of her home and life. The particular performance was given during that brief period in Miss Barrymore's life when critics had generally agreed that her career was ended. The feeling that swept through that summer-theatre matinee audience was ample indication that this great actress still possessed the genius that had given her recognition. Not long after that, she proved it to even the most dubious critic in her brilliant interpretation of Miss Moffat in *The Corn is Green*.

Watch how the actor builds within a speech, a series of speeches, or merely by pantomime to a climax or crisis. This was so evident time after time in Maurice Evans' performance in *Richard II;* and no one who saw this actor play the role of the Dauphin in Katharine Cornell's production of *Saint Joan* will ever forget the climactic moment so quietly portrayed as he completed his questioning of Joan, meekly walked to his throne chair, and dropped in it, emphasizing his weakness as a man and as a ruler, in contrast to the strength of Joan of Arc.

Note how the actor sustains his role. Does the character grow and change as the play progresses? In Clifford Odets' *The Country Girl,* the attitude of the audience toward the two leading characters is completely reversed from the first act to the last. Much of this, of course, is in the lines, but a generous portion must come from what the actor does to gain or lose our sympathy. The change in the character of the young coal miner in *The Corn is Green* requires great deftness on the part of the actor.

Many times an actor will give all he has during the first act. This can only mean a plateau or monotony during the remainder of the play. He may also drop out of character when he has no lines to speak. Nothing can destroy the spirit of a musical that has been running for some time more quickly than to catch the disinterested expression on the faces of the chorus or those in minor roles during the song or dance of a featured player.

Much as we have insisted upon technique and important as it is to the actor, there is nothing more dangerous than the acquisition of a little technique. A few successful productions sometimes give the nonprofessional a feeling of confidence and a conviction that he knows exactly what to do on the stage at all times. This dependence on technique is also found in the work of the greatest stars of our stage, particularly after they have played a role for a great length of time. A discussion of the eternal question, does the actor need to feel the role, is not pertinent to this book, but making the *audience* feel it is very pertinent. The element of freshness in the actor's performance is most essential in this respect. It is not difficult to detect that moment when the actor, as artist, walks off the stage both emotionally and mentally and leaves only the physical part of his character on the stage. Eva Le Gallienne has said that the actor's greatest problem is to recreate the original freshness, sincerity, and emotion of his character in every performance regardless of how many he has given or what his own personal feelings may be at that time.

The freshness of a performance is more likely to suffer on the stage than in the motion picture, for in the latter instance the director may take and retake the scene until the actor has given just the performance he desires. This is also true of the television program that has been filmed. Live television can suffer in this respect, though not faced with the problem of the long run as in the legitimate theatre.

Is the actor restrained? Since we go to the theatre to have our emotions touched, and whether the play is romantic or realistic we want it to happen in us, the final test of the actor is: does he make *us* feel the part? The actor's greatest asset in the realization of this goal lies in the matter of his restraint. He must have power within him, but it must be amply controlled. His job is to stir the imagination of his audience. Tears spilling down the cheeks are usually less dramatic than an effort at control. The blubbering close-ups of the motion picture are highly inartistic and far less effective than more restraint would be. The great actor hints at more than he declares. The real strength or power of any line lies in its tone. The good actor suggests, never portrays, the emo-

tion he wants the audience to experience. He builds up to a particular moment, and when that moment arrives his work is done and the audience takes over. Why should an audience exert itself emotionally when the actor is doing all the work himself?

Mae West has frequently been called a great performer, and her work in *Diamond Lil* confirms this statement. Tallulah Bankhead, with the exception of her Regina in *The Little Foxes*, has frequently received the same comment by critics. In each case the actress named has given just that—a brilliant performance—but has not been working with the rest of the cast to present the play or its meaning. In short, she has lacked that aspect we are discussing—subtlety. Brooks Atkinson once pointed out that subtlety is the real difference between a great performance and great acting. This valuable quality of restraint is evident in the speaking of lines, in the handling of the body, in the grasp and expression of an emotion, in the smoothness and integration of all these elements. It involves never overacting or overstating, but always relying on suggestion and the imagination and intelligence of the audience.

Is the actor easy? The audience must be totally unconscious of any effort on the part of the actor. All hard work, so far as the audience is concerned, must have been done before the opening night. In performance the actor must be the master of himself vocally, physically, and emotionally. His technique is there, but it never shows through. Whatever he does *seems* so natural that it is accepted without question. The perfect performance is one that seems to the spectator so easy and so right that he is tempted to imagine that he, without training, could do as well as the artist.

Observe the success of the actor in the "art of doing nothing." This is one of the most difficult phases of the actor's work. It means that he must be on stage and a part of the scene even when the author has given him nothing to say and little to do, although he is still in full view of the audience. It has been said that acting is not as much acting as reacting, and there is no better proof of this statement than these moments of doing nothing. It is then that the actor's integrity, sincerity, and imagination are challenged, calling for great personal control and restraint. To be successful when given a speech and stage center is not nearly so great an

achievement as to be always an important and necessary part of the picture without detracting from it and with apparently nothing to do.

Note the actor's sense of timing, how he uses the element of time through his mastery of pausing, phrasing, and holding. It has often been remarked that the actor's chief secret is his timing—an important facet of restraint. The term "time value" is sometimes given to those moments when words are not spoken, but the emotion and mood of the scene flow on. Anyone who has seen much theatre will remember particularly poignant moments when the actor played upon the imagination of the audience through the use of a gesture, a movement of the head, or some indication of his feelings, suggesting a similar personal experience to the spectator which would have been lost had the actor resorted to the limitation of words.

There is no single distinction more obvious between the trained and the untrained actors than in their sense of timing. The inexperienced actor rushes forward, fearful that the audience will think he has forgotten his next line, but the true artist makes the most of every time value, knowing that there is greater power in the suggestion of an emotion than in its actual delineation, that he can create more in the mind of the audience by the correct pause than by any words he could speak.

Timing is most important in comedies. Watch how easily the actor plants a laugh, builds it, waits for it to reach the exact peak of its climax, and stops it at just the right split second with his next line so that the play can move on. Observe closely the actor's sense of rhythm in this respect. At its best, it resembles a tennis game in the give-and-take between the actor and the audience as he varies his timing with their response, never breaking the basic rhythm of the play.

This sense of timing is of no less importance in the serious play. The actor's command of the pause, his use of the time value, his feeling for the exact instant for speech or silence are his most precious tools for holding and moving the audience. The actor's training in this respect is one of his most priceless possessions. It develops with the years and is the very core of his technique. For

an observer not to recognize and judge each actor's facility in this area is to miss much of his art.

Is the actor convincing? Every item thus far mentioned on the subject of acting contributes in some way to this question. The ultimate goal of every actor is to make the audience *believe* him and everything he says and does. His actions must at all times be rightly and fully motivated. His role must be synchronized with the whole production. There must be no inconsistency in his playing or in what he wants us to believe.

Sometimes characters carry such conviction in their playing that audiences find it hard to accept them outside the part. During the First World War, Eric von Stroheim played many German roles so well that he was often refused service in restaurants. A very intelligent theatregoer refused to applaud the work of a young man who had played Danny in *Night Must Fall,* and Phillips Holmes found it difficult to win back his public after the first filming of *An American Tragedy.* The fault in each of these instances was, of course, with the audience that had failed in its obligation to dissociate the actor from the part he was playing. Certainly the actor could not be accused of not being convincing.

The make-up and the costuming make their contributions to the actor's world of make-believe. So often his inability to apply make-up properly or to wear his costume naturally and with ease prove stumbling blocks in his convincingness. Make-up takes much study and practice and varies with the lights and auditorium that are being used. There is also the problem, especially in the non-commercial theatre, of the young actor or actress playing the middle-aged or older roles. One should make up for the middle of the house but strive not to apply it too heavily for the front rows. It is better to err with too little than too much. The professional theatre, with its emphasis on type-casting, has simplified the make-up problem to a great extent, but make-up is an art in itself and an exceedingly important factor in the actor's being believed by the audience.

Both professional and nonprofessional players are often guilty of allowing their costumes to overpower them. It is most important to wear the costumes of a period play with ease. The Shake-

spearean ruff and cape, the tunic of the Greek theatre, the ruffles and breeches of the Restoration, the bustles and hoop skirts of the nineteenth century, can bring havoc to a production unless the actors have learned to wear them as well as they have memorized their roles.

In a production of a Civil War play presented by an eastern summer-theatre company, the mood was completely destroyed when the young lady arose from the sofa and turned too quickly in her walk to the upstage door. The front of the hoop caught on the corner of the sofa, and the rear of the hoop caught her on the back of the neck. The warm weather had caused her to reduce her undergarments to a pair of red shorts, and suddenly the audience had what appeared to be the Japanese flag thrust before its eyes! A college production of *The Cradle Song* brought forth a situation almost as ludicrous, for college girls were not accustomed to the steady, smooth, and dignified walk required by the length of the nun's habit.

A criticism often made of an actor is simply: "I did not believe him." To avoid this condemnation is a vital part of every artist's work, for belief is a prime requisite of any dramatic enjoyment.

Does the actor fit into the production as an integral part of the whole? Note how he gives a scene that does not belong to him as well as how he takes the scene that does. It is not always to an actor's credit to say that he stole the show. Many times he may have been playing to the audience in a bid for popularity rather than to have been a part of the scene as the author had intended. Famous stars have been small enough to make a movement, cough, drop a handkerchief, or by some other means attract the attention of the audience when the best interest of the play demanded that it be on some other player.

Sometimes someone in a professional production is guilty of up-staging the other members of the cast. This is unforgivable. The same error may be committed by noncommercial players without any intent of stealing the scene, although frequently with a little technique and some knowledge of the stage they too have been known to do it deliberately. Part of the critic's work is to study each actor and understand his importance in the scene, and then as-

certain any indication he may show of being either the selfish actor who would stand out from the group, or the cooperative one who realizes that he is a part of the picture and is wholly conscious of just what contribution he should make.

A story is told that we shall suppose is fiction rather than fact, concerning three equally prominent and popular actors who found themselves playing a scene together. Actor A, who was downstage right, suddenly realized that Actor B at the apex of the triangle was receiving most of the attention and edged upstage in order to share the limelight. Actor C immediately realized that his back was on the audience and managed to get upstage of both the other two actors. Actor B became frantic and once more returned to the apex of the triangle. The same procedure was repeated, and before the scene was ended, all three actors were lined up against the back wall, turning their heads as they spoke each to the other. Once more we would emphasize that the story is probably not true, but it could have been, and unfortunately there are actors who could be guilty of such an indiscretion.

The preceding six questions must always be asked if theatregoers would observe the art of the actors. Without asking them and observing how successfully each actor has met each one of them, we are denying him his technique and robbing him of his profession.

By now the reader may have found for himself some more honest standard for his decision on the actor's contribution. Although acting does grow out of nature and is based on biology and all the human attributes and characteristics, the average man is no better equipped to evaluate the actor's art than any other art without proper training. Without such background he takes for granted that the actor's ultimate goal is to produce life so realistically that one could mistake the acting for reality. Nothing could be further from the truth artistically. Such duplication in any art is only deception. This deception was the chief reason for abandoning the extreme naturalism of André Antoine, Zola, and David Belasco.

The actor's worth as an artist should be based on our understanding of what he says in addition to the lines he speaks, for merely giving them their literal meaning cannot be considered acting. He

must, in addition, *imply what he and the character are thinking.* Then he has, as an artist, begun to interpret. If he also portrays how *he and the character feel* concerning these lines, he has arrived at what we may call the art of acting.

A final and superior description of good acting comes to us from John Dolman, who says:*

> Good acting is neither wholly realistic nor wholly unrealistic. It is sufficiently realistic to be intelligible and suggestive and to arouse the necessary empathy; it is sufficiently consistent to be convincing; and it is sufficiently unreal to preserve *aesthetic distance* and to leave something to the imagination.

When we, as an audience, have come to appreciate the art of the actor, we shall be able to distinguish between him, his art, and his role. With this artistic intelligence we shall no longer belong to those who insist that any character whose death occurred during the play's action should not appear in the curtain call.

---

* John Dolman, Jr., *The Art of Play Production* (New York: Harper & Brothers, 1946), p. 227. Copyright, 1928, by Harper & Brothers.

The Background

and Technicians

From the very beginning of the organized theatre, the drama and the actors have been integral parts of the picture. Audiences have praised or blamed them, but were always at least conscious of their presence. In this chapter we shall give some thought to another group of individuals whose identity, with a few exceptions, has been lost in our theatre history and whose work in contemporary times is unfortunately taken for granted by the average playgoer. In the modern theatre these workers are constantly making their own very important contributions to the final success or failure of a production, and the more subtle and unobtrusive these efforts are, the more appropriate and satisfactory their work. The names of these persons may not even appear on the printed program and are

not often known or mentioned by many of the audience. They are the people who do all their work behind the scenes—the backstage personnel, the scene builders and painters; the stage, property, sound, costuming, lighting, and, sometimes, make-up crews. Rarely are we conscious of their work in a production, unless a stage hand is accidentally caught on stage, a lighting cue is missed, a property misplaced, or some other blatant error occurs.

It is common knowledge that the stipulations of the labor unions who control these backstage workers in the professional theatre are frequently preposterous and that the weekly salaries of the workers themselves often make bank presidents wonder if they have chosen the right profession. The numerous stories of utterly ridiculous union demands could go on *ad infinitum*. They have too often worked hardships on productions to the point that the closing notice has had to be posted, and equally as often have made it too expensive even to open a very worthy production. They, more than any other single factor, brought to an end the artistic hopes that all theatre lovers of this country had for the American Repertory Theatre, headed by Eva Le Gallienne, Margaret Webster, and Cheryl Crawford. This, however, is not the place for dwelling on what is considered by theatre people to be one of the major causes for the diminishing Broadway stage.

This same group of workers is found in the noncommercial theatre, and here also the value of their contribution too often goes unnoticed. They, however, are not compensated by the lucrative financial returns of their professional brothers. Instead, they work countless hours and with infinite pains to give the actors the proper background and mood and the play its most effective production. All this is done without hope of public praise or pay, for they seek only their own artistic and creative satisfaction and the sheer delight of just being a part of the production. They are true lovers of the theatre, highly important cogs in the wheels that turn out our noncommercial productions. It is this group of "forgotten men" who make it possible for thousands of audiences across the country to know the joys of the theatre experience. Their goal is a smoothly running, well integrated, perfect production, and, strange as it may seem, they get just as much thrill by standing in the wings and

counting the curtain calls as do the actors out front, taking the bows and smiling to the audience. These are craftsmen of the theatre who must also be artists.

The Technicians

Throughout history the scenic background, the costumes, and the lighting have varied in importance. At times each has been utterly ignored, while in other periods and productions one or more have overpowered both actors and play. Although the individual artists involved, with a few exceptions, have been forgotten, it is only within comparatively recent times that we have come to consider the work of those artists known as:

The Scene Designer

The Lighting Designer

The Costume Designer

who are today called the technicians of the theatre. There are other technicians in the motion picture and in television who will be discussed in the chapters devoted especially to those fields. Any conscientious analysis of a dramatic production must take into serious consideration the contributions of the technicians. Such names as Peter Larkin, Jo Mielziner, Stewart Chaney, Donald Oenslager, Cecil Beaton, Jean Rosenthal, Adrian, Motley, Raymond Sovey, and Valentia have thus come to be known by intelligent playgoers along with those of the actors and playwrights.

It is the purpose of this chapter to consider very briefly the historical backgrounds of these technicians and more in detail their individual goals and techniques as they may be observed in any current dramatic production.

The Scene Designer

It is an interesting study in evolution to trace the development of the physical theatre from the campfire of primitive man and his

unconscious drama, through the glorious sunlit outdoor theatre of the Greeks, the spectacular arenas of the Romans, the various stations of the Catholic Church in its liturgical plays of the Middle Ages, the elaborate perspectives of the Renaissance, and the artificially painted backdrops of the nineteenth and early twentieth centuries, to our own "peep-hole" or "picture frame" stage with its realistic scenery. (See diagrams on pages 56-59.)

It is a story that finds the playwright and the actor gradually losing their freedom both in space and emotional expression. The wide open-air stage of the Greeks, with its freedom of imagination and movement, has been traded for the tiny realistic stage cluttered with properties and furniture, and the actor has been forced to think in terms of littleness. He and his emotions have been imprisoned. The move toward realism has also practically eliminated any contact between actor and audience. In our modern theatre, the audience is little more than an eavesdropper, rather than an active participant, as in the theatre of the past. As more and more has been done in the way of portraying locale, it has likewise become less necessary for the audience and actors to exercise their imagination. The price of sharing the intimacy of our next-door neighbor's life has meant trading majesty for the microscopic.

John Dolman in *The Art of Play Production* made an interesting analysis of the scenic background, its evolution, and its various contributions throughout history. His discussion is given brief consideration here because the historical order of scenery is essentially the same as its artistic order of importance in our modern theatre.

Mr. Dolman has pointed out that the one purpose of the "skene" —that small building in the background of the Greek theatre— was to serve as *concealment* for the actors while costume changes were being made or when their presence on the stage was not necessary. It is only natural that the bare surface of such an enclosure would sooner or later call for some means of *decoration*. Undoubtedly the Greeks took some steps in this direction, but it was the Romans who elaborated not only upon the size of the building itself, but also the details of its decoration. The third use or purpose of scenery is *mood*. It did not become an important factor until

the Middle Ages, when the Roman Catholic Church, with the nuns and choir boys as actors and the various stations of the church as stages, turned to the theatre as its means of relating the great stories of the Bible, especially the birth, death, and resurrection of Jesus in the dramas of the Christmas and Easter seasons. It remained for Leonardo da Vinci during the Renaissance in Italy and Inigo Jones in England to develop the perspective in scene painting which for the first time *suggested place*. This element of suggestion gradually evolved into a fifth step, that has come down to the theatre of our day. The creation of the various technicians has varied from the artificially painted backdrops with their attempts to duplicate furniture, properties, and scenic details, to the realistic interior or exterior that may be seen on the stage today. As scene-shifting devices, mechanical equipment, and modern lighting facilities have come into our theatre, it has more and more been the effort of the scenic artist to *portray place*. It reached its peak in this country during the days of David Belasco, whose ultra-realistic settings dominated the stage for years and whose influence is still felt in some phases of our theatre.

Modern Scenic Styles

Before discussing the requirements of scenery, we should consider some of the modern trends in scenic design. Few stage settings would ever fit solely into any single classification, for aesthetic freedom always permits borrowing from any source that will contribute to the total effectiveness of the artist's goal. The scene designer confers with the director and then proceeds to create the scenery that will best fit the needs of the play. Rarely does he think in terms of any particular scenic style. He does what he feels should be done, and after the set is completed, it is the audience who labels it. It is this labeling that presents one of our greatest problems in discussing scenery, and the difficulty lies in terminology. Unfortunately, few authorities are in full agreement as to the exact meaning of all the words they use to describe the settings in our modern theatre.

THE BACKGROUND AND TECHNICIANS

The six most commonly accepted scenic styles are Realism, Simplified Realism, Impressionism, Expressionism, Theatricalism, and Formalism. The first four lean in the direction of imitating life and, in theory, propose to help the actor develop and project the mood and spirit of the play. The last two tend to suggest rather than portray, serving only as a satisfactory background and, in theory, help the actor by staying out of his way. Our interpretation of each style will be presented in an effort to show how that style makes use of line, mass, and color.

Realism. The ultra-realistic set is an effort to portray place consistently, convincingly, and as completely as possible. There was a period when naturalism—which can be defined as extreme realism —would have come first, but it is rarely seen today. There are some plays, such as *Street Scene, Of Mice and Men,* and *The Diary of Anne Frank,* in which realism in the scenery is most necessary. In the realistic set great attention is given to small detail, and every effort is used to give evidence of reality. David Belasco even imported the authentic furniture of Madame du Barry with which he set the stage of the play about her life. At other times he insisted upon running water, a stove that actually prepared food on stage, and such realistic details as knocking radiators. The sunsets he contrived through lighting are still praised for their naturalistic beauty by those who saw them in the theatre half a century ago.

Such duplication of life and such lack of suggestion was and is sure to find criticism among those who accept the premise that all art is selection rather than representation. A further discussion of realism and its effect on the audience will be found later in this chapter. Exciting as it may be and appropriate as it is for some plays, it is not considered as artistic or creative as some of the other styles.

Simplified realism. This is an effort to simplify the advantages of realism so that the setting may meet more accepted aesthetic standards. In the simplified setting no effort is made to fool the audience. If some detail is unconvincing, it is eliminated rather than to continue the search for a more convincing substitute. Some

evidence of unreality may appear, which is not a distraction, but an admission that the setting is only an illusion of reality. The goal of the artist is suggestion of the exact locale rather than representation.

Impressionism. This gives only the impression of locale and carries simplification even further. It is what Jo Mielziner calls "implied scenery" and is more interested in mood than detail or any effort to do more than merely suggest place. It demands more imagination on the part of the audience. Because the element of exaggeration is almost inevitable, most impressionistic sets take on some form of stylization. An impressionistic set normally uses only partial walls and set pieces that are often silhouetted against a plain cyclorama. Doors, windows, and lesser details may be only indicated. This style of scenery is very effective in staging classical plays, or in fact almost any style of drama with the exception of the ultra-realistic. It was used very effectively in conjunction with simplified realism in *Death of a Salesman,* especially in the dream sequences which took place in Willy Loman's mind.

Expressionism. This is the most difficult of all to describe, for it borrows from all the other arts by using music, rhythm, line, mass, color, and lights. The designer distorts the lines of the scenery to express mental or emotional distortion of one or more of the characters. Plastic forms, levels, and sharp angles are used most frequently. It finds its greatest use in such plays as *From Morn to Midnight* or *The Adding Machine.* The asylum scene in *Peer Gynt* is a perfect example of the use of this style.

Whereas impressionism appeals principally to emotion, expressionism appeals more to the intellect. Very common a few years ago, the latter is used less frequently now except in combination with other styles.

Theatricalism. This is both the oldest and the newest style. Until the realistic theatre came into existence, it was the accepted practice in any theatre experience. This was especially true after the development of perspective in scene painting. It reached its height during the nineteenth century when wings and backdrops were frank admissions of unreality, even though they attempted to sug-

gest the locale with their painted exteriors or interiors, including all minute details. A theatrical set today presents scenery as scenery. It may be decorated attractively and in the mood of the production, but it makes no pretense to be more than scenery. There is no attempt at any illusion of reality. It is only background. It is found most frequently in musical revues.

Formalism. Formalism makes use of the natural background belonging to the building, the theatre, or the auditorium where the play is being given. It employs neither representation nor suggestion. Perfect examples are simple draperies, the pulpit of a church, or an outdoor stage. Such a set is ideal for poetic tragedy. It was the only stage or setting used by the Greeks in their outdoor theatres or by Shakespeare in the Globe. Background is only background and not even expected to be considered as scenery. Formal backgrounds are very effective with the classics or in modern unrealistic plays suited to the presentational form.

In the following illustrations Don Swanagan, New York designer, has envisioned a realistic setting and then imagined how that same setting might appear if the generalizations concerning simplified realism, impressionism, expressionism, and theatricalism were carried out. Formalism does not appear, because that style would use the natural locale and, therefore, no scenery, as we have here defined it.

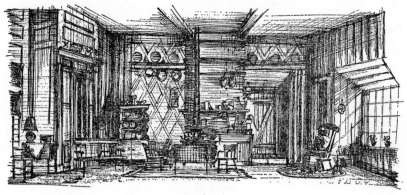

Realism

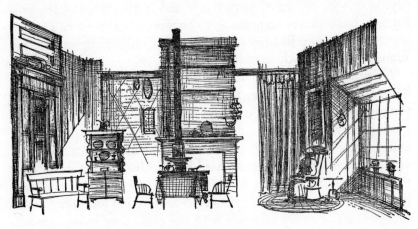

Simplified Realism

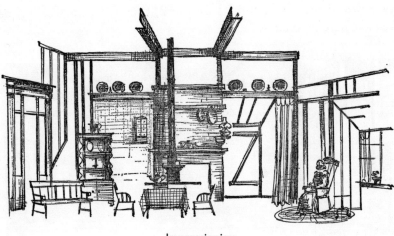

Impressionism

THE BACKGROUND AND TECHNICIANS

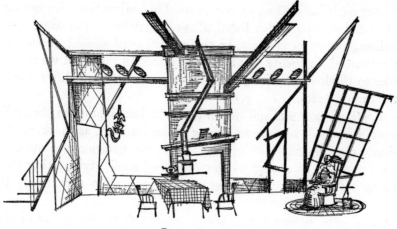

Expressionism

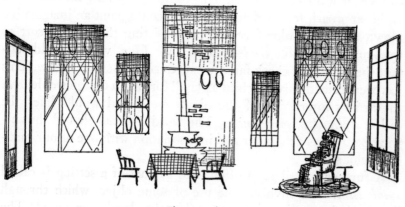

Theatricalism

Contributing Factors to Scenic Styles

Three contributing factors may be used in conjunction with any one of the six scenic styles listed above. They are stylization, symbolism, and space staging. In the confusion of scenic terminology the most abused word of all is "stylized." In this book we should like to think of it primarily as an adjective that modifies one of the major styles.

Stylization works and depends on the imagination of the audience. It appeals to the emotion or to the intellect, as the scene designer may desire. Its chief technique is exaggeration of some kind with a special treatment of an established scenic style, rather than being a style in itself. The very term stylization must imply illusion.

The scene designer may stylize according to the *period* of the play or the *mood* of the play. The first might involve designing a near replica of the old Globe Theatre stage for the production of a Shakespearean play. In Shakespeare's day this would have been a formal setting, but it would now be *stylized formalism*. An equally imaginative designer might conceive a series of backdrops and wings to represent the various settings in *Ten Nights in a Barroom* as it was done in 1890. This could be *stylized theatricalism*. In his approach to mood another artist could paint an imaginative blown-up water color forest scene, depicting the wildest sort of trees and flowers for *Androcles and the Lion*, which would suggest the tongue-in-cheek fantasy expressed by Bernard Shaw. This has been termed "artistic child's play," for such a design would give the artist's impression of the play's mood and would likely be called *stylized impressionism*. The word *stylized* should thus always be used as a modifier and in association with one of our modern scenic styles.

A further contribution often used as part of a setting is called *symbolism*. This involves the use of some object which through its association will establish the thought, locale, or mood. The imagination of the audience will then fill in the remainder of the setting. Such symbols may be used as a judge's bench for a court-

THE BACKGROUND AND TECHNICIANS

room, a blackboard for a schoolroom, a figure of the Virgin Mary for a religious mood. Further objects of symbolism could be a flag, a church window, a jail door, etc. Concrete symbols may become *symbolic impressionism*. Abstract motifs of a similar nature may thus lead to a *symbolic expressionism*. *Our Town* could be said basically to have used a formalistic background, but when the church window was projected on the back wall, or the soda fountain was implied by the use of two chairs and a plank, or the ladders suggested stairways, the scene designer was using a *symbolic formalism*.

The third contributing factor is called *space staging*, and if the director possesses sufficient lighting equipment and a satisfactory cyclorama—preferably black velours—he can do some remarkably artistic and imaginative work. Space staging involves a dark stage with a spotlight picking out of the void the characters and scene involved. The lighted area may indicate anyplace or everyplace. Space staging is usually found most practical and effective when a drama calls for a great many short scenes or when it is necessary for the action to move from one locale to another very rapidly. As much or as little as the designer may wish in the way of properties and scenery may be used to indicate locale. When, through space staging, an effort is made to suggest an exact place, the scenery is referred to as a *simultaneous setting*, and more often than not is impressionistic in style. Any number of locales may be found on the stage—a country store, the pulpit of a church, a bedroom, an office —all adequately equipped to give a definite impression of place. Each can be brought into focus merely by concentrating the light on that particular area. A second and somewhat simpler effect is known as *multiple setting*. The principle is the same except that there is no effort to suggest exact locale. The stage may be practically bare of scenery or properties. It follows more nearly the staging in an Elizabethan theatre with its outer and inner stage, balconies, etc. As then, the lines are depended upon to indicate locale if that information is necessary. With multiple staging little more than light and characterization are used. Space staging can be used effectively in many plays but is less effective in the ultra-realistic play.

We would emphasize that the styles in scenic design are constantly changing and that audiences should no longer expect standard sets, but instead look for imagination and artistry on the part of the scene designer. Experimentation with its possibilities is exciting and audiences can encourage it. Much has already been done by the educational and community theatres in this direction, and the scenic contributions of the professional theatre have shown marked progress in the past decade.

With this explanation of modern scenic trends, the chart on page 159 may help to summarize and further clarify the goals and means of the contemporary scenic artist.

The motion pictures are rarely concerned with the subject of scenery as we have here discussed it. Their surface realism demands the real thing. In television there have been some remarkable uses of all the styles we have discussed and thus some highly imaginative settings.

These six modern trends in scenic art, plus the three contributing factors and combinations of any or all, are the tools of the scene designer.

The Requirements of Scenery

Borrowing from much that has been written on the subject of scenery, we may say that there are four rather generally accepted "musts" that make up the basic requirements of stage scenery.

The scenery must fit the action of the play. The modern play will call for great detail and localization. The setting itself must tell much of the background, social position, and life of the people who live in it. It must have the proper doors, windows, stairs, and furnishings to fit the action of the players. The décor may consist of the five hundred items in *You Can't Take It With You* or the bare essentials of a hut.

In plays of another period, such as the Greek or Shakespearean, less emphasis is placed on detail. A Greek play may be done in front of a stone façade, with a set of natural drapes, or even more effectively in an outdoor theatre. Because of its formal style, it does

CONTRIBUTING FACTORS

Stylization
Exaggeration to
suggest
period or mood

Symbolism
One object
represents another—
or a great deal more

Space Staging
A light picks a scene out of a void and illuminates a portion of a multiple or simultaneous setting which may suggest or represent a specific or a generalized locale—anywhere or everywhere.

MODERN SCENIC STYLES

Realism (Naturalism)
consistent—convincing—complete

Simplified Realism
no effort at completeness;
unconvincing details eliminated

Impressionism
less detail—only essentials
to suggest locale and emotion

Expressionism
still suggests, but by distortion;
tries to portray feeling
in physical set

Theatricalism
Background decorated and
used as background only

Formalism
Building or surroundings
as they are

PURPOSE OR GOAL

Helps actor to

portray

mood—

spirit—

emotion

by assisting him.

Helps actor by

staying out

of his way.

not require much scenery. The imagination of the scene designer may play around with the script and devise some steps, platforms, or pillars, but simplicity is always his keynote. Almost the same holds true for Shakespeare, although many interesting settings have been devised through the use of a unit set and varied multiple settings made up of arches, levels, pillars, or columns whose flexibility permitted the suggestion of the various scenes demanded by the script. Here also simplicity is important.

In the production of plays from the Restoration through the eighteenth and nineteenth centuries, the action invariably demands the use of the painted backdrop and wings with few furnishings, and great use of the front or apron of the stage.

It is the scene designer's first obligation to understand the action and the relative importance of all scenes so that his setting may be used most effectively by actors and director.

The setting must portray the type, style, mood, and spirit of the play. On the rise of the curtain, through the scene designer's use of color and light, the audience should have a clear indication not only of whether the play is fundamentally tragedy or comedy, but even some clue as to whether it is farce or melodrama.

The setting should likewise suggest the style, whether or not it will be realistic, classic, romantic, or fantastic, and the mood or spirit of the scene itself, all of which have already been discussed under the trends in scenic design.

The scenery must help the actor to tell his story. The background should never at any time get in the actor's way or distract from what he is trying to say, do, or make the audience feel. It may do this either by contributing or staying out of his way. Either goal is accomplished only after the scene designer and the director have come to a clear understanding on the style, spirit, purpose, and mood of the whole production. It is then that the designer chooses from the various methods we have described and decides exactly what he can do with the scenery to accomplish the desired artistic impression.

The scenery must never attract attention to itself. The only time the audience should ever be conscious of the scenery is when the curtain first rises. The moment the play begins the scenery

THE BACKGROUND AND TECHNICIANS

should fade into the background so completely that it is forgotten by the audience. Often the work of a scenic artist and his assistants is applauded on the rise of the curtain. This display of appreciation on the part of the audience is commendable, but if at the end of the act we find the setting being discussed in the lobby rather than the play and the acting, then we may know that artistically the setting is wrong. This often happens with the realistic setting, which the audience notices throughout the play in an effort to find either how the artist has attained his effects or erred in his portrayal. Such distractions are the severest criticism of realistic stage settings.

Two examples of such inartistic design may help to illustrate the point. The first concerns an all-school production of *H. M. S. Pinafore*. Costumes were in the hands of the sewing class; the scenery was designed by the art department and constructed by the boys in manual training; the vocal instructor spent months in developing the solos, duets, and choruses; the women's physical education department devised dances; the physics teacher supervised the lighting; and the instrumental music director developed a thirty-six piece orchestra. Truly, it was a cooperative all-school event. The setting was perhaps as complete and realistic as any noncommercial production this operetta has ever had. A near-perfect replica of a ship was built on the stage, and the backdrop portrayed a skyline with almost photographic accuracy. On the evening of production, just before the audience had begun to assemble, the scene designer and director made one final inspection of the setting. They agreed that it was most appropriate and effective. The scene designer felt that the total picture might be enhanced with one additional detail. He suggested punching a hole in the tower of the painted lighthouse on the backdrop and placing one of the stage crew on a ladder with a flashlight that would, by being intermittently turned on and off, suggest the revolving light in the tower. This was done—and with it so was the artistry of the production, for when that small light flashed on and off each thirty seconds during the evening, *H. M. S. Pinafore* all but ceased to exist. When the performance was over, and to this day, there has been little mention of the music, the story, the costumes, the setting, the acting, or even the over-all production. The star of the

evening was the boy with the flashlight. It was summed up most pointedly by a little old lady several weeks later: "I couldn't take my eyes off that lighthouse. It was so realistic. I timed that light, and it came on every thirty seconds. How on earth did you do it?" The elimination of this distracting detail in the scenery could have directed the emphasis where it belonged—on the production.

One more example of ultra-realism should make our point. In Maxwell Anderson's *Winterset,* one of the scenes takes place in the rain. In a college production of that play, a very ambitious senior boy, whose enthusiasm at that age surpassed his artistic evaluation, conceived the idea of arranging a series of pipes above the stage, properly attached to the water supply backstage. Sufficient holes were then made in the pipes themselves to supply the necessary rain. In the scene between Mio and Miriamne where Mio has the line: "I feel the rain in my face," the supreme artist at the water spigot let him have it, and rain, first in a sprinkle and later in a downpour, drenched these two actors, whose real job it was to interpret the lines of Maxwell Anderson. The moment the water began to fall, the audience forgot what the actors were saying and began to think: "Why, that is real water!" "Where is it coming from?" "Those people are getting soaking wet!" Then, with much craning of necks, they began to ask their neighbors: "Where is the water going to?" Many persons confessed afterward that they were unable to enjoy the remainder of the play because subconsciously they had the thought in the back of their minds: "It's raining, and I didn't bring an umbrella."

The three great arguments against realism in the theatre are: (1) it detracts attention from the actor and the play; (2) it weakens illusion by challenging the audience to compare the make-believe of the set with life itself; and (3) it destroys aesthetic distance. Either of the illustrations above should furnish sufficient evidence of the validity of these three criticisms without further amplification. We would point out again, however, that these arguments against realism apply to the theatre and some television programs far more than to the motion pictures, where scenery serves a different purpose.

The proponents of realism contend that the unreality of ex-

pressionism, the exaggeration of stylization, or the artificiality of theatricalism often prove more distracting than realism itself. We can only say that, as in all phases of life and art, moderation, taste, and compromise are necessary to attain the best results regardless of what medium is being used.

The first requirement of all scenery is that it must be functional and a part of the production itself. When *Our Town* first appeared in New York there was great fear among the advocates of scenery that a trend might develop toward its elimination. A clever cartoon appeared in *The New Yorker* in which two of the Helen Hokinson characters were seen at a box office inquiring: "Is this a play with or without scenery?" No play is ever without scenery. The real question should be: "Is there any theatre in the scenery?" How theatrical, how functional, how helpful, or how detrimental is the scenery that is being used?

Frequently professional productions have given their performances with the most elaborate and detailed scenery and décor that could be devised. When these same productions went on the road, it was necessary to simplify to the extreme. Scene designers who have at first felt that it would be impossible to eliminate details in their design have been amazed, when by necessity the deletion was forced upon them, to find not only that the scenery was equally satisfactory in depicting locale, but that it also enhanced the production by demanding more of the audience so far as its imagination was concerned. This was especially true in the settings of *Abe Lincoln in Illinois,* when Jo Mielziner discovered that the simpler design allowed more of the play to come over the footlights than had been possible with the original New York settings.

The Lighting Designer

In our discussion of the scene designer, the lighting was frequently mentioned, and it is not uncommon for the scenery and lighting to be designed by the same artist. In any event, the electrician must work in close cooperation with the scene designer as well as with the actors and costumer, for not only do the lights affect the set-

tings, but they are also often instrumental in altering both the make-up and costumes of the actors.

Historically, the lighting designer is one of the youngest artists in the theatre. The Greeks and Romans, as has been shown, worked under the light of the sun. Even Shakespeare's theatre had no roof and performances were given by day. After the theatre was taken inside, the candle was the only means of illumination. Color was supplied by placing bottles of different colored wine between the flame and the object illuminated. Later gas supplanted the candles and various hues of silk gave the color. It was possible for the first time to alter the quantity of light on a given scene. Neither the color nor the odor from these lights contributed much to the appearance of the actor or the pleasure of the audience. It was discovered in the middle of the nineteenth century that a combination of burning chemicals placed on a cake of lime would produce a strong white light, and this soon became an important part of stage illumination. The phrase "in the limelight" still suggests the actor who holds the brightest area of the scene.

Shortly before 1900 the arc light was invented. This was soon followed by the incandescent lamp and its development. It can safely be said that no single item has more affected the course of theatre art in the past century than has the electric light. It was David Belasco and Steele McKaye who in America did the most in adapting this new invention to the theatre. Since 1920 it has been so improved and refined that today lighting facilities and equipment are a major factor in the design of any building that is to be used for theatre production. No longer is a scene lighted flatly and the same illumination used throughout an entire act or play.

It is in the lighting of its productions that the noncommercial theatre more often surpasses the professional than in any other single area. This is due principally to the absurd exactions of the professional electricians' unions regarding not only the equipment that may be used, but the salaries and exorbitant cost of overtime, the number of personnel required, and the unions' strict rules regarding membership. The strangling effect of nepotism in the unions has for the most part made it impossible for those persons to "get a card" who have been especially trained in the art of stage lighting.

The electrician and the audience who sit in judgment should realize that our theatre today offers three means of controlling the lights—the quantity or amount of light that is being used, the color of that light, and its distribution over the stage. Psychologically, each of these qualities can affect the audience in countless ways. Some knowledge of human behavior and a feeling for the mood of the scene, coupled with artistic design, can lift a dramatic scene to an effectiveness never envisioned by our forefathers. The theatre electrician literally paints with light! It is not unusual for a production to have several hundred light changes during a performance, all of which when well done are so subtle that the audience is hardly aware that they are being made. They may have served to emphasize a character or a scene at the psychological moment when that emphasis was needed, create or change the mood in numerous ways, shift the direction of the audience's attention, relieve eye or nervous tension, alter the color of costume or set, suggest weather or season, give an appearance of life and vitality to a weary actor, unify one group or set it off in opposition to another, or indicate fantasy or reality or a dream sequence. The possibilities of lighting in the modern theatre are limitless in the hands of an artistic lighting designer who takes the time, and possesses adequate equipment and the faculty for taking infinite pains. To realize what has been done and how we have been affected by the lighting is one of the most fascinating phases in analyzing a modern theatrical production.

The Requirements of Lighting

The stage must at all times be sufficiently lighted to make for visibility without strain. This does not mean that every square inch of the stage should be equally lighted as was done by the old-fashioned footlights. The walls and upper corners of the set, or any part of the stage that is not going to be used by the actors, should be given less illumination than those areas where the action will take place. In this respect, the visibility should always be selective. This is impossible with general illumination. It is attained only by

the specific control afforded by the spotlight whose beam can be directed.

Good lighting will select and emphasize that aspect of the production which needs pointing up at any given moment. It would be unnecessary to keep a doorway lighted throughout an entire act, but it may be highly important to light that opening just as an important character makes an entrance. In *Death of a Salesman, A Streetcar Named Desire, The Glass Menagerie, Cat On a Hot Tin Roof, Our Town,* or almost any modern play, this use of directed attention by means of light is basic in its importance. At the same time, the entire stage must be lighted evenly enough for the illumination on the darker area to eliminate distraction in the audience when the actor passes from one emphasized area to another.

Artistic lighting accentuates the proper emotional and psychological qualities of the play. Through the use of color, light, and shadow, a mood is established and an audience is properly affected. Mystery, impending disaster, the supernatural, time of day, and season of the year can all be suggested by lighting. Quite ordinary plays have been lifted almost into the realm of greatness by the effective use of lights. In the same way, a distinguished play could be robbed of its inherent greatness by ineffective lighting. The electrician has the power to establish a mood even more quickly than the playwright or the actor.

This was done especially well in an early production of *There Shall Be No Night.* The impression of the Finnish winter and deep snow was instantly established by the cold white light which streamed through the large window on that New Year's Day.

In *Rose of the Rancho* David Belasco so completely simulated the hot sun of a Mexican afternoon at siesta time that the audience actually became uncomfortable to the point that men loosened their collars and the women began to fan themselves.

In addition to adequate visibility, proper selection and emphasis, and the creation of a mood or atmosphere, the designer must choose between realistic lighting, which would represent nature, or lights used purely for their theatrical effect. If the lighting on the stage is to represent nature it must seem to have a natural source, such as a window with its sunlight, a lamp, or a fireplace. These

THE BACKGROUND AND TECHNICIANS

areas must be in brighter light than other parts of the room, for the lighting must follow the laws of nature.

For those plays that are basically theatrical, it is not necessary to consider the light source. Needless to say, such plays are the joy of the electrician. His imagination can go the limit, and with our modern equipment tremendous effects are achieved in any nonrealistic play.

Theatrical lighting was used with great success in *Death of a Salesman* as Willy Loman moved about the stage, both in reality and in the enactment of his thoughts. By the use of space staging and a combination of simultaneous settings, seven or eight completely different locales were so vividly suggested that the audience never questioned their authenticity.

This theatrical use of lights is most valuable in the production of any style other than the realistic. There it may prove somewhat distracting unless some reasonable motivation is supplied.

It is equally as important that the electrician eliminate any distracting elements, such as a spill of light on the proscenium, teaser, or tormentor, or a light leak from backstage. A poorly illuminated room, supposedly just off stage and into which characters are to pass, can quickly destroy the illusion. An audience can be greatly disturbed by a flickering lamp due to a loose connection or the reflection of some light in a mirror or picture. Extreme care must be given to the light outside windows or when the impression of distance or sky is required.

In our theatre the lighting designer is an artist, and each of his effects is the result of careful planning, knowledge of human emotions, the specific needs of the script, the flexibility and limitations of his instruments, and his own creative imagination. Not to recognize and appreciate his contribution is to miss some of the most artistic achievements of the modern theatre.

The Costume Designer

It was not until the eighteenth century, when David Garrick insisted that his actors dress in the costumes appropriate to the role

and the play, that any special thought was given to the actors' apparel. The players of the Elizabethan period wore the castoff clothes of the lords and ladies under whose patronage they were appearing, and consequently the costumes were always contemporary with the period in which they lived. There are stories of the audience becoming almost hysterical with laughter when the actors in *Julius Caesar* first appeared in authentic Roman costumes. This occurred in both France and Germany well after 1750.

As an integral part of the unified production, however, the costumer in our modern theatre has taken equal rank with the other technicians. He must realize the vast range of color meanings and their psychological effect on an audience. He must be conscious of various combinations as well as the effect of light on pigment. Color must be considered with an eye to harmony, unity, and contrast. Conflicting dramatic forces may wear opposing colors, either warm or cold, or those that clash. Whichever technique is used must, above all, be done subtly. The good costumer knows that the actor must stand out against the set but that no actor, unless for a special purpose, must ever wear a costume or accessory that clashes with the set. In life we may not consider the color of the hostess's draperies in our choice of a tie or dress, but on the stage this factor must be taken into consideration.

The actor's personality must be given special thought, both as it is and as it is to be in the play. The Chinese have pointed out an interesting classification which they call the Yin and Yang theory, applicable to both men and women. The Yin is the sweet, quiet, sensitive, introverted individual, and the Yang the forceful, strident, confident, forward extrovert. The first may seem to lean in the direction of those qualities which we class as "feminine" and the latter in the direction of those we consider "masculine." This theory further suggests that the proper dress for each personality is to emphasize his own type, such as ruffles or softer hues for the Yin, and tailored or more positive colors with an emphasis on the dark for the Yang. At the same time, each should borrow from the other with a median as the goal, rather than to go completely in either of the two directions. To do the latter might have a comedy value, and in some instances be exactly what was needed to portray the extreme masculine man or woman, or the extreme feminine.

THE BACKGROUND AND TECHNICIANS

The same femininity or masculinity could be lessened, given its proper status, or perhaps eliminated by the proper costumes in both color and design.

The costumer must possess great originality in designing and in styling, for pictures of clothes only suggest what others have already done, and exact copies have no place in the life of creative artists. Clothes are as personal as any other aspect of a character. Not only must they be agreeable to the temperament of the wearer, but they must also fit the part he is playing and all it entails. They must have the proper effect on all the other costumes of the company, and, of course, on the audience.

If the play is a period play, the costumer is faced with further problems. There must always be ample evidence of those characteristics which we associate with the costumes of a century. The designer must be reasonably authentic, although he may sacrifice some authenticity for comfort and design. In period plays the emphasis is more concerned with centuries than with decades or shorter periods, although frequent use must be made of those elements which we associate with a period. These would include such details as the midline decoration of the Egyptians, the chin ruffs of the Elizabethans, the immaculate collars and cuffs of the Puritans, the hoop skirts of the Civil War, the bustles and leg-of-mutton sleeves of the late nineteenth century, and so on. The good costumer takes these constant elements and simplifies or exaggerates as his artistic nature and the demands of the play may dictate.

The costumer, in the final analysis, must never forget that there is one essential that must be behind all his work, namely, that every detail on the stage must possess dramatic significance. As in the case of the other technicians, he has certain requirements which must be observed.

The Requirements of Costumes

All costumes must fit the period, season, locality, time of day, occasion, and mood of the scene. Each of these details has either been discussed or needs no further elaboration at this point.

The costume must have the correct line and color to do the most for character projection and for the person wearing it. The character may have to dominate, be dominated by, or blend with the others in the scene.

In this respect the costuming of a modern play is sometimes the most difficult. As an example, it might appear that in staging a scene portraying a college dance in a university theatre production, it would be logical to ask the girls in the cast to wear their own gowns. To do this would quickly show the director and the costumer how sharp is the demarcation between life and art. The result could be chaotic in losing the effects of color values to distinguish between those who have leading roles and those who should be considered as minor characters, and in the general overall blending of colors and setting. To get the right costume for the right person and to blend them all into a balance of color that will tell the story dramatically in such a scene is a most formidable problem. Yet the same girls could wear their gowns at a college dance on the campus with a highly pleasing effect.

Each costume must be stageworthy in that the lines and design are sufficiently exaggerated to carry over to the audience. A costume that might be considered very attractive and highly suitable for street wear could be completely unsuited to the stage. Either distance or lighting could eliminate or alter the design so that it lost all dramatic meaning. Rarely is it possible to use, on the stage, a costume that was actually worn by some friend or relative in an earlier period. It may be very authentic, historically, but lack the theatrical or dramatic qualities so necessary in a production. Likewise, the costume that looks most attractive on the stage could appear too exaggerated or theatrical for street use.

The costumes must be worn with ease. We have already cited examples of occasions when actors, because of inadequate rehearsals, permitted the costumes to distract from the performance. It is essential that each actor have his apparel for a sufficient time to become accustomed to it. If even after such rehearsal the actor lacks the very important freedom of movement, it is then the problem of the costumer to find some substitute. It is the costumer's prob-

lem to see that all costumes blend harmoniously into the performance.

In conclusion, we as an audience in evaluating the work of the
costumer must consider his originality in creation and execution as
well as his understanding of the dramatic significance each costume
has for the audience.

Technical Coordination in Theatre

Regarding the work of the three technicians—the stage designer,
the lighting designer, and the costumer—there is always the final
question: Is there a technical smoothness and integration that
makes the average audience wholly unconscious of these contributing elements? We would again emphasize that because of the technicians' work our theatre has become more and more a visual rather
than an auditory experience. Some of this emphasis has grown out
of our two visual mediums, the motion picture and television. They
have influenced the stage to some extent just as they have been influenced by the stage. The importance of this visual emphasis today in contrast to the theatres of the past is pointed up when we
pause to compare. A blind man in the Greek or Elizabethan
theatres could have enjoyed the play and its beauty almost as
much as the man who could see, for those plays were addressed
primarily to the ear. A blind man in any of our modern theatres
is greatly handicapped. In this sense it can be said that ours is less
literary. Whereas the poetry of the drama was once expressed in
the lines, it is now found in the pictorial phases of the stage and the
integration of all its many parts. Our theatre calls for less imagination from the writer and the audience, but more from all the other
artists.

It is this change of emphasis, plus the unification of the whole,
which prompts many to say that, even though the drama itself may
have declined, the theatre, as the separate institution it is, has the
opportunity to display greater artistry today than at any other
time in its history. The basis of this argument lies in the definition
of poetry given in the first chapter: "Poetry is that happiness

which overcomes us when we become suddenly aware of the presence of the beautiful." With this definition in mind, we readily understand that our modern theatre need not have lost its poetry; that all poetic beauty did not die with Ben Jonson. There can be just as much poetry in our theatre today as there ever was in the theatre of Shakespeare. Only the emphasis has been changed. The poetry of that theatre lay in the drama, in the spoken line; the poetry of the modern theatre lies in the coordination of all the many theatre elements. Without any control of the lighting or the sound, minus scenery or authentic costumes and with a noisy and uneducated audience in the pit, the Elizabethan theatre attempted to create its illusion, and illusion was even more important in the theatre of Shakespeare than it is today. The possibility of mastering all these theatre elements belongs to our modern theatre. It remains only for the workers to prove themselves artists worthy of being a part of the theatre. One individual, more than any other, is responsible for the unification of all their contributions and the possibility of artistic greatness. That individual is the director, and he with his own particular problems and responsibilities will be considered in the following chapter.

THE BACKGROUND AND TECHNICIANS

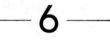

— 6 —

Direction

and the Director

*D*uring its long history the theatre has belonged variously to each of its many artists. The playwright, actor, scenic artist, electrician, costumer, and director have each, in turn, had their "hour upon the stage." At present the pre-eminent position belongs to the director. During the twentieth century he may have seemed to be jockeying at times with the electrician or the inevitable star actor, but in America it has been he, more than any other, who has gradually and surely been growing in importance.

Although the average audience may remember the acting, praise the play, and discuss the artistry of various technicians, it is invariably the director whose planning, selection, and interpretation have been the determining factors in the design of the over-all production. Nonetheless, few of even the most informed theatregoers could name the director of five plays they saw last season. They may not have even recognized his contribution to the produc-

tion. This, many directors would agree, is as it should be, for the very best direction is that which is so integrated in the coordinated work of all the artists that it cannot be detected.

George Kaufman, both author and director, says there are not three persons who can observe a play and then say definitely what is direction, what is the play, and what is acting. Worthington Miner, Broadway director, points out that in the ideal theatre the director would not even exist.*

> If the playwright turned out nothing but completely stage-worthy plays, if all actors had the intelligence, the integrity, and the skill to work together and interpret the plays perfectly, the director would have no function to perform. But our theatre is not ideal. It is necessary for some one to help the average actor appear better than he is, to help the average author appear like a playwright. Hence the director.

Some would question whether the director is a creative artist or merely an interpreter, but to the audience this distinction is not too important. We must realize only that the director in our theatre is the leader, coordinator, guide, and unifier of all diverse elements that make up the theatre, and that any play that has passed through his imagination will contain something of him. It is this that has made many of us declare that interpretation *is* creation.

Alan Schneider, New York director and teacher, once wrote in *The New York Times:***

> If you ask a theatregoer what he thinks a director does, you really have him . . . He sees the director as a combination stage-manager and traffic policeman. He knows vaguely that the director tells the actors where to stand and how to say their lines; conceivably also informing the crew when to put on a light or take down the curtain. In evaluating a director's work, the theatregoer may muster a "good" or a "bad." Occasionally an especially discerning soul will say that the pace seemed too slow, or that the direction was "uneven." But only rarely does this self-made critic take time to explain—even to himself—just what he means.

---

* John Gassner, *Producing the Play* (New York: The Dryden Press, 1953), p. 211.
** Alan Schneider, "The Director's Role," *The New York Times*, August 8, 1948.

Actors must have always had someone who told them where to go or what to do on the stage after an entrance. For long periods, we know, it was the star actor himself who made all these decisions; and invariably placed himself stage-center! There were centuries when it was not an uncommon experience for members of the acting company to hear the lines of the leading character spoken for the first time together with the opening night audience. The Drury Lane actors were highly incensed when Edmund Kean, a newcomer in the role of Shylock, asked for a rehearsal. In the past even when stars deigned to "run through" the play with the cast, it was not unusual for them to hear only the cues of their speeches and rarely, if ever, to give any indication of their interpretation.

It was David Garrick in the mid-eighteenth century who first began to think of the production as a whole. After him we hear little of the subject until just before 1900, when the Duke of Saxe-Meiningen established in Germany the idea of the director's discipline over the production. His company influenced the great Stanislavsky in Russia, who in turn adopted many of Meiningen's ideas in the famous Moscow Art Theatre. Max Reinhardt followed in the tradition, and there emerged in Europe the *regisseur;* or as he is called in America, the artist-director.

This country was quicker than England to revise and develop the idea of the director's responsibility. Even before 1900 we read of such directors as Augustin Daly whose emphasis was on the whole production, and all are familiar with such directors as David Belasco, Lester Wallack, the Frohman brothers, and many others.

With the advent of the noncommercial theatre, which had its beginnings around 1912 to 1915, the prominence of the director has grown rapidly, and today it is of utmost importance that some careful attention be given his contribution to the production.

What Is Direction?

Harold Clurman, one of our most capable and sincere directors, has said that the director might be called the author of the stage production. He goes on to say:*

---

* John Gassner, *Producing the Play* (New York: The Dryden Press, 1953), p. 273.

Though the director does not act, he is, or should be, responsible for the kind of acting we see on the stage; though he does not usually design the sets, he is, or should be, responsible for the kind of impression the sets make; and this applies to everything else on the stage.

In one sense he is comparable to the director of a symphony orchestra, for although he plays no instrument himself, he does unify the work of many individual performers into an artistic whole. He regulates tempo, commands every variation in the emphasis, and creates an interpretation. He must think of the complete effect. The director is not merely a "coach" working with individuals. His concern is with ideas, with scenes, character relationships, the strategy and tactics of the play as a whole.

The director is the author's representative. In a very real sense he must see that each actor not only portrays the voice and actions natural to life and to the character he is playing, but also *translates, interprets, and expresses this reality so that it conveys the playwright's attitude* toward the scene and the characters he has created. This may be called theatricalism, for it involves playing a scene as farce, high comedy, melodrama, or tragedy. It involves playing it up, throwing it away, putting it across—it involves the style, the interpretation, and the very spirit that the author is trying to point out. In short, it is the director's responsibility to see that the actors not only *play the characters* they have been assigned, but that they also *play the play* that has been written for them. Therein lies the true art of the director. It is he who decides *what* is to be done, and the actor who determines *how* that direction will be portrayed for the audience.

Types of Theatres in America

The living stage in this country is divided roughly into three groups—professional, community, and educational—and two general classifications—the commercial and noncommercial. The term "noncommercial" is used in this book in preference to "amateur," because of the unfortunately derogatory connotation of that word.

There are, of course, various shadings that make it difficult sometimes to classify accurately.

The professional theatre. This includes the companies centered on Broadway and the touring organizations that emanate from there. During the summers there are approximately four to six hundred "straw hat" theatres, many of which are professional. During the remainder of the year there exist fewer than fifty professional stock companies in various areas. The majority of these groups are recognized and operate under the rules of Actors' Equity Association, the union of professional actors. There are in addition some non-equity companies, classified as professional because their entire personnel receive regular salaries and the company is maintained solely through the box office.

In the theatre the actual distinction between "professional" and "amateur" is many times only a matter of attitude, and the amateur or noncommercial performance, with its high purpose and sincerity, often matches and sometimes excels the work of many professional groups. A majority of our summer theatres, a few of our road companies, and an occasional New York production would suffer greatly by any artistic standard when compared with the best work of these noncommercial organizations. The noncommercial theatre falls roughly into two classifications, community and educational.

The community and educational theatre. Such well-established groups as the Pasadena Playhouse, the Cleveland Playhouse, and prominent theatres in Houston, Dallas, Indianapolis, Charleston (South Carolina), New Orleans, Rochester (New York), Tulsa, Erie (Pennsylvania), and many others too numerous to be listed here are included in the community category. In addition there are thousands of church, fraternal, civic, and other drama groups which exist as art theatres, community enterprises, service organizations, etc.

The educational theatre, as implied in the name, comprises the high school, college, and university dramatic endeavors, all of which are related to, and usually underwritten by, the educational institutions of which they are a part.

The Director's Goal

As our premise in artistic evaluation is based on the three principles of Goethe, a director should be measured by the same criteria as the other artists. In the discussion that follows, it may appear that more space is given to the educational and community theatre than to the professional stage. This is based on the belief that the vast majority reading these pages will find that at least ninety per cent of their stage experience now and in the future will be in the non-commercial area. Statistically the educational and community theatres are by far the greatest single influence in our legitimate theatre. Their opportunities to save or develop an audience for the stage are unbounded. The danger lies in that they are often controlled or influenced by the uninitiated and immature director who has had little experience in the actual theatre world. In his enthusiasm for *great* theatre he wants to go too far too fast. Caught in the web of his own intellectual and literary background, he forgets that both his actors and audience may not have had his educational advantages, and in so doing he can lose forever those young theatre enthusiasts who could eventually come to appreciate the stage if given the opportunity of growing up dramatically and theatrically.

Every good director, regardless of the organization he represents, realizes there is only one standard of excellence in theatre art. He will not try to excuse the less-than-successful production by "lack of experience," "not enough time," "poor facilities," "very good for beginners," or any of countless other rationalizations. The inexperienced participants in an educational or community theatre may not come as close to scaling the artistic heights as does a professional group, but the first goal of each should be the same—a complete artistic success.

In addition to this common goal of every producing group, each director has further obligations to the audience that will attend the performance and to the active workers in the theatre. He must challenge both audience and participants in a manner that

will broaden their dramatic horizons but not out-distance their understanding, for it is his duty to keep the theatre both popular and alive. Finally, every director has a major obligation to the playwright whose script he is interpreting as well as to the play itself. Each is deserving of as sincere, as artistic, and as faithful a production as is humanly possible. These are all obligations common to every director regardless of the theatre concerned. Furthermore, the professional, the community, and the educational theatre each has its own separate goals and each individual theatre its own local needs. Unless we have given some thought to all these demands, we have not been wholly honest in our evaluation of the director's work.

In the professional theatre the director must attract to the box office a sufficient audience to pay all production costs and salaries, with some margin of profit for those producers who underwrite the production. In addition he hopes to win the approval of a large portion of playgoers and the commendation of professional dramatic critics.

Although many of us feel that the professional theatre often falls short of its obligations as an art form, we should constantly remind ourselves that it is also a profession and a business, and as such the economic element is inextricably interwoven with the artistic. Realizing this, we may be a little less prone to dismiss a production because it is mere "show business." Theatre workers and producers must live, and the professional theatre must therefore give the audience what it will buy.

In contrast, community theatres are usually organized not for the purpose of making money, but to satisfy the creative desires of their members, to occupy leisure time, and to bring together persons of the same artistic interests in a community or group. The community theatre, interested as it is in the artistic success of its productions and in balancing its budget, exists also as a creative and social organization for the benefit of its members and its audience.

Any director who serves such a theatre is responsible to his organization for fulfilling these *additional goals*. They are not only justified, but are a vital part of the organization itself. Every

member of the audience has a right to demand as fine an example of theatre as this group can give, but in his criticism he must not forget that the community theatre does have further obligations of its own.

In both the community and educational theatre the director must be ever cognizant of the primary obligations to play and audience, which have already been listed. Bringing the living theatre to his audiences is especially significant, for frequently these groups furnish the only source of live theatre for their respective communities. The educational theatre, particularly, must serve as a teacher if it is to justify its existence as part of the institution it represents. As such it possesses a special obligation to the student body who will attend the performances. The educational theatre director must give that group an introduction to and eventually an appreciation of the best in dramatic literature, as well as good theatre. In addition he has a further obligation to the individual student who wishes to work in any phase of the dramatic program. The desire must, of course, be accompanied by sufficient talent and ability, but students who possess these three important qualifications must be given an equal opportunity to participate on a strictly competitive basis. Type-casting can thus be eliminated and replaced by a far superior method for both the training of actors and the future of the theatre—the midpoint between type-casting and miscasting. Emphasis will also be put upon a greater number of participants, rather than listing the same actors over and over again. The same is true in all other areas of the theatre—carpentry, costuming, make-up, lighting, painting, designing, or writing. Truly, in the educational theatre lies a gigantic opportunity to teach cooperation, teamwork, loyalty, and responsibility. Nowhere is each better realized than in the well-rounded dramatic production. The educational theatre director has a great opportunity to develop his students physically, vocally, intellectually, emotionally, culturally, and socially.

The director also has an obligation, as a representative of the educational system and to the theatre as an institution, that the plays selected should not only represent the best in type, style, structure, and form, but that they should come from every period

of dramatic literature. His program should be a sort of living library, and at the same time he must not reach beyond the depth of the students involved or the audience that he will attract. They must be challenged, but failure to meet the challenge can not only harm the participants but disappoint and lose the audience as well. The choice of play is of vital importance in every way. It must attract the audience as well as appeal to it after it is there. It has always been necessary for the theatre to build or create its audience. Today, if the stage is to survive, this must be accomplished by the directors in community and educational theatres. A theatre program that is too heavy can prove disastrous. If people are to be taught to love the legitimate theatre, their early experiences must be exciting ones. To start on a solid diet of great literary masterpieces can but play to empty seats, create dissatisfaction on the part of cast and staff, and lose a potential audience.

Nor is this learning process ever complete, for each September brings to the campus a new group and the process must begin again. A director in an educational theatre should not be judged on the choice of a single play or a single season. The programs can be more fairly evaluated only by considering three or four consecutive seasons, or whatever comprises the student generation.

In addition to the general and theoretical questions discussed above, the director in the noncommercial theatre must face many specific and practical problems in the choice of plays season after season. It is proportionately more difficult each year to choose a program that will meet the following requirements.

Each play must:

. . . have been released for noncommercial use;

. . . not have too many or too complicated settings for local physical facilities;

. . . come within the budget, including all royalty, costumes, scenery, and production costs;

. . . meet artistic standards, be interesting, entertaining, timely, worth while, and truthful, and uphold the prestige of both theatre and producing group;

. . . fit the available actors in number, sex, and talent;

. . . not have been done in the area in recent years;

. . . fit local conditions in a given week or season and have adequate variety to round out a full dramatic program;

. . . have sufficient appeal to all levels of class, education, and age;

. . . satisfy at least a majority of the patrons; and last, but *not least:*

. . . have publicity value and draw sufficient audience through the box office to pay all expenses involved in the production and keep the budget balanced.

Finally, there is the ever-important and not-to-be-forgotten obligation of the theatre director *to himself*. He must satisfy his own artistic as well as educational standards. It can be done only after he has first considered positively the other demands, although at times it may be necessary to compromise here and there.

The director in the noncommercial theatre, community or educational, has five distinct obligations beyond bringing the best in live theatre to his audience and presenting an artistic production faithful in its interpretation of the author's script. They are:

1. To entertain and educate the audience and build an audience for the theatre of the future.

2. To develop the talents and further the creativity of active participants in the production.

3. To further the aims or purposes of the particular organization he represents.

4. To contribute artistically to the theatre as an institution and an art.

5. To satisfy himself as a director, an artist, and a teacher.

Directors in countless noncommercial theatres throughout America are meeting these obligations most successfully. These organizations are the legitimate theatre's greatest hope for the future. The creed of one university theatre summarizes excellently what these groups are trying to do.

> Our Theatre shall endeavor always:
> . . . to develop its students as individuals—vocally, physically, emotionally and culturally—rather than for the professional field;

. . . to train both audience and students to appreciate the living theatre;

. . . to present plays that picture all phases of life and dramatic literature;

. . . to approach perfection in its own realm without attempting to imitate Broadway;

. . . to entertain but to contribute something more than mere entertainment;

. . . to encourage creative work in every phase of the dramatic arts;

. . . to add stature to the theatre in general, and to the college theatre in particular; and

. . . to be *educational, challenging,* and *artistic!*

We must not dwell over-long on this subject, but if each noncommercial theatre and its director is to receive the same honest critical evaluation we would level on all artists, it is necessary that some of the particular problems and specific goals be understood by the critic.

What the Audience Should Look For

Many good authorities feel that a clear distinction between acting and direction is not often possible. Nevertheless, there are listed here some areas that seem to belong especially to the director in his present position of authority. There will, of course, be an inevitable overlapping, but this listing should help the beginner in his study of what the director may have contributed to the production.

The choice of play. Considerable discussion has already been given this subject insofar as noncommercial theatres are concerned. In this respect their responsibility is greater than that of the professional field. In the commercial theatre a director is hired to direct a particular play and can be held responsible for its selection only in that he did accept the assignment. If the play is wholly unworthy, then he as well as its producer may justly be criticized.

Every theatre is a case in itself and calls for a different program of plays. The fact that a play was successful in New York does not

mean that it is a great play, and by the same token that a play fails in New York or has not played there is no indication that it is a poor play. The great hit of 1925 may or may not be right for a given theatre in 1960. The type of theatre demanded by the audience in a metropolitan center or on a midwestern college campus or a Texas community theatre is not at all the same. Locale and time are both involved in choosing the play that will attract the audience and do the most for it and the theatre at any given time or place. Audiences are often not ready for a particular play. To misjudge the temperament, desire, and understanding of the potential audience in any locality can only ask for empty seats or an unenthusiastic audience, and either is equally harmful to the theatre and to the producing group.

Casting. Here the director can be largely responsible, although there are exceptions. Producers in the professional theatre do sometimes insist upon special friends for certain roles, and actors have been known to produce plays only so that they might play a coveted part, even though they were not equipped to do it well. Nevertheless, the province of casting is normally considered to be that of the director. He may choose to type-cast and thus make his production easier to direct and more believable to the audience. On the other hand, he may choose to develop someone in a role by permitting the use of make-up to alter that actor's appearance and personality.

There also enters the element of interpretation. The director decides what the role demands, and with thousands of actors—and good ones—begging for parts, it is not unusual to read that the production of a play has been postponed because the director was unable to cast it. Suppose a playwright has pictured a specific character as shy, retiring, bashful, or reluctant to speak up and express himself. Such a character could be interpreted by the director in any one of several ways, accompanied by all the shadings of a human personality. He could arouse a warm sympathy by his quaint, shy, and lovable quality; become a broad comedy character at whom the audience could laugh boisterously; or be a stupid individual whom the audience might prefer to boot right off the stage.

Harold Clurman put it another way when he said that the whole meaning of *Golden Boy,* by Clifford Odets, depended on whether the director saw the leading character, Joe Bonaparte, as a fighter who had a gift for music, or as a musician who had a gift for fighting. Either is a matter of interpretation, the director's idea of the role and how he sees it in relation to the play and the other characters.

We may further consider the director's success by observing any obvious miscastings, actors who do not give evidence of being what they would have us believe they are because of their physical, emotional, or mental stamina.

Allied with the choice of play and the casting there is a special problem faced by most directors in the noncommercial theatre. They are often limited in the number of capable actors, both in experience and in age, and this can limit their choice of program. Shaw, Chekhov, Pirandello, Shakespeare, Sophocles, Molière, Corneille, and even many of our present-day writers make some rather extravagant demands of the actor. It would be unwise to choose a play, great as it may be, for which an adequate cast could not be found. Good theatre, regardless of what period it represents, can be exciting, but it must be well done if it is to excite the audience. The television and motion picture fields have been very careful in this respect, and they have the distinct advantages of both unlimited talent and apparently unlimited funds to pay for it. If the stage is to attract this new audience, now accustomed only to movies and television, its productions must be equally as exciting. The director who constantly strives to uplift the stage in the face of such competition is to be commended, but as a wise theatre man once said: "We are all for elevating the stage, but those of us who love the legitimate theatre would not suggest doing it by depressing the audience."

The emphasis on the theme and style or treatment. There are directors whose greatest ability may lie in serious drama or tragedy, and others who find their strength in comedy or farce. To know the professional stage is to identify immediately the names of certain directors with specific types of plays. Producers are always desirous of choosing the right director. In the non-

commercial theatre the same director may be called upon to handle every type. This fact should be given consideration.

Most theatre people agree that very few directors can make a poor play seem great, although a good director can improve on a poor script. It is also possible that he may not have done as well by the script as it deserved; many a fine play has been ruined by the interpretation of an incompetent director.

No two directors can possibly give the same over-all effect, even with the identical cast and staging. A director's particular style or treatment is always there, evident in shadings of meaning, a change in emphasis, interpretation, characterization, or movement.

Each director may place a slightly different emphasis on the theme as the author has expressed it. He may even point up one of his own that will make the play infinitely more timely and appropriate. This was done most effectively by Orson Welles in his New York production of *Julius Caesar* during the peak of Mussolini's power. By emphasizing the dangers inherent in dictatorships and staging the play in a modern style with the conspirators in black shirts, the whole production took on an exciting, timely, and new meaning.

In such instances the play may resemble the work of its director more than that of its author. Max Reinhardt's *Midsummer Night's Dream* was more Reinhardt than Shakespeare. Any production by David Belasco was obviously a Belasco product. Margaret Webster is always completely honest in her interpretations of Shakespeare, but they also carry the pictorial and colorful contributions that belong to Miss Webster.

Some directors like Welles prefer to do Shakespeare in modern dress. *Hamlet* has been seen with Ophelia drunk instead of insane, and Hamlet in a tuxedo smoking a cigarette. In *The Taming of the Shrew* Petruchio has arrived on donkey, on horseback, on a motorcycle, and in a battered jalopy. Nineteenth century melodramas have been burlesqued or "kidded," and played perfectly straight as they were originally done. So recent a play as *The Constant Wife* could be stylized in mood with the actors playing the parts as actors with tongue-in-cheek and revelling in the wit of Somerset Maugham, or as a realistic comedy, the manner in which

it was envisioned by Guthrie McClintic in the production starring Katharine Cornell. There are infinite styles in which a production might be conceived. This is the province of the director, who is limited only by his own imagination.

We must always ask if every actor is playing in the same style or key. If not, the director is at fault. In a production of *Othello* the whole play loses its meaning if Othello uses all the gusto of the romantic school accompanied by the rant of declamation and Iago is played in a completely realistic style. This error is more common in the noncommercial theatre, due to the varied styles and techniques throughout the cast.

As an audience we should be able to see through all acting and directing to the script itself and determine both its type and style, and then ask whether or not the director has caught, and through his actors projected, the truest and best meaning of the play. It has previously been pointed out that farce and melodrama are built primarily on situation and must be believed while they are in performance, though not necessarily the following day. Sometimes directors and their actors may interpret these pieces so brilliantly that the audience is fooled and believes in them even in retrospect. On the other hand, tragedy and comedy are built on character and must not only be believed while in the theatre but must also stand the test of truthfulness with later analysis. Sometimes the director may so miss the interpretation of the script that the audience does not believe the play even as it is being observed in performance.

These two statements were demonstrated at a recent performance of two one-act plays, the directors being college seniors. The first was a most ludicrous little melodrama. Both cast and director wondered how it could ever be made believable to an audience. However, they attacked it very seriously, gave it a proper background, took great care in lighting, used many shadows and much smoke, incense, gongs, and off-stage effects. They developed a mood and presented the play so seriously and sincerely that it completely fooled many in the audience, who believed it to be a far better script than it really was. The second play concerned a simple situation in which the director himself did not be-

lieve, and he broadened it into farce that bordered on burlesque. Although it was realistic in style, he exaggerated the acting until it became slapstick. The point of the play was completely lost because it was padded with every trick or "gimmick" the director could devise. The audience laughed at the actors and not at the play, did not for a moment believe it, and criticized it most adversely the following day. In both instances the facts of production altered the original promise of the scripts. Whatever those facts may be, it is the director who must shoulder the full responsibility, for he, at least theoretically, has given them his blessing.

Stage movements and business, groupings, and pictures. The word "action" in the theatre denotes only the dramatic action of the play, which is inherent in the lines and story. Change of position on the stage is called "movement"; "business" includes bodily gesture and the handling of properties. While both business and movement are executed by the actors and may have been created by them, the director is basically responsible for having permitted them to continue. Therefore, we may hold the actor responsible for the ease and truth of their execution, but whether or not they distract or are part of the play, scene, or character is dependent upon the director.

The director must always be responsible for furniture arrangement. This will, of course, do much in determining stage groupings and pictures, which must always be the director's work. The famous director and teacher Alexander Dean often said to his actors: "You are the hands of the clock up there on the stage, but I am out here where I can tell the time." Stage groupings are of great importance. They must take into consideration the sight lines in the auditorium, so that every important phase can be seen by all the audience. They must show the different physical and psychological relationships as the play progresses. The stage must at every moment have the proper balance, emphasis, variety, and dramatic meaning to help carry the story, as well as present an agreeable picture. There must always be a focal point to the stage's continuously changing picture, and every movement and every bit of business must have a reason and a specific purpose.

The elements of overacting or underacting may be considered

largely in the director's domain. Contrary to the commonly accepted belief, the noncommercial theatre is more likely to underact and the professional to overact. The director may tone up or tone down any phase of the production, but he must never forget that it is primarily his task to interpret the author's script. A director may have a special flair for creating stage business, ingenious ideas of interpretation, or other embellishments through which he thrusts upon a play more of himself and his own abilities than are good for the production. Worthington Miner has said:*

> If a director with a formula chooses a good play and attempts to apply the formula to it, he cheats the play and the author. The star director works for his star, the clever director and the director with a theory work for themselves, or sometimes . . . for something extraneous to the play. A conscientious director in normal circumstances works and can work only for the play.

There is always the possibility that a company of players too long away from a director may allow much to creep into the play which was not a part of the original direction. Some two weeks after *Death of a Salesman* had been running on Broadway it was completely redirected by Elia Kazan, because he said the mother appeared to have lost her love for her sons. Mildred Dunnock, the actress playing that role, admitted that this was true, that she had become almost afraid of the boys because in their fervor they had actually been so rough in handling her on the stage as to hurt her physically. The subtle expression of her love for her sons was so important to Mr. Kazan that long rehearsals and complete re-blocking of movement and business were necessary to restore this feeling of mother-son affection.

Some good examples of direction and its invariable relationship to acting have been recorded in a splendid article by Howard Lindsay, co-author and co-star of *Life With Father* and *Life With Mother*, he having played the role of Father Day for a total of 3,224 performances. Because Mr. Lindsay says so much so well on this whole subject, it is here included in its entirety.**

---

* John Gassner, *Producing the Play* (New York: The Dryden Press, 1953), pp. 210-11.
** Howard Lindsay, "Confessions of Father Day," *The New York Times,* Jan. 16, 1949. Reprinted by permission of Howard Lindsay.

J. M. Kerrigan tells us of the night he forgot to raise his eyebrows. When another actor addressed a certain line to him, Kerrigan would raise his eyebrows. The audience shouted with laughter. At one performance Kerrigan's mind wandered—he forgot to raise his eyebrows. There came from the audience the same shout of laughter. It was a bitter moment.

In the first months of a run the actor is consciously trying to improve his performance. Herein lies a real danger. He adds much small detail that are elaborations in no way helpful to the audience. They consist of gestures such as Kerrigan's raising of his eyebrows.

As a matter of fact, most of these bits of business that creep in are being done when the audience isn't looking at the character at all, or certainly shouldn't be looking at him. If they are being done when the actor properly has the audience's attention, he is usually adding entirely unnecessary detail that, instead of helping make the moment more graphic, is distracting the audience from the simple value of the spoken line.

There is the oft-told story of the notice that appeared upon a certain theatre callboard:

REHEARSAL CALL
11 A.M. Monday
To Take Out the Improvements
(Signed)   George M. Cohan.

Quite often during the early part of the run of *Life With Father* our canny director, Bretaigne Windust, would point out to me that Howard Lindsay, the actor, was trying to help out Russel Crouse and Howard Lindsay, the playwrights, when they simply didn't need any help. There are, of course, moments when the actor can help the playwright enormously, but there are so many moments when the playwright needs no help whatsoever except to have his lines truly spoken.

Nothing pays off in the technical side of acting so much as economy of method. When we sometimes think we are adding value to our performance, we are merely cluttering it up with insignificant trivia. Perhaps one of the greatest lessons in acting I ever learned was a remark I heard made by that great actress and great stage director, Margaret Anglin: "The insignificant weakens."

The actor's chief problem in the long run is to keep his performance fresh—to preserve what William Gillette emphasized in his essay on acting: "The Illusion of the First Time." This demands a constant and intense concentration. It is when the actor is creating reality for himself that he is creating reality for the audience.

Some actors feel that to keep a performance fresh they must indulge themselves in variations of business and the inflection of their lines. There is no sound reason for doing this. The actor is an interpretative artist. It is his job to find the very best performance of his role and to be able to repeat it with the same precision expected of the pianist, violinist or ballet dancer. Acting is a behavior assumed in order to have a precise effect upon an audience. The actor's reward lies in the consciousness that he is achieving an exact effect. To be able to repeat our best performance is the heart of interpretation.

When playing in a comedy the difference in audiences is most apparent in the frequency and the volume of the laughter. After being used to a nightly hilarious response, there will come an audience that refuses to be greatly amused. The immediate temptation is to broaden the performance. There sets in a determination to make the audience laugh, and the actor assumes a comicality that seldom achieves its purpose.

Prescribing the treatment for the dull audience, Bretaigne Windust laid down for us in *Life With Father* a dictum of profound wisdom: "When you can't amuse them, convince them." Instead of trying to make the sober-minded audience laugh, the actor should eliminate any conscious comedic edge to his performance and set out to create a reality both for himself and for the audience.

Usually it is not long before that particular audience is roaring with the best of them. If not, perhaps you have given that audience a greater reward than laughter. To my mind, for an audience to become so absorbed in a play they forget they are in the theatre is the greatest refreshment of spirit our institution has to offer.

During a long run there is a notable difference between the audiences of the first several months and the audiences that follow. Those who hurry to see the new success are the habitual theatregoers. They are trained in theatregoing. Unconsciously

they know the language of the actor's technique and respond to certain signals.

As we get beyond the habitual theatregoer, a change of interest takes place in the audience. Those out front have less appreciation for the nuances and subtleties of the actor's performance. Their interest is in the story the playwright has set out to tell them.

Too often an audience assembles at a comedy that has been running a long time to find the actors striving more broadly than ever to achieve the laughter they were used to in the early part of the run. In this determination to be comical, the actors go farther and farther away from any truth of characterization. You don't know what has happened to you, but something is definitely wrong and you lose faith in your own performance.

For example, during most of the moments of Father's frequent indignations, there should be always uppermost his sense of incredulity that these things could be happening to him. It was very easy for me to lose this edge of astonishment and become merely exasperated.

Also, there would creep into my explosions an acerbity that was most unattractive. I still recall with deep gratitude a remark Dorothy made to me as we were driving home after a performance. "You know, Howard, I don't think Father is so much bad-tempered as hot-tempered." This thought switched me back upon the track from which I had become derailed.

Lest I sound too damn noble, I wish to add that nothing helped me toward a conscientious performance so much as a conscious interest in the royalties.

Emphasis on the whole production rather than the individual. The director should be primarily interested in the play rather than the separate parts, in scenes rather than particular lines, in the over-all stage picture rather than in the individual actors. His job is to give the complete meaning and mood of the play and the changing relationships of each character to the play and to each other. If he does not accomplish these ends, he is subject to the more uncomplimentary term of "coach" rather than "director." To coach a play is to concentrate on the individual, on special lines or speeches, gestures, movements, or business. This is often necessary in the noncommercial area where the participants lack train-

ing and technique. It is also true that professional actors sometimes choose to receive special coaching on their roles. In this case they usually go—on their own—to a special teacher whom they admire and who, in perspective, can see what they are unable to comprehend either in their role or their interpretation of it. The good director, even though he may have to work with the individual, thinks in terms of the whole rather than any part. He strives for teamwork and unity in the over-all interpretation of the script, so that the audience is not conscious of individual bits or lines or characterizations. He feels and thinks in terms of scenes and meanings, crises, theme, and a unity of the whole. This is direction at its highest level.

Are the correct points being made? Although the playwright has furnished the director with the script, it is the director who must decide whether to emphasize plot, character, dialogue, theme, or atmosphere. After making this decision, he must then translate and interpret the script into dramatic action and sound. If the play fails to show strength in any of these elements, the director may then be forced to turn to spectacle or "gimmicks" or theatrical hokum. The young director mentioned who had to present a melodrama that seemed lacking in material turned to spectacle, and as a result developed a mood that was so believable and effective that some of the audience accepted it as truth and believed the faulty story and characterizations furnished by the script.

If the author has not made all points perfectly clear, it is the director who must clarify and emphasize them in his production. He may do it with movement, line, color, mass, force, or any other attribute he may choose. In short, he is a translator who uses all the arts of the theatre to correct any weakness inherent in the script. He has the final task of making everything clear. In doing so he may push a weak comedy over into the realm of farce or make a farce appear to be a comedy, through his translation and interpretation. This emphasis brings us very close to the earlier discussion of treatment and style.

Rhythm, tempo, and pace. Herein lies the greatest pitfall of the noncommercial theatre, the most difficult aspect of a play to explain. Their combination furnishes the greatest single distinction

between the experienced and inexperienced worker in the theatre. Under *acting* we called this "timing." These elements, when they are absolutely right, will cover a multitude of sins.

Rhythm is defined as the recurrence of an accented beat. Its place in music is easily established and understood. It is quite different in the theatre, where the rhythm is irregular and comes from many different sources. The beat in the lines is, of course, an important part and more easily recognized, but the emphasis may also come from the entrance or exit of a character, the use of a light, an off-stage noise, a brightly colored costume, the gesture or movement of an actor, and many times—especially in comedy or farce—from an audience reaction.

The rhythm of a play is established very early and remains basically the same throughout the performance. The *tempo* alters, though the change may be ever so slight, with the entrance or exit of every character, many times within a scene, and constantly during the evening. The director who senses that a play seems to be running slowly and calls out: "Speed it up!" is utterly lacking in any knowledge of rhythm, tempo, and pace and their delicate balance. To speed a scene is merely to talk faster, to "railroad it" as it is called in the theatre, and all that happens is that the scene gets over more quickly. This, however, is the most frequent criticism of the untrained critic in the audience who proclaims: "The play was slow," "It seemed to drag," "The actors talked too fast," or "They didn't pick up their cues," etc. All these are logical criticisms and may have been true, but the real fault is more basic. The chances are much more likely that the director had failed to point up a defined rhythm.

At the other extreme, the director can become so involved in the rhythm of his performance that it stands out over the principal theme. This has happened in some productions of *The Emperor Jones* by Eugene O'Neill, when the steady beating of the tom-tom has overpowered the actors—not so much in volume as in their failure to cope with it.

Pace is the relationship between the over-all basic rhythm and the ever-changing tempo. It is at its best when these elements are so perfectly integrated and all the speeches and movements of the

actors so well coordinated with the audience reactions that the whole production gives the impression of complete smoothness. Strangely enough, the director finds his success in this respect easier with serious plays. This is largely because he can foresee the audience reaction to drama more easily than to comedy or farce; at least, its reaction is more constant. Comedy, and to an even greater extent farce, are most difficult to do successfully with an inexperienced cast. The comedy lines of the playwright receive such varied reactions from the audience that the actors must constantly cope with those changes and still maintain the basic rhythm that the performance demands.

They must alter their reading of lines or action within a single performance if they are to re-establish the rhythm as it was set by the director in rehearsals. If something unforeseen occurs on stage to alter that rhythm and pace, or the audience contributes a new beat through an unscheduled reaction or fails to supply the one that had been expected, it is only the actors who can once more get the play back on the right track. It is this combination of audience reaction and actors' recognition of it that can make a comedy so much more satisfying on the stage than in either the motion picture or television.

Rouben Mamoulian, famous motion picture and New York director, often establishes a rhythm through the use of a rocking chair, a metronome, or some similar device. He and others have been known to direct the play from out front with a baton. The pace of a performance and its integral parts are definitely in the province of the director, although his work is sometimes almost lost in the hands of an inept cast or the unexpected response of an audience. It is, nevertheless, part of the critic's task to ascertain what the director has tried to do with these intangibles of dramatic production.

The correct balance of empathy and aesthetic distance. These terms were explained and discussed at some length in the first chapter. They have consciously or unconsciously been in the mind of every artist as he went about his work. Early conferences with the director have established exactly what he wanted the production to do in this respect. They have been fundamental in his alter-

ations during the polishing period. Not until an audience reaction has been witnessed, however, will he know whether or not the balance is satisfactory. Many times scenes are pointed up or subdued after the audience response has been studied.

In a college production of *Home of the Brave* this occurred in the scene where the sensitive boy from Texas is ordered by his superior to crush the head of the Japanese soldier whom he has just shot. He obeys the command and then turns his back on the audience, unable to stand the sight. On opening night he had been directed to give the impression of actually becoming ill at this point. It was wholly in keeping with the character and the scene, but the effect on some members of the audience was so distasteful that they left the auditorium. These individuals having shown a desire for greater detachment, the director very wisely subdued this business almost to the point of elimination in the following performances.

This is an area where the audience may be even more likely to disagree among themselves on the quality of the director's work, for it involves so much the personality, experience, or memories of each individual concerned. This personal reaction to the director's selection and balance may be equally true in tragedy or comedy. The final answer as to his success rests upon the director's own sensitivity, his knowledge of human nature and emotions, his good taste, a strong sense of balance, and his stature as an artist.

Has the director shown fidelity to the play's main purpose and in the use of his materials? It is no small part of the director's responsibility to understand exactly what the playwright was trying to say or do. Once he does, he must then do all he can to emphasize these goals through his direction. There must be a fidelity to the central idea. All the artists must subordinate any personal desire to elaborate upon their work by including some personal talent or fetish. Even the playwright may have been guilty in this respect, and if this is true, it is the director's duty to handle the situation or scene so that it will not detract from the over-all meaning.

A most striking illustration comes from Eliot's *The Cocktail Party*. This play proved an enigma to many theatregoers in both

England and America. The lack of clarity was partially due to a scene in the second act just after the psychiatrist had convinced a young lady that she should abandon the immoral life she was living and pay penance for her sins by joining the missionaries in some foreign country. After her exit the psychiatrist and his wife and secretary drink a toast to their accomplishment, but the lines do not indicate either the sincerity or the seriousness we have associated with the characters. It is this scene which has been one of the most difficult to rationalize with the remainder of the play. An unquestioned authority has reported that Mr. Eliot was repeatedly advised to delete this entire scene and that he even admitted it had no particular place in the drama, but added: "It is the sort of thing I do so well."

Every artist could make the same excuse for embellishing his work, but such embellishments would only serve to cloud or destroy the main issue. It is the director's responsibility to keep a strong hand on the reins, and since he has the final authority as to what will be seen and heard, he must possess a greater integrity and artistic sense than any of the others, for he, too, has "the sort of thing he does so well." It is not uncommon for the real heart or soul of a play to be lost through the decorations put there by the director himself and for no other reason than Mr. Eliot gave.

The second test necessitates each artist's fidelity to his materials, and the director once more must make the decision. There are natural limitations to every art. Each artist must recognize and abide by them. He should not try to make a play look like a motion picture, an extravaganza, or a musical. He must not attempt to make a play designed as mere escape pretend to pass as a play of social significance. If he would present a solution to some personal problem, he should not make it appear greater than it actually is. If the play's chief emotion is only sentimentality, then that should be expressed as sincerely as possible rather than making something else of it.

The artist-director will resist the temptation to borrow from the other arts and use beautiful costumes, settings, lighting, or music only because they are beautiful rather than because they help to emphasize his central idea. No artist needs a more consistent ques-

tioning of himself than the director, and if honestly answered this questioning will always take him back to the meaning and purpose of the play and whether or not he projects them clearly and with the maximum honest use of his materials.

Smoothness of the whole production. This has been frequently mentioned in previous pages, but it is in the director's realm of authority. He normally gives full freedom of creation to all his workers, but reserves the right to choose which creation best fits into the picture and mood he has envisioned. It is the director's final selection that we see and hear.

This balance is one of his greatest contributions. Plays have been thrown completely out of focus when a leading actor was far superior to the remainder of the cast. The wise director, therefore, may not permit an actor to give his most brilliant portrayal of an emotion if the player opposite him is unable to rise to that height. The director must also balance the work of all the technicians. If the audience remembers setting, lights, or costumes at the expense of the play, the proportion has been faulty.

The director in our modern theatre is responsible for every phase of the production. It is he who determines the emphasis, mood, tempo, tone, the pointing up of some speeches or business and the easing of others, the balancing of forces and characters, the elimination of distractions, simplification of lines or action that are not clear, unifying the contributions of technicians, a complete new observance of rhythm, tempo, and pace; and, of course, the four tests—Is it fresh, restrained, easy, and convincing?

His influence carries through even to the curtain calls at the conclusion of the play. Some directors do not permit them at all. If they are used, curtain calls can be either most distracting or an integral part of the performance. Distraction comes through lack of rehearsals, for each actor should know exactly what he is supposed to do. The director plans the curtain calls, which often show great originality and may even be remembered for themselves. The only two requisites are that they must be taken in character, with dignity and humility. One tradition that has fortunately disappeared from all reputable productions is the absurd passing of flowers through the proscenium opening or from the tormenter

entrance to some actress who must step out of character, grimace to the audience, and leave a final impression that is completely out of key with the production.

Has the director sufficiently challenged artists and audience? Finally, the director must challenge all participants in the production, as well as the audience itself. So far in this chapter we have considered the director's work with the artists. It is equally important that he give careful thought to the audience. He must neither overestimate its capacity in his choice of play or in its direction, nor underestimate its understanding by playing down to it.

New York directors sometimes feel that when they are producing a play for the road, all jokes must be labeled and acting broadened to the extent that any illusion of reality is destroyed. Educational theatre directors all too frequently direct down to their audience by inaccurately judging its dramatic intelligence. The reverse is likewise often true when plays have been produced for which the audience was neither intellectually nor emotionally prepared. In either instance, an injustice has been done to the theatre as an institution. No director who respects the theatre would agree that the audience should be pampered or given only dramatic fare that demands little or no intellectual capacity. The wise and competent director is aware that the spectators must constantly be challenged as well as emotionally moved, stirred, excited, and pleased. If the audience does not realize these experiences, then the theatre has failed as theatre. If it does, the theatre will have triumphed and merited applause. As Horace once said: "He who joins the instructive with the agreeable carries off every vote."

In summary, it is the director who must answer to the artistic fulfillment of those seven pillars of the fine arts—Unity, Emphasis, Rhythm, Balance, Proportion, Harmony, and Grace. If we, as the audience who evaluate and judge, will give serious consideration to these specific areas of direction, it is logical to believe that we might do what some authorities have said could not be done—recognize the art of this most powerful figure in our modern theatre.

To cite personalities in any area of the arts can only invite dis-

cussion as to why one appears and another does not. There are countless directors in the community and educational theatres whose work would merit the placing of their names on any list of outstanding directors. Here, however, we must think in terms of the national rather than the local picture. In the professional theatre, the following artist directors have won places of distinction in New York: Harold Clurman, Morton Da Costa, Peter Glenville, Tyrone Guthrie, Jed Harris, Garson Kanin, George Kaufman, Elia Kazan, Robert Lewis, Joshua Logan, Rouben Mamoulian, Guthrie McClintic, Jose Quintero, George Schaefer, Alan Schneider, Margaret Webster, and Bretaigne Windust.

Because we have emphasized the great importance of the director in our modern theatre we have presented, in the picture section, the photographs of several outstanding directors of stage, motion picture and television. Each director has listed the names of those productions which he feels were most successful so far as his own goals were concerned.

A Preface to Cinema and Television

*T*he following two chapters are placed toward the end of the book not as an afterthought, but rather because cinema and television naturally follow the stage both historically and in their basic techniques.

Since 1915 the motion picture has been vastly more popular than the stage in attendance. Its popularity with the masses has never really been approached, except by radio for a few short years, and then by television since approximately 1952. Today we know that forty to seventy million Americans go to the movies weekly and that an estimated one hundred million watch television nightly. It is a matter of record that eighty-eight per cent* of our population have accepted television as a normal part of their daily lives.

These figures reveal the fact that the theatre is being more widely enjoyed today than at any other time in the entire history of the world, not even excepting Greece at the peak of her power. Indeed, it can be said that for the very first time we have a truly American theatre, reaching every segment of our citizenry, both economically and intellectually.

However, these two powerful forces, born of Art and Science, must, not only because of their age but by their very nature, borrow and constantly adapt to their own use from the vast storehouse of knowledge and experience acquired by the stage in its three thousand years of existence. They must adhere to the principles discussed in the previous pages, which are the foundation of any dramatic understanding in any medium. The techniques of the motion picture and more especially of television are essentially those of the stage. Any deviation is one of degree rather than of kind. With the background of these stage precepts in mind, let us now consider in the following chapters the motion picture and television as they are related to the stage, showing some of the differences, advantages, handicaps, problems, and requirements of these two younger areas of theatre entertainment.

---

* Walter Kingson, Rome Cowgill, Ralph Levy, *Broadcasting: Television and Radio* (New York: Prentice-Hall, 1955), p. 148.

—7—

The Cinema

and the Stage

*F*or almost half a century motion pictures have been growing in popularity and prestige as a medium of dramatic entertainment. When the week's attendance slumps ever so little, great consternation stalks the studios, offices, and the pages of the trade journals.

In the early days of the motion picture, and again when the element of sound was introduced, there was much talk of the stage and motion pictures being competitors. In the rivalry for the dollars at the box office this always will be true to some extent. However, their purposes and artistic goals are worlds apart. Each is truly a dramatic medium in its own right. Perhaps the cinema more than any other form of art expresses, records, and interprets the changing philosophies, moods, and fashions of its own time. It is

202

magnificently equipped to portray action, everyday life, imaginative but realistic make-believe, visual beauty, and reality in all its
surface aspects.

The stage, with its slower tempo and physical restrictions, must
turn more to intellectual themes. It can handle the more intricate
ideas or thoughts of mankind. Its goal is to reflect and interpret
man's more basic, subtle, inner personal thoughts and feelings and
the more permanent truths of life. Even if the admission fee to the
two mediums were the same the screen would surely be the more
popular, for feelings and emotion have always united a greater
number of the population than thoughts or intellect. Because of its
lower admission prices and its dramatic appeal, the motion picture
has broadened the base of dramatic entertainment. The demise of
each legitimate theatre has been coincident with the rise of many,
many motion picture houses. Millions of persons, once denied the
theatre by the lack of proximity or financial means, found at least a
substitute in the cinema.

It is not the purpose of this chapter to debate the relative artistic
merits of the stage and motion picture, for each is an equally satisfactory means of relating a story, so long as neither tries to imitate
the other. Nothing could be as sad as the experience of a group
some years ago who conceived the idea of taking Broadway to the
hinterlands. In theory the idea was good, but in practical terms it
proved a fiasco. Maxwell Anderson's play, *Journey to Jerusalem*,
had been what is called an artistic failure on Broadway. There were
many who felt it might have a huge audience throughout the country, especially through the churches, the schools, and many literary
or educational organizations, if it could be taken to them at an admission they could afford to pay. Accordingly, the proper lights
and sound equipment were moved in and the cameras were set up
in approximately the fourth row center of the Broadway theatre
where the play was running. A motion picture was taken of the entire production. On film the story lost all the beauty, meaning, and
poetry it might have had on the stage. The dialogue seemed dull.
The acting appeared most amateurish in the worst connotation of
that word. All the artistry of the stage technicians was completely
lost. The audience soon grew weary of the limitations placed on the

actors' movements and the scenic background. In short, the whole event was a colossal bore, and it is doubtful if anyone trained in either field was able to sit through the entire picture. No better illustration could have been presented to prove that these two mediums are fundamentally different, though there are many superficial similarities.

Before starting an analysis of basic differences, let us turn to a definition of the motion picture by Rouben Mamoulian. In an article entitled "The World's Latest Fine Art" he said, "The motion picture is a dynamically and rhythmically organized series of moving images expressing a story, character or mood in a dramatic way which appeals to our sense of the beautiful." This definition will be amplified further as we discuss the work of each artist.

The Audience and Dramatic Criticism

Jean Cocteau has pointed out that the audience viewing a motion picture is seemingly enclosed with the actors in a room lacking a fourth wall. It has a feeling of equality with the actors that is lacking in the legitimate theatre, where the players are observed as if through a keyhole. In the theatre there is a greater sense of detachment, as the scene is outside the spectator. On the surface it would appear that this might make for greater empathy in the motion pictures. Undoubtedly this is partially true, since the films can show so much more detail and give at least the surface realism that may transport the audience physically as well as emotionally to the exact scene. It is unquestionably this ability that has greatly limited, if not eliminated, the use of imagination on the part of the audience in the motion picture theatre, whereas the imaginative element is one of the stage's greatest assets. While the cinema is far superior in its ability to picture realistic detail, it cannot compare with the stage in its illusion and imaginative qualities; at least it has not done so.

The theatre audience is always conscious of flesh-and-blood actors, while in the motion picture, even in the peak of an emotion, there is always the consciousness of the inanimate. All of which

means that in one the audience is primarily concerned with people and in the other primarily with pictures. Mr. Mamoulian has emphasized this point in his explanation of the great differences between stage and screen:*

> How often a shadow on the wall, a closeup of a door-knob, an ash tray or a crashed bottle can be as effective as the best acting. I have seen an Eleanora Duse or a Chaliapin, surrounded by pitiful mediocrities and shabby production, lift the evening in the theatre into the realm of exciting, unforgettable experiences through the sheer magic of their individual performances. But I have never seen a bad film saved by one performer. Indeed, the Stage is the kingdom of the actors, the Screen, the kingdom of the pictures.

Few would debate the difference in mental age and attitude of the two theatres. A dearth of children attending one and the abundance of them in the other cannot but have its effect on both the artists who have prepared the play or picture and the audience reaction. This audience reaction is important in the individual critic's subconscious mind and does have its effect on his critical analysis. However, audience reaction in itself is not as important in the motion picture as in the theatre, for there, as has been pointed out, this reaction may affect the actors' performances and thus alter, if ever so slightly, the spirit or tone of the performance.

One need only stand at a box office to see that hundreds of motion picture goers will purchase tickets and enter without even knowing what picture or actors they will see. This is a rare occasion in the legitimate theatre. In the first instance, they go for the sake of going; in the second, they want to see that particular event. This fact alone has an inevitable influence on the audience. Furthermore, the avid followers of a given star are sometimes interested in his or her artistry, but more often are attracted by some physical appeal.

The motion picture, far more than the stage, is able to supply vicarious satisfaction to that "one-third of the nation who are ill-kept, ill-fed, and ill-housed." In the secluded darkness of the motion picture house these frustrated men and women, who have been

---

* Rouben Mamoulian, "Stage and Screen," *The Screen Writer* (March, 1947, Vol. II, No. 10).

denied the love, luxury, excitement, or emotional experiences their natures require, may receive some measure of release and satisfaction. It is little wonder that the producers have tended to favor this huge audience, for the motion picture, as the professional stage or television, is also a business. It is likewise not surprising that its fundamental and principal appeal to the populace is based on the element of sex, the most basic of human emotions. There are, of course, individuals whose chief interest is in sex who seek their theatre in the legitimate houses, but the percentage is so much smaller that they do not receive the recognition given them by the motion picture producers.

An additional item of difference is the matter of censorship. The motion pictures must unfortunately abide by the moral code of an omnipotent group who considers itself as God by the grace of a political appointment. They assume the power to decide what is good and what is bad in the world. They sit in judgment and decide what is moral enough for their fellow men to see, and what they delete often makes one wonder by what quirk of the mind they could have found evil where few others can see it. Save in an occasional instance, the stage has not suffered such humiliation.

The very important matter of coordinating the audience reaction with that of the production and thus establishing the correct rhythm is almost impossible in the motion picture, due to the wide range of audiences both in size and response. We sense it when, with a full house at a comedy or farce, we miss many lines due to the laughter, or in a partially empty house, the lack of an expected response destroys the basic rhythm.

One of the major contrasts is the difference of appeal; that of the motion picture is principally to sight and that of the stage more to hearing, although as has been pointed out, the latter throws more emphasis on sight than ever before. Mr. Mamoulian in "The World's Latest Fine Art" has said:

> The essence of a picture is and always will be in the visual. A motion picture does not exist for a blind man, no matter how well he can hear the words—we are using too much dialogue on the screen. The formula should always be: express everything in

the visual image and movement, and only when these are inadequate, use spoken words.

Professor Allardyce Nicoll has emphasized the same note by saying, "Whereas in general a stage play demands constant talk, a film requires an absolute minimum of words. The essential basis of the cinema lies primarily in the realm of the visual images." This comes home more vividly when we recall how easy it is to follow a foreign film even when we do not know the language.

One small but final difference can be pointed out. When we attend the theatre we normally purchase an exact location for our seat and we view the stage from that distance and angle throughout the performance, having a free choice of what we want to see. In the motion picture our viewpoint is constantly changing. One moment we are even closer to the event than the front row, and the next may find us at the rear of the gallery. There are both advantages and disadvantages in this. The artists can emphasize more easily what we are to see, and the requirement of physical projection on the part of the actors is practically eliminated. Some of the audience may have the feeling of being constantly jerked back and forth in their seats. At least, the effect can prove distracting unless it is handled extremely well.

In criticizing or discussing the dramatic effectiveness of a motion picture, the earlier chapter on "The Audience and Dramatic Criticism" can be found helpful, especially the "Ten Commandments of Dramatic Criticism." The suggestions made there as well as the entire text have been designed to fit all three mediums. As a supplement we submit the following questions or suggestions which can be of special help in both motion picture and television criticism.

1. Select and describe the most engaging close-up, medium, and long shots; the most pleasing lighting effects; the outstanding camera angles.

2. What cinematic effects are used to establish or maintain the mood?

3. Is there a proportionate use of the close-up? Does it strengthen or slow up the action?

4. Point out places where the camera alone tells the story.

5. Discuss the use of music to introduce a situation, establish locale, identify characters, as mere background, and as atmosphere or mood.

6. List the various sound effects. Was each in harmony with the situation, making the maximum contribution?

7. Trace the change in tempo, building of suspense, increase or decrease of audience response achieved by the cutting.

8. Discuss the dissolves, fades, cuts, montages, or any other types of transition that were used.

9. Discuss the director's distinctive style. Select points where he relied upon photography rather than dialogue to project story, ideas, situation, or characterization.

10. Describe his choice of backgrounds in relation to dialogue and situation.

11. Discuss the director's selected camera positions in relation to interesting angles, lighting, included subject matter, and length of clips.

12. Explain the director's over-all interpretation of this segment of life that he has presented. Could it have been given better treatment in another medium?

The Play and the Playwright

In its art of telling a story the motion picture resembles the novel far more than it does the drama, although the structure of the story itself does follow the pattern of a play. The motion picture need pay no attention to temporal order or the normal sequence of events. It can show anything that can be photographed and is at its best in pageants, huge sagas, spectacles, historical events, and so forth.

One of the first laws of the screen is that there must be constant change and visual alteration. It is far easier to dramatize a novel for the screen than a play, for in the former it is necessary not only to reduce the dialogue, but to add many scenes that actually show

what on the stage may be only discussed or related. This very free-dom can also prove a handicap, but it does mark one of the funda-mental differences in the two mediums. Because the scene must con-stantly be changing, the motion picture cannot pause long enough to allow the significance beneath the surface to sink into the mind of the audience. Rarely does it effectively turn inward to man's thoughts. The projection of subtle characterization or psychologi-cal aspects of character are impossible. These are left for the better stage presentations. Characters far too often prove to be merely types rather than the individuals sought in the theatre. This, of course, makes it much easier to cast the leading personality of the day or the actor with the strong box-office appeal. The audience is left to fill in all the crevices without demanding that the character be clearly drawn by the playwright. This laxity also makes it easier for those frustrated individuals mentioned earlier to identify them-selves with the appropriate character in the motion picture. There is much less need for realism of characterization and for motivation or plot. The audience is satisfied with mere surface realism. Alan Reynolds Thompson has stated it very well:*

> Anybody who can see and hear can check the accuracy of surface realism, but to notice poor characterization, flimsy moti-vation or melodramatic plotting requires of a spectator some knowledge of life and art, some capacity for reflection and anal-ysis, and some training in good taste.

Often a great stage success is made into a powerful film, but one need only have seen both productions to sense this very im-portant emphasis on subtlety of characterization, evident on the stage and lost in the motion picture.

One of our best motion picture directors, Alfred Hitchcock, has said that the pictures are more interested in atmosphere, mood, and movement than in character, and he made a very interesting com-ment on the importance of the chase. A careful analysis of all the pictures we may remember will leave but few where one faction was not somewhere in the picture in physical pursuit of the other—by foot, horseback, motorcycle, boat, automobile, skiis, airplane, or

* Alan Reynolds Thompson, *The Anatomy of Drama;* Univ. of California Press, Berkeley, 1942), p. 22.

by some other means. It is not unusual for the chase to last through one-fourth to one-third of the picture.

Ample proof that the motion picture scenario is an art in itself is borne out by statistics compiled by *Variety Magazine*. They show that of 9,561 full-length cinemas made between 1935 and 1955 the source material was as follows:*

6,052	Original Screen Stories	63 %
1,687	Novels	17.6%
594	Stage Plays	6.2%
560	Short Stories	5.9%
476	Miscellaneous	5 %
114	Source Unknown	1.2%
79	Biographies	.8%

Regarding the type, style, structure, theme and plot, literary and journalistic qualities, or the moral aspects of the motion picture, the discussion in Chapter 3 is adequate. In these areas the two mediums are practically parallel.

Acting and the Actors

Although the names of the actors are used as an attraction to bring an audience into the motion picture theatre, the careful critic will realize that the actors themselves often contribute less to the motion picture than it would appear on the surface. Unlike the stage, the major contribution is often made by the other artists and by other means than acting.

Whereas the theatre is the art of collective acting, the motion picture is the art of individual acting and moving images. Not often is there need for much group work. We are excepting, of course, the many mob or crowd scenes that are so familiar. When an individual or small group becomes important, the camera moves in and we have the close-up. This eliminates all except those few involved in that particular sequence. This is not possible on the stage.

The motion picture actor is often incidental to the background, while in the theatre he must always be superior to it. It is not un-

* *Variety*, Anniversary Issue, January, 1957. Page 8.

usual for the inanimate object to be equally, if not more, effective than the actor. A close-up of a crushed hat or flower or a broken glass can express stark tragedy. The camera can pan down on the turning of a doorknob and produce near panic in the audience. The impossibility of this on the stage is obvious. Herein lies a very important facet of the motion picture art which we should recognize and appreciate when it is done well. Sergei Eisenstein, famous Russian director, has called it "the process of arranging images and feelings in the mind of the spectator . . . A broken ladder, a woman weeping, and a grave . . . these can tell a complete story and create an emotional response." In the theatre an equal result could have been acquired only through much dialogue and acting. Unless we are aware of this great assistance given the actors by the imaginative work of the director and technicians in the development and the projection of emotion, we shall have lost one of the principal elements of the motion picture art. Emotion, yes; but we must not confuse it with acting.

The motion picture actor must work without any audience reaction, but he has as many chances as he may need to "get it right." The stage actor, on the other hand, inspired by the audience's response, has but a single opportunity in each performance. This does assure the assembled motion picture audience that it will see only the finest performance of which the actor is capable. On the stage there is always the possibility of human error—failing memory, a misplaced property, accidents of any kind. These deviations bring with them a new set of circumstances to be faced by the actor and an increased interest and element of surprise or enjoyment on the part of the audience. The tests for freshness and ease are not as valid in the cinema, for the two-dimensional photographs we observe may have been made months or even years ago. They are crystallized and changeless. In making those photographs the artists had many opportunities to get the exact effect they wished, and we see only that result. As Mr. Mamoulian has very aptly said, the audience watches the "future become the past" in a stage production and the "past becoming the present" in a motion picture.

From the actor's viewpoint there are further factors of differentiation. The stage actor must sustain a role over a long period of

time, but he does have the opportunity of building an emotion logically from its very beginning through its crisis. On the screen few scenes last more than two minutes and more often are a matter of seconds in length, and they are not taken in sequence. The motion picture actor need not sustain his character except for a very short time, but he must be able to catch any degree of emotion at any time and without the opportunity of developing it from the beginning. He must start each scene cold. In addition there is the matter of projecting from the stage to the very back row, both vocally and physically. The microphones and cameras solve this problem in the pictures, but the mental concentration must be far more perfect. The very proximity of the camera means that a single extraneous thought passing through the actor's mind during a close-up may register through some minute facial expression. Such details would be unseen by even the front row in the theatre. On the screen the actor must project and enlarge his gestures and facial expressions on the long shots and show great restraint on the close-ups. On large motion picture screens an eyebrow may be many feet in length, and the least quiver can destroy a complete mood. The actor must constantly adjust his work to the camera. It would follow, then, that our tests for restraint and convincingness might be equally valuable in either medium.

Actors on both stage and screen have found it possible to be successful in the other medium, but the techniques of each require study and concentration, both by them and by those of us who sit in the audience.

The Background and Technicians

We have already called the motion picture the offspring resulting from the marriage of art and science. It is obvious that its very birth was dependent upon the camera and the science of photography. Never for a moment must we allow this one essential difference between stage and screen to escape our minds. The two elements of the stage are performance and audience. The screen presents a third factor, often more important than either—*the cam-*

era. Motion pictures are possible without a story, without scenery, or even without actors, but never without the camera. That eye guides the audience to see just what it would have them see and interprets that material for them. In this sense it is both the creator and the spectator, for it not only determines what we may see but how we may see it. In its development the contributions of light and sound and their coordination have at times lifted motion picture productions to the level of an art. This medium has unquestionably produced aesthetic achievements that would have been impossible in any other form of expression.

Turning to Mr. Mamoulian once more:*

> Let us remember that this is an age of science—a sort of scientific renaissance as compared to the artistic renaissance of old. Ours is becoming more and more a man-made world. In the past, science followed the dreams of artists. Today, incredible as it seems, the situation is reversed, and the artist is following the actualities of scientific inventions. Motion pictures are truly a modern art, and present an unprecedented phenomenon in history because they were brought to life not by the artist, but by the scientist. The most naive picture begins where the most advanced science ends. It is the highest achievement of scientific genius that makes possible the photographs that move, the shadows that talk, the mere a b c's of the screen.

> Those who do not acknowledge motion pictures as an art because of this scientific and mechanical element seem to forget that all art in the world is subject to mechanics. After all, what is a piano, paints, chisel and marble, but the mechanics of musician, painter, and sculptor? Yet, of course, it is not tools that made such men as Wagner, Goya and Rodin, but the artistic result they achieved through their tools. The mechanics of a motion picture are merely the tools through which an artistic creation is expressed.

The *cameraman*, then, should receive our first consideration as a motion picture technician. We have shown how he can build a dramatic sequence without the use of actors, solely through photographic images. It is possible for him to create an intimacy through the close-up with its naturalness in both vocal powers and facial

* In *The Screen Writer*, March, 1947.

expression. This is an advantage denied us on the stage, where the element of projection to the back row is so important. Color and light and their very shadings are all within his province. Their psychological effect can be tremendous. At times the whole art of the motion picture comes closer even to painting than to the stage. These distinctions we must recognize.

There are occasions when we find ourselves praising the photography more than any other part of the picture. This is wrong, if we are to follow our initial principle that the theatre is a synthesis of the arts. We must learn to appreciate the photographer's techniques and his ability to use his camera. We should understand the *cut*, which is an abrupt shift from one angle or distance to another, or the *fade*, which acts as a curtain on a stage production to disconnect one scene from the next or denote the end of a sequence. We should appreciate his use of the *dissolve* to connect one scene with the following one and yet to show the passage of time, or be conscious of the emotional strength in the *montage*, that rapid sequence or series of pictures, which can build to a specific crisis. We should appreciate the kinds of shots, the variety, the angles, and their total effect on the dramatic significance of the film. We should recognize his art, but only as it contributes to the total effect of the picture. (For further treatment of the camera and its use in television, see pages 233-235.)

The three stage technicians are also found in the motion pictures. The *costumer* must be far more accurate in detail than on the stage and the *electrician's* contributions are of vital importance, though often his work is credited to the cameraman.

It is the *scene designer* who has the real problem. On the stage, the artist works in a field of frank make-believe. The audience accepts the scenery as artificial—a painted mountain or seascape are just that. Not so in the motion picture; they must either go to the actual scene or reproduce it so perfectly and so realistically that no one in the audience is able to detect the difference. Although the audience realizes that the story is make-believe and that the actors are only actors and that pictures are all it sees, the demand is for the "real" in scenery, sound effects, and properties. The elements of "illusion" and "seem" upon which we put such emphasis in the

legitimate theatre are handicaps to the technicians of the motion picture and especially to the scene designer, for the least inaccuracy diverts the attention of the audience. This, of course, is another aspect of the surface realism we have already discussed, but it does mark a further fundamental difference.

The constant change in background compared with the very few stage sets is sometimes an advantage, but not always. The intimacy and confinement of a play are occasionally a great part of its charm and meaning, but few motion pictures dare confine the whole production to a single set. The urge to move and the ability to do so can detract from the full impact of many stories, just as it can prove a great asset to others.

In addition to the four technicians mentioned, there are at least four others in the motion picture whom we must recognize: the *music composer*, the *sound man*, the *make-up man*, and the *editor*.

More than ninety per cent of our pictures carry with them a full musical score, what was once a distraction having come to be accepted as an integral part of this medium. That it has been raised to an art in itself is proved by the fact that while we may not notice the music as such during the performance we will praise it as a separate recording. The use of a familiar tune may prove a distraction, either by its very recognition or because of its association with some personal experience. A further distraction occurs when in a very realistic sequence the music is not adequately motivated as to source.

Music at its best serves not as a mere substitute for dialogue, but as an emotional asset to the long periods of pantomime. Many times this lack of dialogue is not even noticed. To realize the preponderance of music and scarcity of speech in a motion picture, one need but listen without watching for some length of time. To be praiseworthy, however, the musical score must always supplement and never supplant the acting. The less it is observed, the finer the artistry of the composer.

Only those sounds with dramatic value are included in either the stage or motion picture, but in the latter the element of sound takes on a different dimension. As an example, we cite the condemned prisoner in the death cell. To him the ticking of a clock takes on a very distinct meaning which the sound man is able to

give the audience just as the prisoner hears it. On the stage this dramatic value would be lost.

One can readily see the tremendous empathic possibilities that lie within the province of an imaginative sound man. His contribution is even more important in the proper adjustment of the equipment as it relates to the musical score, the dialogue, or the combination of the two.

Cecil B. DeMille once criticized the make-up man by saying that regardless of what a young man or woman looked like, all were made to look exactly the same in Hollywood. This has been one of the most serious criticisms of the industry for many years.

On the other hand, the make-up artists have achieved great heights. Rarely are we able to discern make-up as such even in extreme age or the most difficult character make-ups, despite the closeness of the image to the camera lens. This is far more than can be said of much of the make-up in the living theatre.

It is the editor in the motion picture whose work most closely concerns us. In the ideal situation his work is done at least in cooperation with the director, but it is the editor who has the ultimate decision as to what we, the audience, shall see. His artistry selects and chooses from all the pictures that have been made those which will be used. He arranges them as to sequence and length—in short, he builds or makes the picture. It remains only for that pedestrian state or local censorship board to step in with its straight-laced scissors and alter the work of this experienced artist who has determined the arranging, cutting, and editing that best express the story and meaning of the picture.

Direction and the Director

We have just mentioned the great powers of the editor and would not lessen his importance in this discussion. We must point out, however, that working side by side with him is the director who has been, even more than on the stage, the final authority from the writing of the scenario throughout the making of the picture. First

216   THE CINEMA AND THE STAGE

he must supervise the writing of the scenario, the casting, and the planning of the picture. It is then his responsibility to direct the actors and all technicians with as many retakes as he may desire until the exact intonation, flavor, expression, and meaning he has envisioned are on the film. A stage production, after the opening performance, is often out of the director's hands, and his interpretation may be altered in future performances, but in the motion picture there is no such possibility. It is always exactly as he wanted it, or as nearly so as it is humanly possible to make it. The same is true in the contributions of all the technicians.

It would seem logical that if we as an audience were to choose our motion pictures because of the director rather than the actors or even the title, we would be far more consistent in selecting pictures we would most enjoy and longest remember.

The motion picture director must first be a creative genius with a tremendous imagination. He must know a story when he sees it, and have a keen interest and a great desire to do it. He must bring to it an original and personal interpretation. He must know what the camera can and cannot do, what it ought to do and what it ought not to attempt. He must know the art of story telling and play structure in detail. He must be absolute master of the story and know exactly what he is trying to do with it. He must be able to convey these ideas to the players and technicians and to inspire them with a desire to interpret the meaning as he wishes to express it. He must know how to edit the picture to acquire the proper effects, and of course he must always be a master in his knowledge of human emotion and the psychology of an audience.

These are the marks of a really fine director, and we have seen the work of many excellent ones, such as John Ford, Alfred Hitchcock, John Huston, Billy Wilder, Sam Wood, Frank Capra, King Vidor, Wesley Ruggles, George Stevens, Joseph Mankiewicz, Leo McCarey, William Wyler, and Cecil B. DeMille, known primarily for their motion pictures, or Rouben Mamoulian, Elia Kazan, Josh Logan, and John Cromwell, who have directed successfully for both the stage and the motion picture. These are but a few of the many who might be listed.

Criticizing the Motion Picture

We must always remember that these two different mediums of the stage and motion picture can never be compared as works of art. Filet mignon and roast turkey are both entrées, corn and asparagus are vegetables, but no one would dream of making comparisons. We may personally prefer one or the other, but when there is no choice, we take what is presented and confine our discussion to the deftness of the chef and the perfection of preparation.

Foreign films from France, Italy, Germany, and occasionally Japan have won acclaim for their imaginative conception and artistic realization. Art theatres specializing in these films have flourished in the larger cities. The motion pictures from England have broken into the more popular field and have proved strong competition for our American films, even in the smaller communities, to the extent that many moviegoers have come to prefer these to the home product. For the sake of fairness let us remember that in this country we see only the cream of the foreign productions. If we were to attend only the best two or three per cent of our own pictures, we might make a fairer comparison. On the other hand, we have both enjoyed and profited by these foreign films. Their success should have given some valuable training to our own producers. One of the most vital lessons that should have been learned is that there are tremendous values inherent in utter simplicity, in absolute truth, and in complete consistency.

The oft-used term "gone Hollywood" has taken on many meanings, but originally it meant—and means even yet—undue luxury, overdone, gilded beyond recognition, out of proportion, exorbitant, untruthful. No observing individual would deny that much progress has been made, but unfortunately this criticism is still applicable to some extent. With unlimited financial means, material properties of every description, the opportunity and ability to do anything desired, and a free rein to all the artists, especially the technicians, it has proved so easy to "pull out all the stops," when only a few would have proved more harmonious in truth, effectiveness, and artistry. For example, a musical may be given the locale

of a legitimate theatre, and an early shot shows the curtain going up, the proscenium arch, and an audience in attendance. As the picture progresses, the stage dimensions take on the proportions of Madison Square Garden. Or again, a timid little girl starts to sing in her attic room, alone and unaccompanied, or to audition with a single piano in some producer's office, when suddenly from nowhere we hear a full orchestra in the background. So many times the whole story is allowed to stop while some comedian injects his particular specialty. Such instances could be multiplied a thousand-fold in every area of motion picture production.

Since Aristotle we have accepted the fact that the least valued of all the elements that compose drama is spectacle. It is used only after the script has proved to be barren of story, theme, character, dialogue, or mood. However, our motion pictures have too often valued the spectacle above all these others, and for no other reason than just that they had the facilities and ability to do so. They have also played fast and loose with the well-accepted principles of drama types and styles, and far too often they emphasize and exploit mere personalities rather than artistry.

Many other general criticisms could be listed, but it all comes back to the glaring truth that the principal reason for these violations was and is that we as the audience would buy them. No one seems to like a double feature, but this monstrosity is still with us. Just as soon as the audience refuses to pay the admission price, we shall be free of double features and all the other weaknesses that this very popular medium may possess.

The motion pictures today are better than ever. The influx of foreign films and lessons learned from them, coupled with the pressure of the television competition, have put them once more on the defensive, and, although the future may not look so bright in millions of dollars, the artistic heights and possibilities are still limitless.

— 8 —

Television, the Cinema,

and the Stage

*W*hen we consider that the stage has been with us for more than three thousand years, the motion picture since approximately 1900, radio for about forty years, and television since roughly 1950, we can begin to comprehend the tremendous growth of this infant in the theatre family. Some continue to look upon the child with disdain, consider it only nuisance value, refer to it as "cheap clap-trap" or "the chewing gum of the eye." There is no doubt that this youngster has grown faster than clothes could be supplied and has attempted to do many things before it was really prepared. It has pushed its way into every avenue of communication—many times when it had nothing worth while to say.

We must recognize these childish traits as part of its growing up, and not permit them to blind us to the potential power the

220

youngster commands. It is foolish to discount its competition with all three of its relatives for the favor of the populace, and it would be just as absurd to imply that the present popularity is only a fad. Television, like the "horseless carriage," has a more than reasonable chance of being with us and playing an important role in our lives for many years to come.

From the beginning many recognized television's potentiality in the entertainment field so far as variety acts—a revival of vaudeville—and the lighter musical programs were concerned. Its strength in the sports world, as a news agency, a lecture platform, and even in education were also early realized. The full extent of its influence on the stage, cinema, and the radio was debated at length. When the infant began to really spread its wings, it was the radio and cinema that felt the first pinch of this new competition, for its appeal and early programs were to their audience rather than to that of the legitimate theatre.

In this book we do not propose to give much thought to the radio drama. To be sure, there were occasional successes and undoubtedly radio's use of the musical bridge and background has had great influence on the merging of music with stage and cinema for mood effects. We are well aware that millions of women found their morning and afternoon emotional outlet via the soap operas and that countless children revelled between four o'clock and seven o'clock in the horse operas and radio's various attempts at historical, crime, and adventure stories or their out-of-this-world fantasies and an occasional educational program. Nevertheless, the radio drama has never been considered a serious substitute for either stage or motion picture. As another offspring of stage and science, it developed, but never really grew up artistically. Due, undoubtedly, to its physical handicap of blindness, it never quite found the answer for producing effectively the dramatic literature of any type, style, or period. In all fairness we should recognize that radio did develop a drama of its own, but it has never shown a permanence or significance sufficient to be included in this discussion.

With television it has been a vastly different story. From the situation comedy it was just a step to serious drama. Fortunately, considerable power fell into the hands of some stage personnel

who had both artistic standards and integrity and were willing to experiment. In a commercial world they found numerous obstacles and fought many battles, both mechanical and artistic. Occasionally they managed to edge in a program of real artistry, and the audience response was enthusiastic enough to make other productions possible. One of these experiments was the Maurice Evans production of *Hamlet* early in 1953 when it was estimated that seventeen million viewers saw that play, perhaps more than had witnessed a live performance of it in all the 350 years of its existence.

This experimental phase also brought out the need for a technique that would fit television. Which of its relatives would it follow—stage or screen? The commercial interests readily recognized the magnitude of the tool at hand, and another gigantic battle began between the west coast and New York. Hollywood with its motion picture knowledge and equipment fought for the filmed television which would resemble the motion picture, and New York for the live television which would follow the techniques of the stage. During this experimental period the two vied with each other, and the public benefited by the excellent productions of dramatic literature from the Greeks through Shakespeare down to the best in our realistic theatre, as each tried to show the merits of its case.

Even today the discussion is not resolved, for we have with us both filmed and live shows. In the meantime this new medium has developed some techniques that fit its own particular needs.

Television's growth in the presentation of drama has without question been responsible for the decrease in the attendance at live theatre productions across the country. Broadway has lost ten to fifteen legitimate theatres to television—a loss it could ill afford.

The television screen, live or filmed, still lacks the person-to-person, flesh-and-blood qualities of the stage. The live show cannot possess the complete fluidity, size, spectacle, and range of the cinema. There is also absent that very important ingredient common to both stage and cinema—the joy of just being part of an audience participating in the birth of a dramatic production.

Balanced against this loss is the tremendous personal comfort of relaxing at home in an easy chair and seeing some of the top names in the theatre world perform in a variety of three or four

programs in a single evening. This involves a greater degree of physical comfort than to come home weary from the day's work, wash, dress, hurry, drive through heavy traffic, find a place to park, walk to the theatre, pay an ever-increasing admission, sit in the same seat for two hours, then again fight traffic and arrive home very late.

Another aspect of television we often hear criticized is the ever-present commercial. However, we must not forget that television, even more than the professional theatre or motion picture, is a business as well as an art, for television must sell something besides itself. We should therefore accept the commercial as inevitable. The average cost of a television drama is $40,000, and someone must pay the bill. Since we rarely consider the cost and upkeep of the set itself, our admission is measured by the minutes we give the sponsor. Certainly this is small enough payment for many of the fine dramatic productions available.

It cannot be said that television has brought about a renaissance in the quality of dramatic entertainment, though it has greatly increased the quantity. Perhaps seventy-five per cent of the dramatic programs are far beneath a reasonable standard of excellence, but this might also be said for both the stage and motion picture. They, too, have a high percentage of failures and of productions that fall far short of our desires. In any instance, we do have the right to choose what we see, and in television we have a singular advantage; we can with a flick of the finger eliminate it entirely or we can, in an instant, turn to another program. We do not have this immediate relief in either of the other mediums. Even when they prove to be less than we had hoped, comparatively few of us get up and walk out. More often than not we sit through to the bitter end, either because of the time and money already expended or because there is no other place to go.

The Audience and Dramatic Criticism

Perhaps the greatest single difference between television and the two other mediums is in its audience. We are not now concerned with those in the broadcasting studio, but rather with the individ-

uals viewing the performance before millions of sets. There may be one, two, three, or any number in homes, bars, restaurants, service clubs, hotel lobbies, or wherever people may be gathered before a television set. Their ages, background, health, experience, and demands run the gamut, more varied than for either the stage or cinema. Even the time of day is not constant. A program wholly satisfactory for adults at ten o'clock in New York could be displeasing to the seven o'clock children's audience in California. Each television artist must think of himself as an additional guest in each of these groups, but the generosity usually afforded a guest cannot be depended upon, for the program can be abruptly ended at any moment.

In spite of this wide variety of viewers, the producers are well aware that the vast majority of their audience is at home. They also know that there is no more personal or intimate relationship possible. Each member of such an audience is completely free from the sophistications or pretenses he may don when in contact with the outside world or when part of a crowd. A man alone is sincere, and he demands the same sincerity and truthfulness from every aspect of the television production. He may wish the drama or comedy to be amusing, shocking, frightening, mysterious, or exciting, but it must present unmistakable truth, whether in the imagination of fantasy or in the characterizations of realistic theatre.

It is far easier to detect falseness and cheapness under these intimate circumstances, for the characteristics of an audience that differentiate it from the individual are no longer present. The viewer is not swayed by his neighbor nor by a feeling that he must like what he should like. As a further disadvantage his interests are divided. There are the distractions of the home never present in the theatre—the telephone, visitors, letting out the dog, watching the baby, attending the furnace. These interruptions all play a part in his over-all evaluation of the program.

To criticize justly we must always ask if this is a live or a filmed program. The live show is more limited in its dramatic time (the period covered by the story's action) as well as in costume or set changes. It has the possibility of human error, but it also holds

the excitement of the "future becoming the past" before our eyes. The film with its greater variety and fluidity has eliminated all possibilities of error, and as in the cinema, we merely watch the "past become the present." Frequently there are parts of each which complicate judgment somewhat. The kinescope is a third possibility, but since this is a picture of a picture—usually of a live production given at some previous time—we shall not consider it separately. In any event, the points on criticism made in Chapters 2 and 7 on stage and motion picture are equally valid. We would especially call attention to number seven of the "Ten Commandments of Dramatic Criticism" on page 50, and to the twelve questions for the motion picture or television critic on pages 207, 208.

There is an additional advantage and responsibility that is peculiarly ours as members of a television audience. This is the immediacy and the tremendous effect that our reactions can have on the sponsors and on the broadcaster. The air which carries any program into our homes belongs not to the station nor to the producer, but to *us*. We need only voice our complaint or our praise. Vast millions see a program on a single evening. It would take months or years for the same number to see any given cinema or stage production. What was said earlier about the power of the audience is more poignant in television than in any other medium. Truly the calibre of television entertainment lies largely in our hands, for the program that emanates from any studio can be of our choosing. It behooves us all to choose wisely and with discrimination, and above all to make our desires known.

Any honest evaluation of television will find that the vast majority of programs must be approached on the third level of dramatic criticism, which we have defined as "show business." We may rationalize or wish for more, but by its very nature it must appeal to the mass audience. Bound by all its purely commercial restrictions —the necessity of appealing to many, time limitations, available material, expense of production, necessity for financial return on investment—we must accept the fact that television *is* show business. This does not mean that it should not strive to be the very best of its kind, and it is the duty of an intelligent audience to demand just that! Frequently a program does rise to the second level of criti-

cism by creating the theatre magic or aesthetic enjoyment that that level implies. Our overt praise of such an effort can bring more of the same. Occasionally the medium has really distinguished itself, and by so doing demanded that it be considered on the highest level of dramatic criticism. It is on these all too rare occasions that our joy and enthusiasm are dampened only by the extremely low audience response as reflected by the professional ratings. (A further discussion of these national ratings appears in the summary of this chapter.) There is a very great need for personal praise, directly to the producer, of those programs that can be evaluated on the first or second level of dramatic criticism. Only by such action can we hope for continued artistic growth in the medium.

The Play and the Playwright

Television was still in its infancy when it became evident that its major problem was material, and that the writer would be the most sought-after individual in the whole of its personnel. Not only did this infant devour new scripts as fast as they could be supplied, but it also consumed the dramatic literature of the past at an alarming rate. Coupled with this problem of finding the material to broadcast was the fact that it demanded a particular and specialized diet, in the form of its writing. The novelist was given far too much to description and covered too vast a field; the playwright designed his work primarily for talk and for a larger stage with little or no limitation on the number of characters.

The radio writer was even further from base, for he had been forced to portray vision, characterization, action, sound, reaction, plot, and everything in words, words, words. Furthermore, his product rarely got full attention. Cooking, scrubbing, reading, studying, bridge, conversation, or any other human activity shared the hearer's interest. This necessitated repetition—more words— and placed a greater importance on the exact vocal quality than on the development of characterization.

And so for television a new writer has been developed, for its needs lie somewhere between the stage and the motion picture.

The ages and the nature of the audience have made many subjects taboo. Politics, race problems, religious beliefs, deviations from the generally accepted way of life must either be eliminated or given a very special care in their treatment. Ideas that can be discussed openly or with few restrictions on the stage and with somewhat less freedom in the cinema dare not be suggested to this vast and varied audience. Certainly sex has little of the freedom of discussion that is permitted on stage or in the cinema. Furthermore, the camera rather than the dialogue tells a large portion of the story, but there must be more dialogue than in the cinema. The limited physical time of the script means that each speech must be packed with meaning as well as dramatically effective. It must characterize the person speaking it, furnish some background of the existing situation, and push the story forward toward its major conflict. In this respect it resembles the stage. The television dramatist must work very fast. His situation and exposition must be rapidly introduced with much use of the camera. There must be a strong crisis at just the proper break for the commercials. The outcome of the conflict must be held a secret until the very end, and the conclusion must be a logical outgrowth of the story's events.

Physical time restrictions are most inelastic. A half-hour show permits just twenty-three minutes for the story. Not more than a single characterization can be developed in that time. The others must resort to general types, which means that only rarely can a half-hour show rise above pulp writing. The hour show is given approximately fifty minutes. Two or three characters can, in the proper hands, be adequately developed in this period. The ninety-minute show allows approximately seventy-five minutes to the story, and in that time a playwright can approach the development found in the average motion picture script of ninety to one hundred minutes, or the two hours to two hours and a half—minus intermissions—usually found in a stage play. An hour-and-a-half television show, however, presents scheduling difficulties. They are very expensive and, though growing in number, comparatively rare. Further restrictions are involved in the limitation on sets and costumes, especially if it is a live program.

In a stage play Act I is usually given to setting up a situation,

Act II to complicating it, and Act III to resolving it. The first two are far easier than the third. Television has taken advantage of this fact in its need for scripts by simply not bothering with the resolution. There are few of us who have not been very much interested in a particular dramatic program when suddenly we were confronted by the closing commercial and realized that the end of the program had come, although the situation had not really been resolved. Those who know the rules of the industry recognize this as a technique evolved to meet the time limits, coupled with the constant pressure on the author to turn out new scripts. These deadlines are a major factor in curbing an imagination that might have created an artistic and moving resolution. They are largely responsible for what many consider hack writing and certainly represent a major criticism of the industry.

Plays of a journalistic rather than literary nature are encouraged. Audiences have come to choose particular programs for the theme or emotion for which they are noted. Writers are frequently advised to watch as many programs as possible and then choose the special style or trend in which they would cast their story. There are specific programs that emphasize suspense, mystery, crime, murder, foreign intrigue, the courts, family relationships or problems, romantic love, sentimentality, sweetness and light, spectacle, or some similar pattern. The writer able to accomplish such a feat may "hit the jackpot" financially, but in doing so he frequently sacrifices any literary aspirations he might have had.

The television playwright is not necessarily doomed to realism, but thus far he has found it to be the most fruitful field. The drama here must be more penetrating than on either stage or cinema. The camera permits a delicacy and a subtleness that are impossible on the stage. Although they can be duplicated on the motion picture screen, both realism and detail excel in television more than in either of the other fields. On the stage there is only the semblance of realism. In the cinema the very size of the screen and the presence of the audience are handicaps. The great secret of television is to find one specific emotional moment or one facet of a character and to portray that so vividly that it will touch the same spring in the mind of the viewer. In real life the man next door or the

completely normal person has little to offer dramatically. However, under the microscopic eye of the camera small details of character can be exposed that will make him a most interesting figure on the television screen.

The purpose of all mediums has been to present the normal and natural, especially in the realistic theatre. Here the motion picture screen, and the stage even more so, have worked under the most abnormal and unnatural situations. Now, in the privacy of home and the intimacy of the camera's close-up, we can seek out the most realistic and exact emotion or feeling that has ever been known. Indeed, if it is realism we want, it is better portrayed on the television screen than at any time in all our history. No better medium exists for the portrayal of personal drama and inner feelings. This ability to speak so realistically for an audience steeped in realism is unquestionably one of the major reasons for its great popularity.

The Actor and the Acting

In television we are primarily concerned with the visual effect, in contrast to radio's dependence on the auditory. When both elements are involved it is necessary that one be dominant. When the audio and the video take on equal importance the audience becomes confused, and this confusion breaks the mood of the story and proves a distraction. The actor is television's chief visual aspect. Let us now consider some of the similarities and differences in the acting of the three mediums.

In the realm of television, the stage and screen actors have each found their backgrounds to be both an advantage and a disadvantage. The great use of the close-up has been advantageous to the screen actor, while the stage actor, with his projection to the back row of the balcony, has found a need for adjusting to these new circumstances both vocally and physically. The stage actor trained to the arena style of production finds this experience most valuable in the area of television acting. The stage actor can

memorize a role or sustain a character throughout a long scene; he possesses a greater consistency in his control of body, voice, and imagination than the motion picture actor, who has always played very short sequences and had the opportunity of repeating scenes time after time until the exact effect was attained. On the other hand, the cinema actor has been accustomed to numerous mechanical devices such as countless lights, numerous microphones, properties, and the ever-present camera. The stage actor must adjust to being the servant of all this mechanical equipment, and to being fenced in by it.

Both are faced with a far smaller playing area, the necessity for following exact movement, turns, and angles, and a most limited rehearsal period. The months usually given a motion picture and the weeks for rehearsing a stage production have shrunk to a matter of hours for the television drama. Television actors are conscious of these and many other details even while they work to develop a characterization and remember the lines, the exact direction, the idea of the play, and the relationship to all the actors, keep one eye on the director, and remember that their audience is really the cameraman, even should there be a studio audience present. Yet they dare not permit the discerning eye of the camera to show any of the frustrations which these technical elements can bring about. Add to all this the constant pressure of the clock ticking away the seconds, the vagaries of the sponsors, advertising agencies, and public ratings, and we can see why television acting is perhaps the most demanding of all.

Knowing all these problems of the television actor is an important background, but we should not allow them to enter into our final evaluation of his work. They are merely occupational hazards. As critics we give them no more consideration than we do the inexperience of the actor in the educational theatre, always bearing in mind that there is just one standard of excellence in any theatre production.

There is a somewhat brighter note, however, for actors have found television a boon to their financial problems. In New York there is more money spent on television acting in any given week than is paid for all the Broadway stage productions in a single

year. In Hollywood the motion picture actor has found television his answer to making ends meet between pictures. Unfortunately, a small percentage of the would-be actors in either city are playing a majority of the roles. The spread is greater, however, than it was in radio, for television requires more rehearsal time and the same actors are unable to appear on as many different programs. Likewise, television actors are far more the victims of type-casting than in either stage or cinema. Both the time and difficulty required to change make-up and the risk involved of its being detected by the camera have eliminated the opportunity of actors playing characters unlike themselves in age or general appearance.

And now we would consider some of the special talents required in this difficult field. Even more than on the stage, the voice on a microphone must have a pleasing quality, a wide range, good articulation, and a diction that does not attract attention to itself (unless it is essential to a particular characterization). It should also possess a style of its own and show rich feeling and intelligence. Through the voice and visually by the actor's body we get the sense of a speech, the purpose or intention of the character. There is no room for generalities in the reading of a line on television—the *specific* must always be in evidence. The actor must be especially careful of his word groupings, his emphasis and pauses. Variety is a vital factor. It is as if he were speaking to us personally, for he is physically so close to us, and our attention is so concentrated on him alone.

Characterization is of central importance. Because of the extreme proximity this can be at once easier or more difficult. A greater control of facial expression and eyes, in fact of the whole body, is essential. The slightest movement can be made meaningful or distracting. The close-up eliminates the possibility of any momentary relaxing that might be possible on the stage. A character in the theatre exists primarily in the imagination of the actor. By that actor's selection of physical and vocal externals he transfers that character to the imagination of the audience. He must know exactly what lies behind each speech if it is to be properly motivated. In any realistic characterization the television actor has a greater opportunity and more details with which to

work, but with that opportunity he also has more responsibilities and a need for greater control.

Motives are the source of all action and reaction in theatre presentation. As viewers we are always interested in the motives of the characters. On the stage our chief interest is on the speaker and his actions. In both the motion picture and the television we frequently see more of the reactions of characters being acted upon. One can detect in any television program the great emphasis the camera, director, and even playwright place on reactions, through the practice of focusing the camera on the face and action of the person being spoken to. This is an aid to both playwright and actor, for it pushes the story forward by telling the audience two stories at once. We are able to look inside the character's mind and to hear his thoughts.

Farce, which in television is often referred to as "situation comedy," is one of the most popular types of program. Here we find the same star appearing week after week in a slightly different situation. More often than not the leading roles are played by the same actors. Within the program each character may have a name, but rarely do we remember or use them. The series is known by the name of the star and exists solely on his or her personality as a showman. Here the word "performance" as Mr. Atkinson has distinguished it from "acting" comes into even better use, for these programs are to television what the comic strip is to the newspaper. Characterizations are based on such simple and single traits as being extremely shy, very bold, most stingy, in search of a husband (or wife), unusually quarrelsome, well meaning but blundering, or just being an "average family." A companion to this situation comedy is found on a long series of morning and afternoon programs. The only difference lies in their melodramatic and pseudo-serious situations.

In either case the script, week after week, is practically the same, the situations varying just a bit from the previous episode. We must not condemn these cartoons *per se*; they may serve some purpose; but they must be recognized for what they are. Individually we may or may not care for the actor as a personality, for the character he portrays, or for his particular acting style, but as critics we must view his work objectively.

The Background and Technicians

Live television is not unlike the stage in its use of scenery, lighting, and costumes, at least so far as the audience is concerned. Technically there are many problems, and they are different for the black-and-white or colored picture. We are interested only in what we see as a result of all technicians meeting these problems.

Filmed television, with its greater freedom, comes closer to the cinema technically, the difference being only that it cannot be as effective with the panorama, the long shots, huge crowds, beautiful settings, or the chase. It is true that some television pictures have tried to incorporate these techniques, but the small screen makes them very difficult. This liability is often apparent when we see a regular movie, prepared for that medium, being used for television.

As in the cinema the most important technician is the cameraman. Due to the time limitations of the program and the size of the screen, his responsibility is even greater than in the motion picture. He is second only to the director, and in some programs there is a camera director as well as the floor director responsible for the staging and acting. The two must constantly work together. If, as critics, we fail to catch the full impact of the camera as playwright, actor, and technician, we have failed to comprehend much of television's art.

As a playwright the camera serves as narrator, capable of prowling about the set and among the characters looking at everything. The smallest gesture, action, or property can become the most important facet of the entire story. The camera can act in a most *objective* manner, as a third person whose purpose it is to show the audience just what it would have the viewer see, yet never becoming a part of the action. The camera can interpret the story, choosing just which character will at any given moment contribute most to the central idea, and making that character appear just as important or unimportant in the total composition as it chooses to make him. In some situations as in a ballet, it can take on the attributes of another participant and move about among the performers as an integral part of the scene. This is called *subjective*

camera technique, which means that the viewer may see the performance through the eyes of one of the characters involved.

As a technician the cameraman must have a keen sense of composition, dramatic values, sensitivity for feelings, and a knowledge of psychology as well as art. He must know that too much movement of the camera can have the effect of making the audience dizzy whereas too little will lead to monotony. There is a very short time, twenty to thirty seconds, when the viewer can look at a single picture without losing interest. The cameraman must know just how much of the subject should be included in the picture for the best pictorial and dramatic effect—full body, from knees, waist, chest, or just the face and head. He must make the choice of angle—from side, front, back, or from below or above the subject. Psychologically and photogenically, as well as dramatically, this angle can mean much to the artistic or dramatic value. A camera shot from below can increase the size and importance of a character, both physically and psychologically; from above it can diminish his importance in relation to the whole picture.

Each angle must have a meaning. A shot taken from high above the heads of two lovers in an embrace or from below could only confuse the viewer, unless it was an effort to use the camera subjectively and give the impression that someone was observing the scene through a transom or from a position of hiding. The cameraman must appreciate just which view of the face is most pleasing, for individuals are often more photogenic from one side than another. He must be especially careful of the extreme close-up, particularly with a woman who may be playing a role younger than she actually looks. Few persons can stand to fill the screen with just face and head. The slightest blemish in complexion, scar, mole, or perspiration can prove a serious distraction. Costumes can be very attractive from one angle and quite ordinary or uncomplimentary from another. The cameraman must be sure that all pictures are adequately framed on the three sides, especially giving characters head room, which means ample room between the top of the head and the top of the picture. To cut a picture at the hair line of an actor or the ankles of a ballet dancer is a serious error. The cameraman must also choose the movement the camera will

make—whether it will move forward or backward, to the right or left, vertically or horizontally. And all his work must be without effort. As with the other artists, we must never be conscious of his techniques. All camera changes must be smoothly done and in complete rhythm with the action and movement of the story. For further discussion of the cameraman, see pages 213-214.

Television, contrary to the stage, has many technicians whose duties vary but who are generally responsible for make-up, set decoration, special sound effects, musical score, and, of course, the sound or audio part of the program. The long list of credits that comes at the close of any program gives some indication of what a tremendously cooperative art this is. Each artist must make his contribution to the sum total or unified effect, if his work is a part of, and never apart from, that single impression. If the scenery, the décor, the lighting, the costumes, the make-up, the sound, or the properties attract attention to themselves as such, then they are in error. Once again, it is the director who does the coordinating. All these artist-technicians are, in a sense, "extensions" of him.

Direction and the Director

The responsibilities of the director in the modern theatre have been emphasized under both the stage and motion picture headings. All that was said in those two chapters about the director's work and the goals he sought is equally true in television. If possible, his authority and influence here are even greater, for he is personally present from the first reading through the final performance. There is no altering of his interpretation as occasionally occurs during an extended run of a stage production. From his control booth he is truly an autocrat—commanding, begging, cajoling, pleading, demanding, forcing, or entreating, but somehow getting as nearly as possible exactly what he wants from all the technicians and actors. Here even more than in the other two areas, with the possible exception of some motion pictures, the production can be the creation of the director more than it is of the author.

There is little more that we need say about the work of the

director that has not been stated in earlier chapters. However, one of the leading men in this field, Mr. Edwin Duerr, has explained that work so well that some of his main points are presented in the following three paragraphs.*

Normally the director is the first to receive the script for study and thought. During this period he must discover the exact characters of the piece; search out their motives and relationships to each other and to the story; understand just where the play begins, how it builds through a series of crises to a turning point and a climax; just where the breaks will come. He must discover the mood or atmosphere; in short, determine exactly what the playwright has sought.

Once the director has made this discovery and has a full command of the script's form and meaning, he must think in terms of actors who will fit into the various roles; of voices and personalities that will blend or contrast properly; of camera movements and pictures; of setting, stage décor, properties, lighting, sound, and many other details that will help to interpret and emphasize this "something" toward which he believes the playwright is moving.

During both rehearsals and performance, the actor must lean heavily on the director's interpretation. There is not the time available in a stage production nor the retakes possible in a motion picture. The actors rarely have sufficient opportunity to study the script adequately. Each actor must now find a true-to-life portrayal of the character he is to enact, but this is not in itself enough. Each must rely on the director to blend this truth into the larger truth of the whole play as he works individually and collectively with the cast to do three things: (a) give an appearance of reality that is (b) so interpreted by the actors as to (c) express the playwright's idea in a distinctive way. This is the form of the play and involves capturing just the right qualities of this particular group of individual characters in just this situation; of choosing and establishing an atmosphere; of developing just the right theatricality, rhythm, pace, feeling, that will project the playwright's *attitude*

* Edwin Duerr, *Radio and Television Acting* (New York: Rinehart & Co., Inc., 1950), pp. 371-81.

toward this situation and life. These last two elements—interpreting and expressing—go well beyond the mere picturing of life. Herein lies the work of the director and the art of the theatre, whatever the medium.

The television director is not denied any of the responsibilities previously mentioned for his fellow directors. He does have some added problems, and considerably less time for solving them. Directors come and go more rapidly in television than in either of the other mediums, for numerous reasons—not all artistic ones. However, as in the other areas, a director's name may often be a greater guarantee of a worth-while production than either the playwright or the actors involved. Many of the names that follow are familiar for their work on stage or motion picture screen as well as in television: Sidney Lumet, George Roy Hill, Norman Felton, Alex Segal, James Yarborough, Jerry Thorpe, Robert Stevens, Lawrence Schwab, Vincent Donehue, Ira Cirker, Don Richardson, Alan Schneider, Delbert Mann, David Alexander, and Ted Corday.

Quality of Programs

The host of panel shows, quiz and parlor games, give-away and amateur hours, athletic shows, and even variety programs are, though classed as entertainment, not the concern of this book. If we do not approve them, we need not choose them and do have the opportunity of voicing our protest. When they cease to have an audience they will disappear. Unfortunately, public opinion polls have never really reflected what type of program the audience actually wanted; they have only reported the popularity of the programs that were available. This is a fallacy which *Time* magazine has aptly pointed out in the following quotation:*

> While the majority rule might be very acceptable in a democratic government, it is folly for television. The viewer is both the unwitting culprit and the ultimate victim of the tyranny. The ratings discourage worthy programs that might make a deeply

* Courtesy *Time;* copyright Time, Inc., 1957, "The Only Wheel in Town," January 14, 1957, p. 72.

favorable—but unmeasurable—impression but that do not attract measurably large numbers. They inspire imitations of high-rated programs, touching off cycles of the second-rate.

We can but wonder how many fine programs have never been seen only because they did not show an immediate promise of a high rating. This is one of television's most serious dilemmas, for these programs, with their appeal to the smaller audience, should have the same right to existence as those with the mass appeal. Each should be evaluated on its own level. This very problem was most poignantly illustrated in early March, 1957, when England's famous Old Vic company presented a ninety-minute version of *Romeo and Juliet*. Its rating as compared with the programs in competition was, as might have been expected, disappointing. The dangers inherent in such a fallacious measure of artistic success were pointed out by the television critic on *The New York Times*, Jack Gould.* With Mr. Gould's permission a large portion of his article is quoted:

> Barbarians in television smugly nodded their heads last week. Juliet Capulet ran a poor second to Lucy Ricardo in the popularity ratings on Monday evening. Culture once again was put behind the eight ball. Video's forlorn executives duly genuflected before the awesome power of variety for the mass.
>
> The Old Vic's brilliant presentation of "Romeo and Juliet" may have had quality and artistry, but not what it takes in television. Shakespeare forgot to dope out the numbers game. He wound up with the short straw in the Trendex drawing.
>
> The viewers who tuned in the romantic tragedy on the National Broadcasting Company were a paltry few in contrast to the audiences garnered by the rival attractions offered over the Columbia Broadcasting System.
>
> According to the research organization, here were the ratings for each evening half hour:

	8:00-8:30	8:30-9:00	9:00-9:30
Romeo and Juliet	15.6	14.8	10.9
Burns and Allen	20.8		
Talent Scouts		26.3	
I Love Lucy			41.6

---

* *The New York Times*, March 10, 1957.

The results spoke for themselves. The sponsors who presented "Romeo and Juliet" only had to wait two days to be advised by *Variety* that "Shakespeare doesn't pay off on TV apparently." From coast-to-coast there ran the same quip in newspapers: "Wherefore art thou, Romeo?". . .

Of course, the lovable Gracie Allen, the wry George Burns, the hilarious Lucille Ball and the durable Arthur Godfrey outdrew Shakespeare. Did any person doubt that they would? They're contemporary popular stars who, with varying degrees of skill and showmanship, are satisfying a genuine need in entertainment.

But what in heaven's name do any of them have in common with "Romeo and Juliet"? Only in television has there been injected the preposterous notion that somehow totally dissimilar attractions can be equated.

In music we do not dismiss Rodgers and Hammerstein because we have Elvis Presley. In literature we do not erase Hemingway because there are poems by Edgar Guest. We do not close golf courses because more people go to horse races.

Yet, because of its unique economic structure, with its dependency on the mass, television subtly tends to compress all art forms into a common maw. The younger generation raised on TV is being exposed to the philosophy that anything or everything must meet a single test of "popularity" or be cast aside. Lucy scores, so Juliet is scorned.

It is time the affirmative side were stressed. That "Lucy" is popular is not news. What is news is that many millions of persons saw "Romeo and Juliet." Conceivably, ten to twenty million saw it. Is this not a magnificent achievement, an exciting conveyance to a large audience of the best our culture has to offer? Judged for itself, which is the only way it can be judged, the Old Vic's "Romeo and Juliet" was a success.

Sooner or later the television industry must reorientate its thinking or there is bound to be a gradual disappearance of the finer things on TV. If a comparative rating is accepted as the only valid measure of success, then sponsors are bound to shy away from "Romeo and Juliet" or anything of quality that may appeal to only a minority audience. . . .

Television's whole concept of trying to equate unlikes must be abandoned or everything is bound to turn out alike. . . . The

reliance on mere figures and meaningless comparisons is not evidence of its power and effectiveness but rather of its crippling weakness. Modern industry lives by the constructive credo of diversifying its wares and investing in research. The same credo has equal validity for the arts and television programming.

The crying need in television is a barometer that makes allowance for initiative and individuality in programming. One can hear howls of pain from the business world if a list of the "top ten" products were the basis for deciding whether a manufacturing firm should survive. Such a comparison might run like this: (1) Bread, (2) Milk, (3) Cigarettes, (4) Soap, (5) Toothpaste, (6) Electric light bulbs, (7) Gasoline, (8) Aspirin, (9) Matches and (10) Clothing.

Yet in television the arts are subjected to just such a yardstick.

How much longer is television going to show interest in such fantastic comparisons that make a mockery of common sense and ultimately threaten to drag the medium down to new depths of infantile behavior? How much longer will a gigantic industry tolerate the wretched business of trying to average out apples and oranges in hopes of discovering a coast-to-coast pear?

The picture, however, is not all black as some of television's most severe critics might paint it. We are fortunate that the medium is not government controlled or subsidized. This could mean only the dullest kind of programs. Commercial television means competition, and competition means faster growth and a more consistent effort to please. Even as this chapter is being written many excellent programs are available and the future looks ever more promising. Daily we read of new developments and inventions, the possibilities of which seem almost unbelievable—even to our generation, which is conditioned to the unbelievable. Few who follow the medium carefully or regularly will condemn it wholeheartedly. That remains for those who do not know what it can do, and what in its happier moments it has done. Most would agree that there are many excellent programs, but the viewer must select carefully if he is to conserve his time or to see the medium at its best.

Some very fine theatre has been made available to the television audience. There have also been some worthy new scripts

written especially for television, and excellent adaptations of novels, short stories, and nonfiction. In contrast to the spectaculars, which would always be a part of so commercial a medium as television, we are grateful for a few programs that in their simplicity have brought to our television screens some bright, imaginative, and artistic moments.

Before condemning this infant of the entertainment world, we must each think for a moment of the many occasions on which we have been privileged to see and hear the greatest musical and dramatic artists of the day, at a cost that is almost negligible. Our parents lived a lifetime knowing such artists only by reading their names in a newspaper, but today there are very few great personalities of the theatre or musical world whose genius has not come into our homes. This is a privilege we should recognize with appreciation.

In its very short life much progress has been made. The techniques have not yet become firmly entrenched, for this new art is still feeling its way, and further developments on the technical side may greatly improve its artistic values as well. Just what television holds for the future few would venture to prophesy. The one positive prediction that can be made is that the type and artistry of the programs that it will bring into our lives is entirely up to us!

9

Summary and Retrospect

With the basic assumption that the word "Theatre" includes, for our purposes, cinema and television as well as the living stage, this book has set out to outline and explain one theory of theatre understanding and evaluation. The concepts and principles on which this theatrical approach to the theatre is based have been used in an effort to set up at least a temporary criterion for the beginner to apply in arriving at an understanding of why he has or has not enjoyed a given stage, motion picture, or television experience. Beliefs and prejudices of the author have been presented as such, with the full realization that any playgoer with further experience and reading may modify or even discard much of what he has found on these pages. This is inevitable—the point is that *in so doing he will have set up his own standards of judgment.* This is the first goal of *A Primer for Playgoers.*

It is said that Shakespeare followed a cycle of first stating what

he was going to say, then saying it, and finally pointing out that it had been said. Whether or not this generalization can be substantiated, the purpose of this chapter is to complete this same cycle, examining this book in retrospect as a whole.

We have from the beginning conceived the fine arts to exist primarily for the purpose of aesthetic pleasure. The theatre has been considered to be a synthesis of the arts, because it is composed of all their elements and may therefore be called the meeting ground of the arts. We have supposed that it belonged to the people and that the audience went to the theatre primarily to have its emotions touched. We have concluded that audiences are different from the individuals of which they are composed, and that accordingly the art of the playwright is the most difficult of all literary work. We have insisted that each artist be ever aware of the fact that the theatre must *entertain* its audience in the fullest meaning of that term; that all entertainment is not art, but that all art is entertainment, and that there is something wrong with the art that does not entertain. In addition to its entertaining, the theatre must, in its capacity as a teacher, challenge the audience in its thinking, improve its taste, increase its knowledge of life and art, and clarify its thinking. In so doing it will thus *create a better audience which will in turn demand better theatre*. This is the second major goal of the book.

All this must be done while the spectators are being entertained, for the theatre has the right to expect only involuntary attention, the attention that comes without effort on the part of the audience. As an art it is the obligation of the theatre to give the audience more than it could have lived in the same period, it must suggest life rather than imitate it, and it should be an illusion of *seeming* real rather than *being* real. This is accomplished through theatrical reality, commonly called theatricalism, which we define as *exaggeration under control* and which is found in every phase of the production. This bigger-than-life quality must never cease to be believed by the audience as long as it is in the theatre.

The vast importance of the audience, its reactions, and its contributions to the production must never be forgotten by any of the theatre's artists or those who would consider themselves critics.

The theatre is in one sense similar to a five-ring circus, with each ring contributing an essential part of the whole production. The five areas are the audience and its reaction, the play and the playwright, the acting and the actors, the background and the technicians, and the direction and director, whose work today is that of an artist and coordinator.

Poetry can be as vital and as alive in the twentieth century as at any time in the past; it has only changed its appearance, and may be found in the unity, harmony, emphasis, proportion, balance, rhythm, and grace that the artist director can bring to the well-coordinated production. We have accepted the belief that all art is selection, and that it consists of substance, form, and technique. We have defined technique as the artist's means of accomplishing his end. It is the measure of his own creative powers for bringing together the substance and form. *A Primer for Playgoers* has tried to explain some of the accepted theatre forms and to point up some of the most obvious techniques of each artist. The artist works not only in the hope of sharing his own aesthetic experience with the audience, but of receiving its approbation for his efforts. Finally, we have considered that all art is life seen through a personality as that artist creates, interprets, portrays, or suggests some segment of life.

Separate chapters have pointed out the basic differences in the technique of the stage, of motion pictures, and of television. Fully conscious that these three mediums of dramatic entertainment can never be compared one with the other, the fact remains that they work with much the same material, employ practically the same artists, and strive for a common goal—that of moving their audiences emotionally through the communication of a story. Therefore, we may evaluate the total effectiveness of each on much the same general standards, which in this book have been presented as ten commandments of dramatic criticism with a few supplementary questions in Chapter 7.

Every individual is moved emotionally or aesthetically depending upon the stimulus, his personal background, and his experience. Unanimity of opinion is never expected or even desirable.

SUMMARY AND RETROSPECT

This book was planned in the hope that it might make the reader understand and demand more of these three mediums of entertainment, education, and communication. It is further hoped that through the influence of these pages he might view the stage, the motion picture, and television with a greater degree of imaginary puissance, and never fail to take into consideration Goethe's three significant and valid principles for evaluating any work of art: What is the artist trying to do? How well has he accomplished his goal? Is it worth the doing? Such an approach demands that our dramatic criticism exist on three levels—the *literary*, which emphasizes the written drama; the *theatrical*, stressing the creation of beauty through sheer theatre magic; and the level of pure *escape* or entertainment commonly referred to as "show business." Such an approach will permit each artist the freedom to create, and in turn will *produce a fairer and more honest evaluation of his work.*

If, then, these pages have (1) helped the playgoer create his own standards of dramatic criticism, (2) provided a fairer judgment of the artists' work, and (3) laid the foundation for building better audiences who will eventually demand better theatre, a contribution will have been made in the realm of dramatic understanding, discrimination, and theatre appreciation.

Questions for Discussion

Chapter 1

1. Apply Goethe's questions to some recent event which, at the time, received your adverse criticism. Does your opinion alter in any way?

2. From your experience with any dramatic event—stage, motion picture, or television—show how it was marred because some individual in the audience did not observe the obligations of an audience.

3. Give some examples of theatricalism that you have found both pleasing and effective.

4. Give a personal experience with empathy and one with aesthetic distance in a stage, cinema, or television production.

5. Choose any dramatic event and distinguish between its substance, form, and technique in the artists' work.

Chapter 2

1. Name some television programs that you would rather observe with a group than alone, and explain why. Name several you would prefer to see alone.

2. Make a list of your own personal prejudices related to the three entertainment mediums of television, stage, and cinema. Make a list of the dramatic events or actors you do not like. Place the two lists side by side and ask: "Is it my own prejudice that causes my displeasure?"

3. Recently a prominent member of the clergy said: "The church's job is not to condemn portrayals of real life; its job is to provide the answers for the problems that they raise." Explain this in terms of censorship.

4. Can you remember a time when an audience either made a poor play seem successful or a generally good play seem less so?

5. Give an example of a wholly unqualified person, from the viewpoint of knowledge of the subject, who tried to criticize a dramatic production.

Chapter 3

1. From your experience choose some humor that fits each of the steps shown on the ladder of comedy. Can you remember material that belonged on one step but was either raised or lowered by its treatment on the part of the artist?

2. Give several examples of thoughtful laughter as contrasted with situation comedy so prevalent on the television screen.

3. Cite an incident in a play where an effort was made to portray reality by imitation. Cite another where the artist has used suggestion.

4. Name several plays or instances where the element of sentimentality has been the source of the emotion. Where was it handled so well that you were fooled by it? Where was it so obvious that it was unpleasant?

5. Choose a play or motion picture that has in some quarters been termed immoral, and either justify or refute that stand.

Chapter 4

1. George Jean Nathan has said: "The playwright must interpret life artificially in terms of reality, while the actor must interpret life realistically in terms of artificiality." Explain.

2. Discuss and explain the following quotation from Margaret Webster, the eminent actress and Shakespearean director:

When an actor rises to the greatness of his vision with the full armory of his physical powers—that, if his vision be great enough, is genius; and only when his physical prowess outruns the fervor and truth of his vision may he be labeled "ham."

Ham acting is technique in excess of emotion. Keep the two in proportion all the way up, and you will finally arrive at a theatre which is as exciting as it is honest, as theatrical as it is true.

3. Think back over five motion pictures, five stage productions, and five television programs. Was it story or acting that you remember? Explain fully why these have stayed in your mind.

4. Give instances of actors who you feel have mastered only the technical area of acting. List some who have largely mastered both the technical and the mental. In your theatregoing, have you ever been conscious of an actor who seemed to have reached the third area? Explain.

5. Make a list of ten actors, and explain a special quality or aspect that each possesses which enhances his artistry; name some asset he brings to a role.

Chapter 5

1. Choose from any available pictures of theatre productions a scene design that will bear the characteristics listed for each of the six modern scenic designs.

2. From your experience in theatre, give several examples where ultra-realism distracted from the main point of the production.

3. Give an example where the work of the technicians has added materially to the success of a production. Where it has detracted in some way. Who was specifically responsible?

4. Give some examples of realistic lighting; of theatrical lighting; of simultaneous setting; of multiple setting.

5. Explain how a costume or a stage setting can have dramatic significance. Two negative criticisms of these technical aspects have been used as follows: "It's a beautiful costume, but it does nothing for the actor"; and "The setting is attractive, but it has no theatre in it." Explain how each statement might have been true.

Chapter 6

1. If the director is responsible for the **what** and the actor for the **how,** separate and discuss the direction and the acting in any recent dramatic production.

2. Give some examples of type-casting in a professional or a noncommercial theatre. Name some castings in a noncommercial production that might be considered "midway between type-casting and miscasting." What are the advantages in each to both the actor and the production?

3. Debate the two opposing theories of the noncommercial theatre: (1) To expose the actors and the audience to the very best in great drama even though their abilities to perform or understand them may cause the produc-

tion to fall short in quality compared to the script; (2) to choose somewhat lesser dramas but to produce them in a more professional manner.

4. This book has emphasized the belief that there is only one standard of excellence in dramatic art. Many persons believe there should be various standards depending on the producing groups. Present arguments on both points of view.

5. Have you ever seen the same drama in two different productions? How did they vary in technical aspects? In acting? In direction and over-all interpretation?

Chapter 7

1. List as many films as you can remember that would have suffered by stage confinement. Why would this be so?

2. Have you ever seen both the motion picture and stage version of a story? What alterations were made in the two versions to make them fit the medium? How would you explain the reasons for such alterations?

3. Choose a recent picture and discuss the camera work with a special note on the angles, methods of changing from one scene to another—the use of cut, wipe, dissolve, montage, and fade.

4. Actors—and other artists—are occasionally criticized because of particular political beliefs or for some aspect of their private lives. Should our disagreement with such ideas or acts have any relation to our evaluation of their work as artists? What is the artist's obligation to his audience beyond his work as an artist?

5. Walter Kerr has said, "In theory the critic places the good of art above the good of the community . . . and the censor places the good of the community above the good of art." Discuss, using some concrete examples from recent productions.

Chapter 8

1. Make a list of your five favorite television series. What particular emotional, intellectual, or entertainment value do you associate with each?

2. List some distractions with which a television program may have to contend in its various audiences. How does it meet these problems in its production techniques?

3. Jack Gould, television critic, has said, "Producers should not be allowed to put on television plays that don't have last acts." Another has argued, "The indecision of television is commendable. It leaves the end in doubt, and isn't that the way it is in life?" With whom do you agree? Why?

4. What developments or improvements do you see for television in the future? What new discoveries have most recently been announced for its use?

5. Choose some recent television program and distinguish between the work of an actor and that of the director by pointing out specific instances of each.

Glossary of Theatre Terms

Most of the following terms are frequently used in discussions involving the stage, motion picture, or television. A knowledge of their meaning is essential. Generally, those which were defined or discussed in the text have not been included here.

Abstract set . . . . Drapes, single units of doors or windows arranged for music or ballet numbers. No effort at realism or locale. Common in television.

Actors' Equity Association . . . . Union of professional legitimate theatre actors with headquarters in New York City.

A.F.T.R.A. . . . . American Federation of Television and Radio Artists. Union for television and radio actors with offices in New York City and Los Angeles.

Angel . . . . Individual who furnishes financial backing for a production, whose name rarely appears in connection with it.

A.N.T.A. . . . . American National Theatre and Academy. Congressionally chartered organization for serving the theatre in all its branches. Supplies advice and various services. Offices in New York City.

Annie Oakley . . . . A pass or complimentary ticket to the theatre, so called because of the habit of punching holes in such a ticket in the pre-rubber stamp days.

Antagonist . . . . The character most in opposition to main character (protagonist) of the play.

Antoinette Perry Awards . . . . "Tonies," awarded each season for outstanding work in writing, acting, and design in the New York theatre. An award in honor of Antoinette Perry, actress and director.

Apron . . . . Space on stage in front of main curtain; very wide in Restoration and eighteenth century. Much of the play took place here.

Arena stage . . . . A form of center staging with audience on three or four sides. (**See** "Theatre-in-the-round" and "Penthouse theatre.")

251

Arras setting . . . . Half circle of neutral draperies which serve as formal background for the stage. (**See** "Cyclorama.")

Artistic failure . . . . Play that may have artistic qualities but has received poor notices and is a failure at the box office.

Aside . . . . Words spoken by the actor in a lower tone. The audience, but not the other characters of the play, is supposed to hear them.

Audio . . . . Sound portion of a television show.

Backdrop . . . . Large flat surface at rear of stage, painted to suggest locale and used with wings in seventeenth, eighteenth, and nineteenth centuries. In present-day theatre usually represents sky. (**See** "Sky-drop.")

Backing . . . . A series of flats or drops placed behind doors and windows to mask backstage area.

Backstage . . . . The entire area behind the proscenium arch, but normally during the action of the play that area which is not seen by the audience.

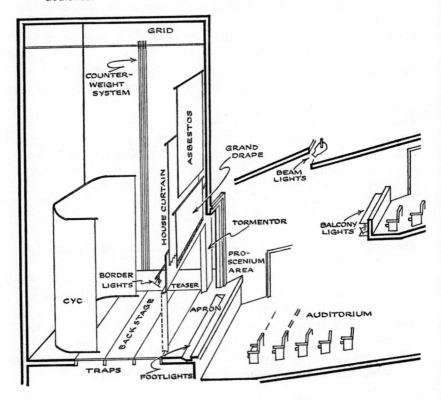

Bit part . . . . Very small role, described by one actor as "two speeches and a spit," such as "The carriage awaits, milady."

Blooper . . . . Error by some member of cast or crew. Sometimes called "goof" or "boo-boo."

Border . . . . A short curtain hung above the stage to mask the flies when a ceiling piece is not being used.

Borderlights . . . . A series of lights above and at front of stage to light the acting area with general illumination.

Box set . . . . Standard setting of today with back wall, two side walls, and usually a ceiling to represent the interior of a room.

Broad comedy . . . . Slapstick bordering on farce or burlesque. Overdone for sake of "groundlings," and lacking subtlety.

Bridge . . . . A transition from one scene to another. In radio it is usually music; on television the use of a small object such as a letter, picture, or fan to allow change from one set to the other by an actor.

Burlesque . . . . An exaggeration in character traits, stage business, or movement, so overdone that the sense of reality or its illusion are destroyed. Emphasizes humor.

Cheat . . . . To turn body or play toward audience while appearing to be in conversation with other players on the stage.

Clambake . . . . A poorly constructed or rehearsed program that is much below standard.

Claque . . . . A group in the audience (friends or especially hired) who applaud or react vocally to give the impression of great enthusiasm for the performance.

Commedia dell' arte . . . . A pantomime or drama without any set literary form. The theatre of common people in Europe beginning with the fifteenth century. It gave us such characters as Harlequin, Pierrot, Columbine, etc.

Conventional theatre . . . . Indicates accepted theatre building with raised stage, scenery, lights, and proscenium, with auditorium and audience out front as we know it.

Critic's Circle . . . . A group composed of all first-line New York critics for newspapers and magazines (about twenty-eight) who by secret ballot award prizes to best American and foreign play and musical each spring.

Cross-fade . . . . **Audio** — to fade out one sound and fade another in. **Video** — to fade out one picture and fade another in.

Cue . . . . The final words, business, or movement of one character before another begins his own.

Cut . . . . **Stage** — to delete a line or omit certain business. **Screen** — transference from one picture to another.

Cyclorama or **"cyc"** . . . . Curtain or canvas usually hung in half-circle to cover back and sides of stage. May represent blue of sky or be plain drape setting. (**See** "Arras setting.")

Décor . . . . Furnishings, properties, draperies, and decorations of setting. (**See** "Inscenierung.")

Dénouement . . . . The moment when the last suspense is eliminated. From the French — literal translation is "untying of the last knot." Usually comes with or after climax and before conclusion.

"Deus ex machina" . . . . See "God from the machine."

Dissolve . . . . The second shot appears on the screen under the first and becomes increasingly distinct as the first disappears. Serves to connect scenes on the screen.

Downstage . . . . The part of the stage nearest the audience.

Dramatic time . . . . The period that elapses in the action of a script. (**See** "Physical time.")

Dressing the house . . . . Scattering the audience by leaving pairs or more of seats empty to give impression of a larger attendance.

Drop . . . . The name given the curtains that are hung from the flies.

Dry-run . . . . Full rehearsal without the use of cameras.

Emmy . . . . Television award given annually. (**See** "Oscar.")

Fade-in and fade-out . . . . Light intensity of first camera shot falls to zero and second rises to normal value. Serves to disconnect scenes.

Film clip . . . . Film inserted into a live telecast.

Filter . . . . Audio effect used to give a metallic quality to the voice, such as talking over telephone.

Flat . . . . A piece of scenery composed of muslin, canvas, or linen stretched over a wooden frame. Used for walls or backing of a set.

Flies . . . . The whole area above stage back of the proscenium where borders, drops, and small pieces of scenery are hung.

Fluffed line . . . . A stammer, stutter, twisting of words, or other faulty delivery by the actor.

Fly . . . . To raise scenery above the floor of the stage by use of ropes, battens, etc.

Fly catching . . . . Movement, business, or sound made by an actor to attract attention to himself when emphasis should be elsewhere.

Forestage . . . . Part of stage nearest audience when an inner proscenium is used. Sometimes used interchangeably with "apron."

Format . . . . Style or make-up of a television script. Also used to describe the method or pattern of opening and closing the program. Usually followed from week to week.

47 Workshop . . . . Playwriting course originally at Harvard and later at Yale under George Pierce Baker. Gave us many leading playwrights of the twentieth century.

Freeze . . . . To stand completely still as if for a picture.

George Spelvin . . . . Name often used by an actor for the second or lesser role he is playing. Sometimes credited to William Gillette, William Collier, Sr., and William Seymour, but generally accepted to have been used for the first time in 1907 in Winchell Smith's and Frederic Thompson's play, **Brewster's Millions.** An actor chose the name for a second role. The critics praised "George Spelvin" for his work and the play was a hit. Smith always insisted on listing the same name on future programs, for luck.

Ghost walks . . . . Used by actors to denote payday.

Gimmick . . . . A device or trick used for a special effect, usually in an effort to get a laugh, athough it may seek any emotion.

God from the machine . . . . From the Latin, "deus ex machina," when Fate (or the author) intercedes to save the action from the logical conclusion.

Good theatre . . . . A quality that makes a play especially effective when presented before an audience.

Grand drape . . . . A curtain above the stage and at the top of the proscenium arch; it hangs in front of the main curtain and decorates the top of the stage and reduces the height of the opening.

Gridiron or grid . . . . Framework of wood or steel above the stage. Used to support and fly scenery.

Ground cloth . . . . Waterproof canvas covering usually used to cover the entire stage floor.

Groundlings . . . . Term used by Shakespeare to indicate the uneducated and untrained theatregoers who sat in the pit, and were highly entertained by broad comedy.

Ground row . . . . Profile at the back of stage representing trees, shrubbery, hills, etc. Masks the meeting of stage floor and cyclorama.

Ham acting . . . . An exaggerated and insincere performance, notable for noise rather than honest feeling or sincerity. Extravagant gestures, choking sounds, and trickery are used for their effect alone. Should not be confused with broad acting or projection.

Hokum . . . . Deliberate simulation of emotion by artificial means, and also the means used. Sure-fire but time-worn theatrical tricks.

House seats . . . . Seats retained by the management to cover errors or to be given to distinguished guests. Released just before curtain time.

Idiot-sheet . . . . Copy, cue lines, or other material written in large letters for television actors, announcers, or others.

Image . . . . Picture appearing on the television screen.

Inner stage . . . . In Elizabethan theatre the small area upstage and enclosed by curtains. It localized action which moved forward to outer stage after the scene was underway.

Inscenierung . . . . German term to indicate the whole visual stage picture, including lighting. (**See** "Décor.")

Light leak . . . . Light that can be seen through a crack or opening in the set.

Light spill . . . . Light that strikes the proscenium or set and thus "spills over" in a distracting manner, rather than striking just the area it is supposed to cover.

Live . . . . Actually present in studio, as opposed to filmed or recorded.

Lock . . . . Term indicating those elements which prevent a character from escaping the results of the conflict.

Mask . . . . To cover from view of the audience with some type of scenery.

Montage . . . . A rapid series of different pictures that build to a climax and in doing so give a single impression.

Moscow Art Theatre . . . . Established by Constantin Stanislavsky in the last decade of the nineteenth century, and until the Stalin regime considered one of the finest theatres in the world.

Muff . . . . To mispronounce or transpose words or syllables.

Musical comedy . . . . A light story with spoken dialogue interspersed with music and dances.

Obligatory scene . . . . The scene of the play which the playwright has led us to expect and without which the audience would be disappointed. Sometimes referred to as "scène-à-faire."

GLOSSARY OF THEATRE TERMS

Oscar . . . . Motion Picture Academy Award, given each year for the outstanding achievement in all phases of the cinema.

Outer stage . . . . Forestage of Elizabethan theatre and used especially for soliloquies and most dramatic scenes. Historically preceded the apron. (**See** "Apron.")

Pan . . . . To criticize adversely. **Screen** — Relates to camera angle as it moves from one position to another without a break.

Paper . . . . Complimentary tickets given out free or at reduced rates to bring in a larger audience. Sometimes called "papering the house."

Penthouse theatre . . . . Name given to the first arena theatre of this century when it opened at the University of Washington.

Peripeteia or **peripety** . . . . A reversal of circumstances which leads to a result contrary to our expectation.

Physical time . . . . The actual minute length of the production, as opposed to the dramatic time.

Plant . . . . Apparently casual insertion of an idea, character, or property to be used more significantly later in the play.

Plastic scenery . . . . Built in three dimensions rather than being painted on a flat surface.

Playwrights Company . . . . A producing organization in New York controlled principally by playwrights themselves. The founding members (1938) were S. N. Behrman, Maxwell Anderson, Robert Sherwood, Sidney Howard, and Elmer Rice.

"The Poetics" . . . . Written by Aristotle (360-322 B.C.). The earliest critical treatise extant dealing with dramatic practice and theory.

Point of attack . . . . That arbitrary point where the writer has chosen to begin his script.

Practical . . . . Scenery that is usable; a door or window that will open, etc.

Producer . . . . In America the individual or group who raises the money or underwrites the production financially. In England usually considered to be the director as well.

Project or projection . . . . **Stage** — To increase size of voice, movement, and gesture so it can be seen and heard in the rear of the auditorium. It "theatricalizes nature," so to speak, by increasing the feeling, but all is done with sincerity. Sometimes called "playing broadly," but not to be confused with "ham acting." **Screen** — Throwing the picture on the screen.

Properties or props . . . . Any article or piece of furniture used by the actor.

Proscenium . . . . The wall that separates the audience from the backstage.

Proscenium arch . . . . The opening in the proscenium through which the audience sees the stage; the picture frame.

Protagonist . . . . The leading character in the play — the one in whom the audience is most interested.

Pulitzer Prize . . . . Award given each year to the best play on an American theme.

Rake . . . . To place the set on a slant. Usually applied to side walls.

Repertoire, or **repertory** . . . . A list of dramas, operas, parts, etc., which a company or person has rehearsed and is prepared to perform. They are alternated in performance.

Repertory company . . . . Theatrical group that has and performs a repertoire.

Resolution . . . . Method of solving all conflicts presented in the play.

Return . . . . A flat used at extreme right and left of stage and running off stage behind the tormentor. Sometimes it serves as the tormentor.

Revue . . . . A series of unrelated songs, skits, dances, very loosely tied together by the title—usually some topical subject. All pretense of plot is abandoned.

Scenario . . . . General description of action for a proposed motion picture.

Scène-à-faire . . . . (**See** "Obligatory scene.")

Schmaltz . . . . Overly sentimental material, usually with the use of music in the background. Sometimes applied to overacting or production.

Screen Actors Guild . . . . Union of motion picture actors.

Script . . . . The written drama from which the play is built.

Set pieces . . . . Scenery that will stand without support. Used especially in nonrealistic productions.

Show business . . . . Name applied to theatre productions pandering to a nondiscerning audience and emphasizing escape or box-office appeal rather than literary or theatrical merit.

Skeleton setting . . . . Rudiments of a setting, appealing largely to the imagination of the audience.

Skene . . . . A small hut in the Greek theatre, used for concealment during a change of costume. It has given us the English word "scene."

Skit . . . . A short scene of dialogue or pantomime, usually in a satirical or humorous vein.

Sky-drop . . . . A drop painted blue to represent sky and to mask rear of stage; hangs from the flies. (**See** "Cyclorama.")

Sneak . . . . To bring in music, sound, or voices at an extremely low level of volume.

Snow . . . . White spots or interference in television picture. Due to low level of the station broadcasting.

Soliloquy . . . . A speech delivered by the actor when alone on the stage. There are two types:

Constructive — to explain the plot to the audience, as in many of Shakespeare's prologues.

Reflective — to show personal thought or emotion, as in **Hamlet.**

Stage right and left . . . . Right or left side of the stage from the actor's point of view.

Static play . . . . One in which very little happens and the characters and situations are essentially the same at the end as in the beginning.

Steal . . . . Getting from one part of the stage to another without its being noticed. Also applied to taking a scene that really belongs to another.

Sting . . . . To punctuate with a sudden musical phrase, shout, or some other emphatic sound.

Stock, stock company . . . . A resident company presenting a series of plays, each for a limited run, but not repeated after that engagement.

Superimpose . . . . Overlapping of two picture frames. The images of two cameras seen together, one on top of the other.

Tag . . . . Final line of the play.

Teaser . . . . Border just upstage and back of the front curtain. Masks the flies and determines the height of the proscenium opening during the performance.

Theatre Guild . . . . Producing organization in New York. It works on a subscription series there and in many other large cities.

Theatre-in-the-round . . . . (**See** "Arena stage.")

The Théâtre Libre (Paris) . . . . Free theatre in France in 1887. Headed by André Antoine, it introduced Naturalism and freedom from artificiality of the nineteenth century.

"The Method" . . . . Name applied to the Russian or Stanislavsky approach to acting; very subjective, introspective, and individualistic.

Tormentors . . . . Flats at extreme down right and left of stage near proscenium and masking backstage area. (**See** "Return.")

Trap . . . . Opening in stage floor, permitting entrances or exits from under the floor.

Turkey . . . . Name indicating the dramatic production that has utterly failed.

Unit setting . . . . Pieces of scenery — flats, pillars, doors, pylons, arches,

etc. — that can be put together in various combinations to furnish different settings.

Upstage . . . . Toward back of stage. For many years the stage was higher in the back and slanted down toward the footlights and audience. This is still true in some European theatres.

Victorian . . . . Applied to the era of Queen Victoria or the second half of the nineteenth century in England. Noted for prudery and ostentation in art.

Video . . . . The sight portion of a television program.

Washington Square Players . . . . Amateur group, which grew into the present successful Theatre Guild.

Well-made play . . . . A name given those plays written in mid-nineteenth century which followed a set pattern or formula in their construction. Now has a derogatory meaning.

Wings . . . . Off-stage space to left and right. Sometimes refers to wing pieces used in series of two or three on either side of stage as part of wing and backdrop set.

Wipe . . . . First camera shot is peeled off, revealing the second as if it had previously been there.

Zoom . . . . A camera movement toward or away from the object — very fast and smooth.

Index

Index

263

Aesthetic styles (*Cont.*)
  types:
    classic, 87, 91
    expressionistic, 89, 90
    fantasy, 90
    naturalistic, 89
    neoclassic, 88-89
    realistic, 89-90, 91, 92
    romantic, 88-89, 91
    symbolistic, 90
Albright, H. D., 98, 98n.
Alice in Wonderland, 14
All My Sons, 65
Amateur, influence on theatre, 2-3
American Repertory Theatre, 147
Anatomy of the Drama, The, 73n., 209n.
Anderson, Judith, 64, 134
Anderson, Maxwell, 34, 64, 65, 66, 68, 72, 96, 102, 162, 203
Anna Christie, 61, 84
Anna Karenina, 68
Antigone, 87-88
Antoine, André, 89, 144
Antony and Cleopatra, 40
Architecture, 8
Arena stage, 59, 251
Aristophanes, 74
Aristotle, 10, 17, 19, 27, 28, 61, 98, 219
  literary approach to drama, 42
  Poetics, 19, 65, 257
  theory of catharsis, 10
Arsenic and Old Lace, 82, 84, 91
Art, 12, 17, 19-21
Art of Playgoing, 34n., 36-37, 128n.
Art of Play Production, The, 44n., 145n., 149
Atkinson, Brooks, 12, 19, 19n., 46-47
Audience:
  characteristics, 34-35
  and dramatic criticism, 32-51
  effect on performance, 37
  elements, 35, 36, 37
  estimate of, 38-39
  how to judge actor, 131-45
  joy of, 33
  motion picture vs. stage, 205-208
  obligations, 15-17, 108-109
  TV, motion picture, stage contrast, 223-26
  what to look for from director, 183-200
Auntie Mame, 51, 82, 91

B

Backstage personnel, 146-72 (*see also under* Name of type)
Bacon, Francis, 17

Balance, 45
Bankhead, Tallulah, 40, 124
Barrie, J. M., 55
Barrymore, Ethel, 123, 135, 138
Beaton, Cecil, 27, 148
Beauty, defined, 10-13
Beaux' Stratagem, The, 74
Bacque, Henry François, 89
Beethoven, Ludwig von, 19
Behrman, S. N., 34, 76, 100-101, 102, 134, 134n.
Belasco, David, 127, 144, 150, 151, 164, 166
Bentley, Eric, 11, 34, 37, 46, 47, 48, 119
Bernhardt, 3, 25, 55, 120
Blithe Spirit, 47, 51, 75, 82, 90
Blood Wedding, 62
Blue Bird, The, 14, 90
Bolger, Ray, 82
Booth, Edwin, 31, 124-25
Brecht, Berthold, 34, 37
Broadway, 2, 43, 105-106, 147
Brown, John Mason, 34, 34n., 36, 40, 65, 117, 128-29
Browning, Robert, 54
Burbage, Richard, 3, 54
Business, 188

C

Cameraman, 213-14
Candida, 85
Capra, Frank, 217
Catharsis, theory of, 10
Catherine Was Great, 40
Cat On A Hot Tin Roof, 65
Censorship, 206
Chaplin, Charlie, 28
Chapman, John, 40
Charley's Aunt, 51, 82-83
Chase, Ilka, 38
Chase, Mary, 90
Chaucer, Geoffrey, 19
Chekhov, Anton, 37, 61
Cheney, Sheldon, 80, 80n., 88, 148
Cherry Orchard, The, 61, 91
Cicero, 98
Cinema (*see* Motion pictures)
Circus, 28
Classicism, 87-88, 91, 97
Cleveland Playhouse, 177
Climax (*see under* Structure)
"Closet dramas," 54
Clowns, 28
Clurman, Harold, 175-76, 185, 200
Cobb, Lee J., 62

C

BILLY WILDER. Motion Picture
Credits: *Double Indemnity, Lost
Weekend, Sunset Boulevard.*

WILLIAM WYLER. Motion Picture Credits: *The Big Country, Wuthering Heights, Mrs.
Miniver, Best Years of Our Lives, Roman Holiday, Friendly Persuasion.*

GEORGE STEVENS. Motion Picture
Credits: *Giant, Shane, A Place in the Sun,*
The Diary of Anne Frank.

KING VIDOR. *Photo by Berko.* Motion
Picture Credits: *War and Peace, Duel in*
the Sun, Northwest Passage, Our Daily
Bread, Street Scene, The Big Parade.